HE AM WHAT HE AM!
JACK MERCER
THE VOICE OF POPEYE

BY FRED M. GRANDINETTI

Published in the USA by:
BearManor Media
P O Box 71426
Albany, Georgia 31708
WWW.BEARMANORMEDIA.COM

ISBN 1-59393-096-8

Printed in the United States of America.
Book design by Brian Pearce.

TABLE OF CONTENTS

ACKNOWLEDGEMENTS

First and foremost I wish to thank the late Virginia Mercer, wife of Jack Mercer, who wrote letters and shared conversations with me regarding her husband's career.

This book could not have been written without the efforts of historians who have spent years researching (and documenting) the field of animation and the characters Jack Mercer was involved with:

Mike Barrier
Jerry Beck
Mike and Debbie Brooks
Leslie Carbarga
G. Michael Dobbs
Mark Evanier
Leonard Kohl
Ken Layton
William Mailing

Also, I would like to thank, Jerry Alvarez, Steve Bierly, Dan Braun, Tom Hatten, Mark Kausler, Bob McFadden, Tom Moore and Don Oriolo.

Dedicated to the memory of Jack and Virginia Mercer.

Jack and Virginia Mercer in 1984 (from the excellent DVD, Popeye Original Classics produced by Steve Stanchfield and Thunderbean Animation Studios).

INTRODUCTION

This is not a comprehensive biography of Jack Mercer, nor could it be. In the days of theatrical cartoon production, Jack Mercer would often be called in to provide the sound effect of a car backfiring or a horn, anything which was needed to finish the recording of a particular animated film. As the practice was not to credit voice performers, Jack Mercer's entire contributions to the field of animation are lost. I have gathered together as much information which has become available where Jack Mercer's talents have been given credit.

From my written and verbal correspondence with Jack Mercer's second wife, Virginia, I discovered she was vigilant in setting the record straight regarding the individuals claiming to be the voice of Popeye. How could so many people step in and claim credit?

This is partly due to the media's acceptance of published material without checking the facts, but also Jack Mercer's reluctance to publicize his work is responsible.

While other voice artists have been showered with praise and honors, Jack Mercer's contributions have remained pretty much in the background. When one considers that he provided the voice for Popeye, a character who performed good deeds but didn't accept the accolades to go with them, perhaps this is fitting. Still, through his artistry, storytelling and voice work, Jack Mercer left his creative stamp on the field of animation.

THE FRIENDLY VOICE OF POPEYE

Steven R. Bierly has a unique relationship with Popeye the Sailor. As a pastor he often uses references to Popeye cartoons in his sermons and teachings with students. He grew up in Upstate New York, went to a seminary in New England and now pastors a church in Hull, Iowa. This book would not be complete without hearing from one of Popeye's fans and how Jack Mercer's vocal characterization of the mighty mariner made an impact on his childhood.

Popeye has been my lifelong friend. He's nearly always been around. As I was growing up, I watched his cartoons regularly on TV stations broadcasting out of two nearby cities. Even during my college and seminary years he would pop up from time to time on TV just when I needed him. Beyond seminary to today I have watched him on cable channels and have even used his cartoons to teach lessons on boy/girl relationships to high school students. So Popeye is, and always has been, a part of my life. He's familiar. I know him well.

Another reason the one-eyed sailor man and I are buddies is Popeye's character, which is a genius mixture of the heroic and the comic. I admire him, want to emulate him at times, and yet am able to laugh at, and with, him as well. He brings out the best in me and gives me some chuckles along the way. Isn't this what you want a friend to do?

I could list other reasons why I feel like Popeye is a friend, but the purpose of this book is to focus on the talented Jack Mercer. And that I will gladly do, because I think it was the vocal work of Mr. Mercer which helped make Popeye so amiable.

In the early Popeye cartoons by Fleischer studios, "friendly" wasn't really an adjective you could use to describe the sailor. He was combative, self-centered, and could be even downright mean. His voice sounded to me as if it had a sneer in it. When Popeye sang his theme song in his first screen appearance, there was anger and defiance in it. He wasn't just announcing his arrival to the world; he was also challenging the world to make something out of it and putting an unspoken, but implied, "So there! Noah! Noah! Noah!" at the end of every line. Not that the early animated Popeye was always angry or couldn't laugh, but when he did laugh, it sounded as if it was coming from another character altogether, as though Popeye had a split personality and wasn't just endearingly eccentric but plain crazy.

Speaking of crazy, the Popeye in the Fleischer cartoons was known for muttering under his breath and making vocal asides without moving his lips. But in a cartoon like *The Dance Contest*, his mutterings are pretty incomprehensible and are mostly semi-articulate expressions of pain or joy. This makes Popeye seem like he's one of those old, crazy, homeless alcoholics who hang around bus stations talking to themselves and once in a while shouting out something. Rather than befriending him, you want to move away from him.

Like the denizens of those bus stations, the early Popeye seems disconnected from his environment. Even when you can understand the expressions of pain he utters, he seems more like he's just commenting on the action in the cartoon rather than that he's sincerely hurt. We watch this Popeye, but when he says things like, "I guess I have no sex appeal," when Olive leaves him, and "My only friend," when he pulls out the spinach can, his voice is too gruff and matter-of-fact to make us feel anything for him. And we can't empathize and sympathize with a character we can't be friends with. Even his ejaculations like "Wow!" or "Oh" seem more like he's noting that a "Wow" moment is occurring in the plot and that he's providing a sound effect much as he does when he says, "Wham!" before belting someone. If Popeye can't emotionally relate to the world around him, how can he relate to us and be our friend?

But did the early Popeye even want to be our friend? In *Strong to the Finich*, it's hard to tell whether he likes the kids living on Olive's farm or not. In fact, he might be the old guy in the neighborhood who would always be complaining about us kids and yelling at us to stay off his lawn. The early Popeye's gruff, edgy voice, combined with his wrinkled and severe appearance, always made me think of him as being old, and not fun old like my grandfathers, but crotchety and scary old.

This is not to fault William Costello, the first actor to voice Popeye. His Popeye was very much in line with the way the character was first portrayed by his creator, the incomparable Elzie Segar. When Popeye made his initial appearances in the *Thimble Theater* comic strip, though he exhibited the admirable qualities of perseverance and self-confidence which would be part of the character in all of his incarnations, and though he was funny, he was also rude, crude, a gambler, a cheater, and a brawler. He was a rough-and-tough sailor, who had relied on himself for so long that he really didn't seem to care all that much about anybody around him. His home was the docks and the ships and he wasn't very civilized. He would just as soon sock you in the jaw as look at you. I can imagine him sounding very much like Costello. And Costello's voice certainly fit the plots and situations that Fleischer Studios put Popeye in.

But as Popeye became popular with kids, King Features Syndicate, the comic strip distributor, mandated that Segar tone Popeye down somewhat and make him more heroic. Popeye morphed into a guy who would still throw a punch, but now if he'd do it he had a good reason — someone picked on him first or justice was needed for an oppressed underdog. He still was confident in his unique view of the world but came across as more quirky than grizzled or weird.

Giving him Olive Oyl as a love interest and Swee'pea as an adopted son further humanized the sailor. And Segar's plots and characterizations made his readers feel for Popeye and the inhabitants of his world, even as the readers were getting their daily laugh. Fleischer Studios modified Popeye and company and their adventures along those same lines as time went on.

It's a good thing Segar and the Fleischer's did what they did, because these qualities cause Popeye to remain popular today. If Popeye hadn't changed, not only would the creators have run out of ideas for him, but he would have become a mere footnote in pop culture history, just a fad that captured America's fancy during the tough days of The Great Depression and World War II when a no-nonsense tough guy was needed.

In Jack Mercer, Fleischer Studios found a voice to perfectly match the new Popeye. Not that the new Popeye or Mercer's vocalizations burst on the scene all at once, but as time went on the way Popeye was portrayed in the cartoons matched more and more the enduring American icon that was appearing in Segar's strips and Mercer's voice sounded less and less like Costello's.

Mercer's Popeye could still sound tough, but his voice also had a lighter and a more natural quality to it. Now both Popeye's fighting and his laughing seemed to come from the same internal personality and to be two aspects of the same character, not an evidence of schizophrenia. And his laugh was fun to imitate, which was only one of the reasons we kids loved to pretend to be Popeye. The animated Popeye with his Arf, Arf, Arf! lifted from the comic strip or his higher pitched Uk, Uk, Uk, Uk! let us hear what a Segar creation would sound like laughing if such a being actually existed in the real world. While Popeye still had a cartoon, exaggerated voice, it also came to take on an every man quality. Popeye was now one of us. And though he was still drawn as wrinkled, nearly bald, and beaten on by life, his voice made him seem younger somehow. While the local television hosts would refer to him as our old pal, Popeye, when Mercer voiced him he seemed closer in age to us kids than the Costello version had been and maybe not so old after all. This increased his appeal to me immensely when I was a kid, as I had no real interest in watching a show about middle-agers or senior citizens.

As time went on, when Mercer's Popeye would sing his theme song he did so as a celebration of his existence and when he would perform other musical numbers that tied into the plots and moods of the cartoons, he was inviting us to join in on the fun, not daring us to try to stop him. Popeye began scat singing in the cartoons and it was full of joy. It was as if he was a guy having so much fun singing in the shower that he couldn't stop as he went about his daily business, or because he was the eccentric Popeye he didn't know that polite society would want him to stop. And being the rugged individualist he was, even if Popeye knew about society's wishes, he wouldn't heed them. All of which made the character very appealing indeed.

When Mercer's Popeye muttered asides, we could actually understand what he was saying and his under-the-breath remarks were often funny, due to Mercer's ability to come up with great ad-libs. It seemed as though we were being given insights into Popeye's quirky mind and we discovered someone who liked to pun and who had his own amusing way of processing information even when his conclusions were wrong.

The exclamations that Mercer's Popeye made seemed spontaneous and to come from the heart. And when Popeye expressed his emotions he did it, not as a tough guy making grudging concessions to the script, but as someone who was revealing what was going on inside, and either didn't know that society would rather that people always wear masks than be honest, or didn't care and would wear his heart on his sleeve. Not only did this make Popeye very innocent and child-like but it also allowed us to feel with Popeye instead of just observing him. Think of how much less effective Fleischer cartoons like *The Spinach Overture* (Bluto steals Popeye's orchestra away), *I Yam Lovesick* (Popeye convincingly feigns illness in order to get Olive back), *Goonland* (Popeye finally finds his Pappy who doesn't like relatives), *Hello, How Am I?* (Popeye suffers from identity confusion when Wimpy dresses up like him to get Olive's food), and *Fightin' Pals* (Popeye tracks down his lost buddy Bluto in Africa) would have been if we didn't feel anything while watching them or weren't convinced that Popeye did.

Mercer's Popeye wasn't afraid to feel and to connect with his world. So we believed that he had real relationships with Olive Oyl, Wimpy, Poopdeck Pappy, and Swee'pea and didn't view them as plot contrivances that were only necessary to move the stories along to the point where he'd get to hit somebody or destroy something again. As kids we came to believe that Popeye was, at heart, a people person and that if he met us he'd like us as much as we liked him.

Mercer helped make Popeye as likable on the screen as he was in the daily newspapers. But the Fleischers moved Popeye in directions beyond what the comic strip did and Mercer's voice work would prove invaluable in this area too, and would help keep Popeye popular for decades so that the sailor man would still be around while I was growing up.

It was primarily from the cartoons that the idea came that when Popeye is in a jam he imbibes some spinach for a quick boost of super strength. Segar's Popeye rarely resorted to a spinach booster shot. Instead, he was supernaturally strong all the time. One reason for this was that his regular diet included spinach. The animated Popeye however, nearly always needed to down a can of it in order to save himself and/or others from being humiliated, incapacitated, crippled, or even dying. When Costello's Popeye would pull out the spinach, it often seemed as though he was just doing what the script required but that he secretly knew this was all nonsense and that he could have handled what was being thrown at him just fine without it, thank you very much. Mercer's Popeye, however, knew he or his friends were goners unless he got a hold of the green stuff. This allowed the creators to inject suspense in their cartoons. Segar was masterfully able to build up suspense over time in the daily comic strips. But time is something a theatrical animated short subject doesn't have. Hence, the name short subject. So the questions of how will Popeye get his spinach and will he eat it in time brought some tension into the mostly humor-centric Fleischer cartoons. The element of suspense would become even more important as the Famous Studios years rolled on.

Not only did the Fleischer Popeye (and all the animated Popeyes that came after him) need spinach to boost his strength, but in cartoons like *The Dance Contest, Spinach Overture, Let's Celebrake,* and *Me Feelin's is Hurt* it gives him (and in the case of *Let's Celebrake,* Olive's grandma) skills, abilities and competence that he didn't have without it. When the Fleischer's put Popeye in the military in *The Mighty Navy, Blunder Below, Fleets of Strength,* and *Many Tanks,* Popeye can't seem to be able to do much of anything right until he eats spinach. This was also the case in some of the wartime cartoons made by Famous Studios. Popeye would be easily fooled by the enemy or get knocked around until he ate his spinach. Maybe this was a subtle way of reassuring the folks back home that the goofy, bumbling boy-next-door they sent off to war would finally prove himself able to handle the Axis forces when the chips were down. The everyman quality in Mercer's Popeye voice and the fact that the Mercer Popeye could really be confused, befuddled, humiliated, and even endangered was important in selling the cartoons that wanted to portray Popeye as being in over his head before he eats his spinach. And we kids related to Popeye because we often felt we were in situations where we were in over our heads, too. And we certainly embraced the spinach fantasy. As kids, we longed for something magical that could give us instant strength, make us popular, and allow us to triumph over our tormenters, solve all our problems, and transform us into experts at whatever we were doing. I even want such a thing now!

When the Fleischer brothers lost their studio to Paramount Pictures, the operation was moved to New York City and renamed Famous Studios. At first, the Popeye cartoons Famous Studios produced were very much like what the Fleischer's had been doing. This is understandable because most of the same creators were still involved. But over time, the cartoons changed. I like the changes and feel that the Famous Studios cartoons are just as entertaining and enthralling and memorable as the Fleischer films, but for different reasons. Film historian Leonard Maltin has complained that the Famous Studios Popeye cartoons took themselves too seriously. But what he sees as a minus, I see as a big plus. The Famous Studios Popeye cartoons wanted us to take at least the final perils that Popeye and Olive Oyl found themselves in, no matter how outrageous those perils were (for example, Popeye being locked in a bear trap and fired via spear cannon out over the ocean where he was swallowed by a whale in *Snow*

Place Like Home), very seriously indeed. And as a kid, I appreciated the action and suspense and tension of those scenes. Jack Mercer's voice work was invaluable here because over time he had lost none of his ability to convey pain and emotions. When his Popeye yelled, "Yeow!" we felt it and when he expressed worry and hopelessness with lines like "What a whale of a spot I'm in," we were anxious for him. When I think of the Famous Studios Popeye, I think of a friend who is enthralling me with cliffhangers and adventurous tales.

But the Famous Studios cartoons were often filled with another kind of tension as well. Believe it or not, they were filled with sexual tension — a fact I appreciated as I went through puberty and my teen and young adult years all the way up to today. The creators revamped Olive Oyl and Bluto's personalities and looks and turned them into romantic leads and then placed them in plots where having romance was a must. In fact, to me, the Famous Studios Olive Oyl and Bluto (and by the name Bluto I'm referring not only to Bluto himself, but also to Popeye's other male rivals in those cartoons) are the hottest cartoon characters of all time and they practically burned up the screen together. In their presence, poor Popeye could have gotten lost, but Mercer's voice work is one of the reasons he didn't. Mercer expressed heart-brokenness and made us feel for him. And his everyman quality make us put ourselves in his shoes and remember what it was like to be dumped, or to think about how hard it would be to be in a love triangle. As Bluto would heap indignations on the sailor to get rid of him, we would feel for our old buddy. And when Bluto would finally reveal his true colors and subject Olive to indignations which today would get him arrested (i.e. inviting her to his penthouse and then tricking her into putting on a straitjacket in *The Royal Four-Flusher* and turning her into a kissing yo-yo in *Tops in The Big Top*), we rooted for Popeye to come to her rescue.

As the Famous Studios era drew to a close, Popeye and his cast were about to suffer another kind of indignation — they would be rendered according to the budget available for limited made-for-television animation. King Features Syndicate commissioned several studios to produce Popeye cartoons that would be broadcast as kids' fare. Even when I was young, I realized that the characters in these films looked and moved differently than they had in the past and that these cartoons weren't quite as good as the ones that had gone before. However, Popeye, voiced again by Mercer, sounded like himself. So I concluded that these adventures must be legitimate. In the King Features Syndicate cartoons, Mercer's friendly Popeye voice welcomed us to the new series and was put to good use in it, as Popeye's pal Wimpy would be featured more often than he was in the past. Rough House from the comic strip appeared in a couple of cartoons and Castor Oyl and Toar had cameos. Alice the Goon also had chances to do her thing — whatever that is. So Popeye had plenty of opportunities to display his friendliness toward his expanded animated cast. The toughness and determination that Mercer could give Popeye's voice also got chances to be heard in the TV cartoons as Popeye's old nemesis from the comic strip, the Sea Hag, was now a regular, and the schemes and personality of his main male rival, called Brutus, were usually more transparently evil than they had been in the Famous Studios cartoons. Consequently, Popeye tumbled to things faster and took action quicker.

After the production of the King Features Syndicate films ceased in 1961, Popeye didn't star in another ongoing cartoon series until 1978. But that was okay with me because there were always the reruns.

When Hanna-Barbera's version of Popeye appeared, it left me cold. The character's looks were based on the Fleischer and comic strip models, but the cartoons had none of the old school charm. Also, because of political correctness and the changes in children's television programs over the years, it was now forbidden for Popeye and Bluto to hit each other. What's a Popeye cartoon without fisticuffs? And I found it ridiculous that a character with a history of smoking and of being utterly dependent on spinach and of tossing his empty cans wherever he wanted was now lecturing kids on staying away from drugs and protecting the environment. But as least the new cartoons still featured Jack Mercer as Popeye's voice. I took comfort in that somehow. It was good that Mercer, the enduring and endearing voice of Popeye, had been reunited with the character. All was right with the world.

PROLOGUE

Jack Mercer was a talented artist and writer but he is best remembered for his work providing voices for numerous animated characters and sound effects. Animation historian Mark Evanier wrote, on his website Point of View, *on September 27, 1996, an excellent article explaining the history of voice-over performers from the time Jack Mercer began in theatrical films to the production of television cartoons. There is also insight as to how Mercer worked when he got to the microphone to exclaim, "Blow Me Down" as Popeye or "It's the Professor" as Felix the Cat. Courtesy of Mark Evanier is his article:*

The first cartoon voice artist was probably Walt Disney. He made the first sound cartoons and he cast himself, altogether appropriately, as Mickey Mouse. Many of the early makers of animated talkies looked no further than their own staffs, conscripting artists and secretaries to stand, often trembling, before the microphones.

Which is not to say they were all bad. Walt was fine as Mickey — a task he kept for himself until he became too busy with studio matters. Jack Mercer, the longtime voice of Popeye and other characters, was discovered in the Fleischer Studios art department. And one of the all-time great voice artists, Bill Scott (voice of Bullwinkle, Dudley Do-Right and umpteen others), was first and foremost a writer and producer.

The first actor to make a living primarily doing cartoon voices was probably Clarence "Ducky" Nash, voice of Donald Duck. Disney heard him on a radio show in 1934 and quickly signed him to what turned out to be a lifetime gig. When "Ducky" wasn't speaking for The Duck, he was the studio's goodwill ambassador, making personal appearances with a ventriloquist figure of Donald.

Then in 1936, Warner Brothers gave a shot to a beginning radio actor named Mel Blanc. Smart move.

Blanc billed himself as the Man of a Thousand Voices — good p.r. but probably not an accurate count and certainly a misassessment of his talent. It wasn't quantity that made Mel great; it was quality. His "voice characterizations," as the credits called them, were rounded, fully-developed personalities — with comic timing and delivery as skilled as the best radio comics of the day. The cartoon acting field had found its Olivier.

Soon, a few other masters happened along, including Daws Butler, Stan Freberg, Paul Frees and, in a class by herself, the incredible June Foray. Butler — the man Blanc himself called "my only rival" — would later voice Yogi Bear, Huckleberry Hound and most of the early Hanna-Barbera characters.

Between 1950 and 1970 (all dates approximate), a relatively small talent pool supplied most of the cartoon voices in Hollywood. Butler, Blanc, Foray, Frees, Hans Conried, Don Messick, Allan Melvin, Howie Morris, Janet Waldo, Joanie Gerber, Hal Smith, Dick Beals, Walker Edmiston, Julie Bennett, Lennie Weinrib, Shep Menken, John Stephenson and a few others probably handled about 75% of the work. In 1969, a young impressionist named Frank Welker began doing voices and quickly became ubiquitous. If anyone were to ever tally who since then has logged the most hours making silly sounds before microphones, Frank would be the easy victor.

Since about '70, there seems to have been a rush of new voice performers. Some hail from the comedy circuit and from various improv troupes. Others come out of disc-jockeying or on-camera acting. Most grew up on cartoons, dreaming of someday being Mel Blanc or Daws Butler.

Between 1970 and 1990, the field became flooded with new performers and, since then, it's only gotten more crowded. As a result of Disney features, *The Simpsons* and a general depression in Screen Actors Guild employment, it is no longer unfashionable for on-camera actors to do cartoon voice work. Many animated shows have rushed to cast actors who are best known for their work on live-action TV series on the questionable (I think) premise that employing these folks elevates the cartoon to some higher level.

Cartoon voices are almost always done before the pictures. The animation is done to the voice track. (One exception was at the Fleischer Studios where they usually animated first and voiced after. This order of business is what led to Jack Mercer doing all those wonderful under-his-breath mutterings as Popeye.)

For theatrical cartoons, it has usually been the practice to record the dialogue a line at a time. The actor does multiple takes of each speech, doing it over and over until the director is satisfied. Often, when two or more actors are involved, they're recorded at separate times...or, when one actor does multiple roles, they record one character at a time. Mel Blanc would sometimes perform Tweety one day and Sylvester, the next.

Television cartoons are almost always recorded like a radio play, with the entire cast gathered together in one room, everyone doing his or her lines in sequence. The few instances wherein the actors aren't all together, it's usually because someone wasn't available, not because the producers wanted it that way. Usually, the actors all record together and when they can, the procedure goes something like this...

1. The first thing that happens, of course, is the casting. On a new series, they usually have auditions for the recurring roles. Actor after actor is brought in and recorded reading a few lines of copy, then the producers (or network folks or whoever) whittle down the pile and make their selections.

Each episode also has non-recurring roles — one-time characters who are usually cast by the voice director without an audition. Whenever possible, to save money, they'll try to have the regular actors double. The Screen Actors Guild contract says that, for the basic session fee, an actor can do two roles, plus he or she can do a third for a small increase. If an actor does four roles, the "count" starts over and they get paid the basic session fee again.

Not all actors can double. Some are hired for their one wonderful voice and can't really do a few lines as Man #1 or the Policeman in Scene 22. But to the extent possible, the voice director will have the show's regulars cover other roles, then hire as many other actors as necessary to fill out the cast.

After the actors are booked, everyone gathers at the specified time at a recording studio and the real work begins.

2. Voice actors work from scripts that contain all of the dialogue but little, if any, description of the visuals. Each line is numbered. Sometimes, they may be shown a storyboard or other artwork, especially if the episode contains a new character whose voice must be invented.

The director assigns roles and explains the action. He tells the actors what their characters are doing when they go, "Yow" or whatever. He takes them through the script and may have them read it aloud once or twice. (On certain shows with certain actors, there is a value to not doing this. You let them read it the first time with tape rolling, just in case magic happens. Actors have been known to do things on a first read that they cannot replicate once they know what they're doing.)

Actors will usually mark their scripts as the director explains things. They all have their own mysterious codes and symbols. Don Messick, who is unparalleled at switching voices and playing nine people talking to each other, carries an array of colored markers. He'll highlight one character's lines in yellow, another's in green and so on.

3. The actors are placed at individual microphones in a studio. Each has a few pages of script spread out on a music stand before them. It's not a good idea to have the actors turning pages during a recording. Good takes have been ruined by the sound of paper rustling.

4. The director, who sits outside the booth at a console by the engineer, will designate a sequence to be recorded. He'll say, for instance, "Let's do lines 1 through 20 this take." The engineer will roll tape and then slate, meaning that he'll record some information to identify the sequence. He might say, "This is [Name of episode], take one, lines 1 through 20." This will help him locate the proper takes when it comes time to edit.

5. The actors will perform their lines in sequence. If someone makes a mistake, the director will stop them and either start over or try to find a natural place in the dialogue to restart.

6. Once the take is done, the director may give them comments and do it again several times. Then he may do pick-ups of individual lines. Once he's

satisfied that he has at least one good take of every line, he will designate which ones to use. He might tell an assistant, "Let's use 1 through 10 from the second take and 11 through 20 from take three, except that I want to edit in the pick-up of line 15 from take four." Later, the editor — sometimes working with the director, sometimes off the notes — will assemble all this accordingly.

And that's pretty much it. The "gang" method is generally preferred to the system where the actors are recorded separately. Actors like working with other actors. They draw energy and inspiration from one another and the result is usually a more natural flow. Also, this way, the actors have a bit more control over the timing of the dialogue and the pauses between speeches (although even then, the editors may later shorten or lengthen these pauses to suit the animation).

Baby Winfield, better known as Jack Mercer. The future voice of Popeye the Sailor, began performing with his family as a baby.

JACK MERCER:
A CAREER OVERVIEW

JACK'S EARLY YEARS

Born on January 13, 1909, some folks, such as Jack Mercer (who was also known as Winfield Mercer during his younger years), are natural-born entertainers and an examination of Mercer's family lineage shows sometimes it seems to run in the blood. His parents and aunt performed as part of a troupe that appeared regularly at the Palace Theater in New York in the 1910s and 1920s. Besides acting, his father performed as an acrobat and created the sets for the troupe's shows.

Jack, whose family performed as a repertory company (consisting of Jack, his mother, father, aunt and grandmother), first appeared on stage as an infant. In order to get Baby Winfield to cry on cue a pinch was applied to his posterior! Eventually, a bit from Jack's act, in which he stood up on a chair and conducted the show's orchestra, caught the eye of a Hollywood talent agent who wanted to sign Jack to a contract. Jack's uncle intervened via his desire to preserve both his family and the troupe.

Stock characters, such as ingénues and heavies, were added and, after years of performing melodramatic works, the family settled in New York City and became part of the local vaudeville scene, performing in theaters throughout the RKO-Keith chain. As Jack was growing up, his parents became concerned about the unstable nature of employment opportunities afforded to those in the performing arts and suggested that he consider another line of work. Taking his parents' advice to heart, Jack attended art school, but soon dropped out. He then found work with a company manufacturing lace curtains, yet this was also short-lived due to economic hardship on behalf of his employer, Meyer Kiel of the William Becker Studio. Jack, however, received a strong letter of recommendation, which read:

To Whom It May Concern,

The average letter of recommendation is a stilted form given to an ex-employee as a matter of routine. Here is an unusual case and this is written solely for the purpose of calling to your attention the value of the services Mr. Jack Mercer as an apprentice artist. He is skillful in his execution of his work, is

versatile and certainly earnest and faithful. Economic necessity was the only reason for his dismissal and he leaves our
employ with our best wishes and with the hope that a proper
opening will present itself real soon.

Meyer Kiel
William Becker Studio
January 26, 1932

THE FLEISCHER STUDIOS

Jack Mercer explained to animation historian G. Michael Dobbs in 1977
how his next career change occurred. "I was in show business, of course, my
whole family was in show business, and they wanted me to do something else. I
could draw a little bit, and my mother had an agent who booked her vaudeville
act, and he was acquainted with someone at Paramount who suggested I go to
the Fleischer Studios and see if I could get some type of work drawing."

The Fleischer Studios was an American corporation which originated as an
animation studio, located at 1600 Broadway, New York. It was founded in 1921
by brothers, Max and Dave Fleischer, who ran the company from its inception.
The company had its start when Max Fleischer invented the Rotoscope, which
allowed for extremely lifelike animation. Using the Rotoscope, the Fleischer
brothers got a contract with Bray Studio in 1919. The brothers' first cartoon
series was *Out of the Inkwell,* which featured Koko the Clown. The Inkwell
series became so successful it gave the brothers the confidence they needed to
open their own studio.

Jack Mercer recalled to G. Michael Dobbs, "When I first started I was in
the opaque department. I went through all the various departments, the inking department, the in-betweening department. I enjoyed it. I hadn't done any
professional drawing before that. It was just on my own." Gordon Sheehan,
who was also employed with the Fleischer Studios, recalled to animation historian Leonard Kohl, "Jack showed me how to paint cels. We both got promoted
to the tracing department and then we both got promoted to the in-betweening department."

One of the Fleischer Studios' best-known creations was Betty Boop, who
animator Grim Natwick modeled after Helen Kane, a famous singer who also
performed as an actress for Paramount Pictures. Natwick originally made Betty
as an animal, in this case, a French poodle. She was redesigned by Natwick in
1932 to be human for the cartoon, *Any Rags.* With her overt sexuality, Betty was
a hit with theater audiences.

Fleischer Studios historian and author, Leslie Cabarga recalled Elzie Segar's
Thimble Theatre comic strip had been a favorite of Max's. Max thought he could

A photo of a young Jack Mercer from his time performing in vaudeville.

do something with this, what he called a "nutty little creature." The "nutty little creature" Max was referring to was Popeye the Sailor, who made his comic strip debut on January 17, 1929. Max met with a Mr. Gortatowsky of King Features Syndicate, who owned the rights to the comic strip and said, "I want to make a cartoon of your Popeye."

"Out of that ugly looking thing?" Gortatowsky asked.

"The funnier he looks, the better the cartoon will be," Max replied.

Popeye made his animation debut with his girlfriend Olive Oyl (who had appeared in the comic strip since its debut in 1919) and bearded bully, Bluto (first appearing in the strip in 1932) in a Betty Boop entry, *Popeye the Sailor* (1933). Popeye's original voice was provided by William Costello, known profession-

Jack Mercer and his family performed as a repertory company eventually becoming part of the New York City vaudeville scene.

ally as "Red Pepper Sam." Due to the overwhelming success of the *Popeye the Sailor* cartoon, the sailor's own series shortly began production. Costello found himself enjoying a good income and recognition. Success went directly to his head and he became impossible to work with. When he demanded a vacation in mid-production, he was fired. The search for a new voice began, while other actors supplied Popeye's voice for a few films.

Jack Mercer recalls how he got the job as Popeye's voice: "I was imitating various characters in the inking department just out of my own amusement, and everybody seemed to get a laugh out of it. And a lot of people suggested

I try out for the Popeye voice. I didn't know they were looking for anyone. So I eventually went home, and tried to improve the voice I was doing. So I finally got the voice after I practiced a while. I thought I could really do the voice and got the quality I was after. I gave an audition over the phone to someone at Paramount. They heard it and from then on they said, 'Why don't you come over and do some voices.' Which I did. Sort of a breaking-in period, I guess.

A check issued to Winfield (Jack) Mercer for services rendered as an artist for the Fleischer Studios dated May 20, 1932.

They told me I was going to do the Popeye voice. That's how it started. You know, fooling around while I was working at other jobs."

The Fleischer Studios issued a contract to Jack Mercer on April 24, 1935, which read, in part,

> Mr. Winfield Mercer
> 142 West 75th Street
> New York City
>
> My Dear Mr. Mercer:
>
> We are glad to be able to tell you that your services are now engaged for a period of one (1) year from this date, at a salary of $25.00 weekly for the first six months of the year and $30.00 weekly for the following six months of the year. This salary to be paid to you at the end of each week in which you actually render services for our company. You will do artwork in our studios pursuant to our instructions and do such other work, as we shall call upon you to do.
>
> We have observed the quality of your voice and we believe that it can be developed and used as to be of service in the

making of recordings for our cartoons. We shall be glad to test your voice and make reasonable efforts to adapt it for our purposes, and if found feasible, we shall use it at our option and we shall see to it that for every recording in which you represent the voice of Popeye and of other characters, or of Popeye alone, you will receive the sum of $50.00 per cartoon. Should we call upon you to record the voice exclusively of characters other than Popeye, we shall see to it that you receive as compensation the sum of $25.00 per cartoon. You can readily understand that we can not make such arrangements with you unless you agree for a period of a year from the date of this letter to make such recordings at our request and not to use your voice commercially in any way except

A letter dated April 11, 1935 from The National City Bank of New York Compound Interest Department Times Square Branch authorizing Winfield (Jack) Mercer to open a joint account with Max Fleischer.

with our permission and subject to our instructions. Unless
such an agreement is made, it will be impossible to give you
the opportunity of making recordings for our cartoons.

While William Costello's Popeye voice was gruff sounding, Mercer's was
gentler, yet strong when it had to be. His Popeye voice gave greater dimension
and versatility to the character. Mercer's voice soon grew hoarse from the strain
of imitating Popeye and he was plied with candies and soda to soothe his over-
extended vocal chords. Soon, Mercer grew accustomed to providing the one-
eyed sailor's voice that, already, was Paramount Pictures most popular animated
star at the box office.

Mercer's first Popeye cartoon was Fleischer Studios' *King of the Mardi Gras*
(1935). Leslie Cabarga, author of *The Fleischer Story* (Nostalgia Press, 1976),
had the following to say regarding the switch from William Costello to Jack
Mercer: "It's hard to say whether Costello had the intellect Mercer obviously
possessed, that allowed him to make all those witty asides and to go into the
story department in later years. As for Costello, we can only surmise that the
inability to recognize that success had gone to his head (as Mae Questel com-
mented to me), and the absence of any subsequent fame (that any of us know
of) is an indication that Costello might not have had Mercer's staying power. It
certainly does seem as if fate moved to make Mercer the voice of Popeye."

Mercer recalled his relationship with Max and Dave Fleischer, "Dave was
always kidding around. Very jolly. I had no conflict with him at all as far I can
remember. It was always sort of a happy family. As far as I was concerned I was
working for Dave and Lou Fleischer and the animators. Max was always in the
front office. I very seldom saw him. He was always engaged in some innova-
tion for the studio, the technical end of the things, inventing machines like the
turntable for dimensional effects, things like that.* Every once in a while I'd run
into Max and say 'hello.' So as I say I knew very little about him. He invited me
out once to dinner in Miami when he got his new home. I guess that's the only
social event I could think of outside of appearing at the parties. Sometimes he'd
come in and look at a picture or sit in on a recording session or something like
that. He was like the godfather, though. If you had any troubles, you'd go to him
and he straightened them out."

Often by Jack's side in the recording room during this period was actress and
voice artist, Mae Questel. Born in New York City on September 13, 1908, she
won a talent contest at the age of 17 and began performing in vaudeville. She

---

* The "turntable" device was used to create three-dimensional backgrounds in the Fleischer cartoons
using miniature models. This process can be seen to great effect in the following Fleischer cartoons:
Little Swee'pea (1936), *Learn Polikeness* (1937), *Popeye the Sailor Meets Sindbad the Sailor* (1936) and
House Cleaning Blues (1937), among others.

was spotted by Max Fleischer, who was on the look out for an actress to replace the current voice of Betty Boop. Questel's Betty Boop voice was performed in a style similar to Helen Kane, who the sexy animated character was modeled after. She began providing her familiar Olive Oyl voice as early as the Fleischer Studios *I Eats My Spinach* (1933). She often said she based Olive's voice on that of actress ZaSu Pitts.

The most memorable aspect of the Fleischer Studios *Popeye* series was the constant ad-libbing by both Mercer and Questel. Leslie Cabarga recalled, "Much of the dialogue was mumbled by the characters through closed lips. The creativity of Mercer and Questel added to the confusion. They delighted in trying to improve upon the script as they rehearsed, and they ad-libbed like crazy during the recording."

Some of Mercer's memorable ad-libs, spoken where Popeye's lips are closed, include the following:

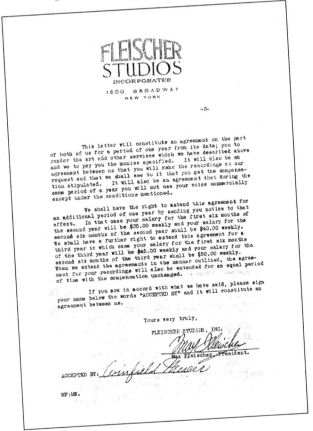

Page two of a contractual agreement letter signed by Max Fleischer, President of the Fleischer Studios, and Jack Mercer for art and recording services from the mid-1930s.

What-No Spinach? (1936) Popeye goes into Bluto's diner to eat. The menu is on Wimpy's shirt (Wimpy is the hamburger moocher from Segar's *Thimble Theatre* comic strip), and it begins with the heading, "Menu" at the very top. As Popeye reads Wimpy's shirt, he mutters, "Menu? I don't want any of that."

Hold the Wire (1936) As Bluto is stomping on Popeye's hands, the sailor holds on for dear life on a telephone wire. Olive screams for him to get his spinach! Popeye mutters, "I never thought of that!"

The Twister Pitcher (1937) After eating a can of spinach, which Bluto filled with grass, Popeye's facial expression twists and turns and he mutters, "This stuff is cut I think."

Proteck the Weakerest (1937) Olive Oyl asks Popeye to walk her dog, Fluffy, which he is embarrassed to do. As the sailor is walking, what he refers to as a "puny mutt," Popeye mutters, "You don't look any dorg to me. You look like a chip-monkey. You see, you're an anemic dog and I like bloodhounds. Pekinese is weak in the knees and I don't like these, ya sees."

Hospitaliky (1937) Popeye and Bluto try to get themselves injured to land in the hospital near nurse Olive. Popeye, on top of Bluto, pulls out his spinach can! Bluto sees it, knowing Popeye's plan, and mutters, "Ah, git' away." Popeye pries open Bluto's mouth and mutters (the sailor knowing, after all, this is a cartoon), "C'mon open wide, you're going to eat the spinach this time!"

A Date to Skate (1938) Popeye is putting skates on Olive's big feet when she mutters, "How do you play this game?" Popeye's mutters, "Oh, it's just like 'London Bridge is Falling Down.'"

Learn Polikeness (1938) Olive Oyl demands that Popeye learn to become a gentleman like Professor Bluteau. The professor greets the pair at his door and says, "Entrée," to which Popeye mutters, "Entrée? I already 'et, young fella." Later, when the professor asks Popeye to escort Olive up a flight of stairs, Popeye mutters, "She was always able to walk up herself before."

Popeye Meets Ali-Baba and his Forty Thieves (1937) Popeye, Olive and Wimpy are walking on the hot desert sands and Popeye mutters, "I wish there was a boardwalk on this beach … if I had some bread, I'd make a sandwich, if I had a which."

Mercer said in 1977, "There's a difference in the thought of the line when it looks like it's just stuck in rather than actually having been written in."

It was reported in the June 1936 edition of the Fleischer Studios' in-house publication, *Fleischer's Animated News*, "Jack Mercer is now a member of the story department." However, due to standard practice at this time, he did not receive credit on the films as either a voice artist or writer. Mercer recalled what a story session was like while employed at the Fleischer Studios. "What would happen would be if there was one story man or two story men, they would get together and try to get an idea for the character that was assigned to them. Everybody got the chance to do various characters.

"We all didn't just have one character to work with, like Popeye. The writer would try to get a synopsis, write that down, and send it to be accepted by the directors who were going to direct the picture. Lots of times they'd all get together, and decide if they wanted to do the story or not. If they didn't like it, you'd try to get another angle, and as soon as they accepted one, then you'd go back and 'gag' the synopsis. Then you'd have to draw it up in storyboards. You'd have meetings with the director, and sometimes the animators would come in, and we'd all discuss the material; if it's funny or not, if it was too long, all sorts of problems. Then, after it was accepted, as far as we were concerned it would leave the room, and we would try to get another angle on another character. Also, we were asked to try to create characters. Now, with the Fleischers, they seemed to be interested in characters with some various capabilities; capabilities different

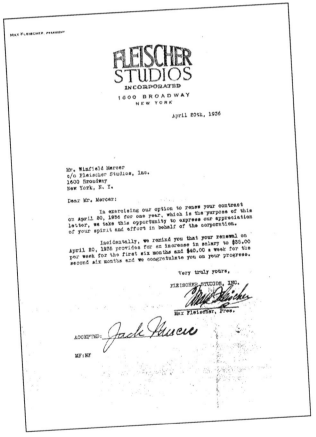

A letter dated April 20, 1936 from the Fleischer Studios exercising the studio's option to renew Mercer's contract and expressing their "appreciation for your spirit and effort in behalf of the corporation." By this time, Mercer was signing his name as Jack rather than Winfield.

than usual characters. For instance, a ghost that could walk through things."

The Fleischer Studios *Popeye* cartoons continued to be a great success and the sailor often beat Mickey Mouse at the box office. A turning point for the artists of the *Popeye* animated shorts occurred in July of 1935 when the Wagner Labor Relations Act (a.k.a. the National Labor Relations Act) was passed into law as one of Franklin Delano Roosevelt's New Deal initiatives. Its passage

Jack Mercer's rendition of Popeye the Sailor Man. Before being hired as the voice of the sailor, he was an artist for the Fleischer Studios.

reinforced the protections of collective bargaining that had been detailed in the defunct National Industry Recovery Act. Spurred by the passage of the WLRA into law in August of 1937, 100 employees of the Fleischer Studios announced they had formed an alliance with the Commercial Artists and Designers Union (CADU) in an attempt to resolve workplace grievances, such as 45-hour, six-day workweeks and a lack of sick or paid vacation time. The employees filed a complaint against the Fleischers after their demands fell upon deaf ears. Soon thereafter, the 100 unionized Fleischer Studios employees went on strike.

Mercer recalled to animation historian G. Michael Dobbs how the strike affected him. "During the strike I was working in the story department, and that was sort of a section all by itself, you might say, and I didn't associate with the others. I didn't notice anything. You see, with the storywriters, we were just one big happy group. It was only the attitude of the opaquers and the inkers that might have been different. As far as I was concerned I didn't notice

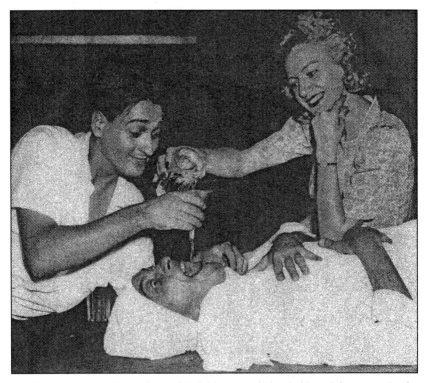

An often reprinted publicity photo of Jack Mercer and Margie Hines (who gave voice for Olive Oyl in the Fleischer Studios Popeye cartoons produced in Miami and the early Famous Studios shorts) pouring water down Pinto Colvig's mouth to create the special gurgling sounds needed for the sea sequences in Gulliver's Travels *(Fleischer Studios, 1939). Little is known regarding Jack Mercer's marriage to Margie Hines suffice it to say it was short-lived and he found later happiness with his second wife, Virginia. Photo from the book,* The Fleischer Story, *courtesy of its author, Leslie Cabarga.*

A drawing of the Fleischer Studios version of Popeye the Sailor, addressed to "Paul and Craig from Jack Mercer."

everything. I did have once incident as one day they asked everyone in there to pitch in and help any way they could. The people on the picket line used to take the pictures of people going into the studio, and threaten you. One night I was going home on the subway and some strange looking characters sat down on the other side of me. There wasn't anyone else in the car at the time, so I felt perhaps they were trying to intimidate me in some way. It was very funny. These two fellows would come in and sit on either side of me. At the station before the one at which I usually got off, I got off the train real fast and left them sitting there! The door closed, and the train went on. That's the way I got rid of them. Maybe it was just my imagination, I don't know. That and the fact they would harass you as you entered and left at work, and that they would take a photo of you going past their picket line."

In 1938, the Fleischers announced the studio would be moving to Miami,

A studio portrait of Jack Mercer.

Florida in order to both capitalize on a law passed by the Florida State Legislature that granted tax-exempt status to motion picture studios within the state for several years and to produce feature-length-animated films. Another benefit for the studio was the anti-union atmosphere prevalent throughout the state and promoted by its government; thus its employees would be less likely to go on strike. Mercer was initially hesitant to relocate, but decided to make the move. Once production began on the Popeye cartoons in Miami, the films took on a brighter appearance. When produced in New York, the backgrounds looked gritty and run down, which became a trademark of the series.

Mae Questel didn't make the move to Miami and she was replaced as both the voice of Betty Boop and Olive Oyl by Margie Hines (also referred to as Heinz). Mercer and Hines fell in love and married, but precious little is known about the relationship. Virginia (Carroll) Mercer, who married Jack in the summer of 1953, recalled many years later, "*The National Enquirer* asked if Jack had ever been married before and he turned white. I explained that it was a painful part of his life and we'd appreciate it if they not mention it in their article and they obliged." Virginia Mercer remembered the marriage took place after the Fleischer Studios moved to Florida and ended immediately after Jack's return from the Army, October 1945.

Mercer said that after the move to Florida many new faces joined the studio and gave it sort of a "Disneyland" atmosphere. He said, "All of those guys were crazy, and they brought a bit of Hollywood to Miami. I suppose that's why people thought it was all a party and I suppose there was, but I didn't get involved with it."

While in Miami Mercer voiced the character of King Little (and other incidental characters) in the Fleischer Studios first animated feature film, *Gulliver's Travels* (1939). He went on to provide the voices for both Mr. Bumble and Swat the Fly in the studio's second animated feature, *Mr. Bug Goes to Town* (1942). He was billed as the third voice performer for Mr. Bumble and fifth for Swat the Fly in the opening credits. With the *Popeye* film, *Fleets of Stren'th*

A cartoon of Jack Mercer and his new bride Virginia Carroll from the staff of Famous Studios, dated July 24, 1953.

(Fleischer, 1942), Mercer began getting an on-screen writing credit (along with his co-writers who, at various times, included Dan Gordon, Jack Ward, I. Klein and Carl Meyer). Change was in the air at the Fleischer Studios. The *Betty Boop* series was dropped shortly after the studio moved to Miami. Attempts to create another successful series included the *Stone Age* series and *Gabby*, who was a main character in *Gulliver's Travels*. Nothing jelled with movie audiences until the Fleischers began work on the *Superman* animated series. Though extremely popular, the cartoons were in production at a time when brothers Max and Dave were barely on speaking terms. Their conflicts and the failure of *Mr. Bug Goes to Town* at the box office, led Paramount Pictures to take over the Fleischer Studios, renaming it Famous Studios and moving everyone back to New York in 1942.

FAMOUS STUDIOS

The *Popeye* series continued with Famous Studios and others were added including *Little Lulu*, *Screen Songs* and *Noveltoons*. The *Noveltoons* featured films which, if the characters were successful enough, would branch out in to their own series. One of the break-out characters was Herman the Mouse, who would later team with Katnip in the long-running, *Herman and Katnip* series.

Popeye (Jack Mercer) has his boat snagged by a pirate ship in Popeye and the Pirates *(Famous Studios, 1947). Mercer was not in favor of changing Popeye's uniform in the* Famous Studios *cartoons.*

Mercer was not only co-writing (or entirely writing) animated cartoons featuring Popeye, but many others produced by Famous Studios during this period. As Virginia Mercer recalled, "When Jack was no longer with the Fleischers, people called for Jack to redo others' work and freelance. They referred to Jack as the 'story doctor.' I don't remember who said that. While Jack was still with the studio [Famous], they were looking for new characters that might develop into a series. Jack wrote a story about an Italian mouse, made him a chef and since he was an Italian chef, Jack had him singing. Jack wrote a song for him to sing. They asked Jack to do the voice and sing the song. Now, the last thing that's done is the music. Musicians were on strike and Winston Sharples [who composed the music for Paramount's animated cartoon productions] asked Jack to play the background music! So Jack had to rent an accordion and practiced all weekend. Jack had had an accordion but gave it away when we bought a piano. Later, someone wanted a story that included Penguins in the North Pole. I dropped off the story on my way to work and the producers (I don't remember whom) said, 'I wanted the penguin in the North Pole.' He was very disappointed that Jack had put him in the Antarctic. I said, 'If Jack says they aren't in the North, then they aren't,' and off I went!"

When Jack Mercer was in the Armed Service, Famous Studios got others to fill in as Popeye's voice, most notably Harry Welch, whose rendition was heard during the fight scene at the end of 1946's *Rocket to Mars*. Mercer's Popeye was heard prior to this climatic battle. Virginia Mercer remembered, "Jack did many of the Popeyes while in the army. The studio saved them until he got home on furlough. When he was overseas, that was different." Though not the Popeye voice during this period when Jack was overseas, his lines were often dubbed in while Welch and others were doing the primary Popeye vocals. For example, in *The Island Fling* (Famous Studios, 1947), Popeye pulls out a treasure chest, pours the contents on the floor and, in Mercer's voice, says, "Gee thanks for the tip pal."

For the record, the non-Jack Mercer-voiced *Popeye* films during this period were:

> *Shape Ahoy* (1945) Mae Questel (with a mechanically-controlled raised voice) is rumored to be the voice of Popeye in this cartoon.
>
> *For Better or Nurse* (1945) Harry Welch.
>
> *House Tricks* (1946) Unknown performer, possibly Harry Welch or Mae Questel.
>
> *Service With a Guile* (1946) Unknown performer, possibly Harry Welch or Mae Questel.

Klondike Casanova (1946) Harry Welch.

Peep in the Deep (1946) Unknown performer, possibly Harry Welch or Mae Questel.

Rocket to Mars (1946) Begins with Jack Mercer, ends with Harry Welch.

Rodeo Romeo (1946) Harry Welch.

The Fistic Mystic (1946) Harry Welch.

The Island Fling (1946) Harry Welch.

Abusement Park (1946) Harry Welch.

As for Mercer's service in the army, Virginia Mercer recalled, "As for the army, when they learned of Jack's background they offered him the USO. He said no, he trained with these guys and he was going on with them. He was in the Signal Corps. He altered his own uniform to fit and did many things to make life comfortable for his buddies. Jack Mercer entered the Army on August 4, 1943 and was discharged on October 21, 1945."

With Famous Studios in New York, Mae Questel returned to providing the voice for Olive Oyl, but a new voice for Bluto was needed. For a long period, the bully had different voices, with Mercer filling in on occasion, but he found switching back from Popeye to Bluto difficult. Jackson Beck, born on July 23, 1912 in Manhattan, was an American actor who had a radio, television and animation career dating back to 1931 with *Myrt and Marge*. In 1943 he became the narrator for radio's *Superman* series; it was Beck who intoned the famous prologue, "Strange visitor from another planet."

In 1966, he would recreate his role as narrator for the *Superman* TV-cartoon series and provide the voice for *Daily Planet* chief, Perry White. Starting with 1944's *Anvil Chorus Girl* for Famous Studios, Beck began a long association with Popeye, providing the voice of Bluto. Beck told animation historian Leonard Kohl in 1998, "I miss doing Popeye cartoons and I miss Popeye himself, Jack Mercer. He was marvelous! He did a great job at it - there's nobody else that can imitate him as an entertainer, he was an absolute wonder!" Beck confirmed that Jack Mercer was very shy and, unlike other actors voicing a popular character, he didn't make it readily known or ham it up in public. Beck said, "Oh my gosh, you have no idea! He was anything but a ham. He was so quiet and self-effacing. I had to talk for him and say, 'For heaven's sake, you're the star of this piece!'"

Beck recalled how a typical recording session was done. "Somebody would tell us what the heck is happening and generally it was Jack because he wrote the stories. So he'd say, remember this scene, this and this is happening and we'd say, okay and we'd play it that way. We'd do what had to be done to fit the picture that was coming. They were smart, they did us first [record the soundtrack dialogue] and then the pictures, so that the lips would synch more or less."

New Popeye cartoons were released by Paramount Pictures throughout the 1950s with Mercer's name appearing as co-writer or sole writer. The sole writing credit increased from 1955 to the end of the series in mid-1957 not only on the *Popeye* series but other Paramount animated theatrical films. Famous Studios became known as Paramount Cartoon Studios in October of 1956. Paramount, in need of a cash infusion, sold the Fleischer/Famous Studios Popeye cartoon

A letter from Sam Buchwald of Famous Studios (successor to the Fleischer Studios) sent to Private Jack Mercer, while he was in the armed services, dated December 23, 1943. Note, according to the letter, other Famous Studios personnel were in the service and Mercer was still married to Margie Hines. The letter indicates the completion of the first Little Lulu *cartoon,* Eggs Don't Bounce, *which Jack Mercer co-wrote with Carl Meyer and Jack Ward.*

While Jack Mercer was providing voices for two cartoon series for television in 1960 (Popeye and Felix the Cat), Jackson Beck (center) was doing the same, providing the voice of King Leonardo for the lion's self-titled Saturday morning series, in addition to his voice work on the made-for-TV Popeye series. Veteran voice artists Allen Swift (left) provided the voice of Itchy Brother while Kenny Delmar (right) gave The Hunter his Southern drawl.

library to television distributor Associated Artists Productions in 1956. While this changing of the guard was going on, Mercer continued to be busy with non-Popeye productions at Paramount, probably thinking his voice association with the sailor was at an end.

THE TELEVISION YEARS

While continuing to work for Paramount Cartoon Studios as voice artist and writer, opportunities in the fairly new medium of television came Jack's way. Felix the Cat was an incredibly popular star of silent animated cartoons produced by Pat Sullivan. Felix's heyday was during the 1920s, but he was still visible in comic books and a newspaper comic strip by the late 1950s. Joe Oriolo, who worked with both the Fleischer and Famous Studios, gained the rights to Felix the Cat and, with distribution by Trans-Lux, planned a new cartoon series for the feline specifically for television. Many talented craftsmen, employed by both Fleischer and Famous, were hired and began working on these television productions. Jack Mercer was hired to provide all of the voices in the entire

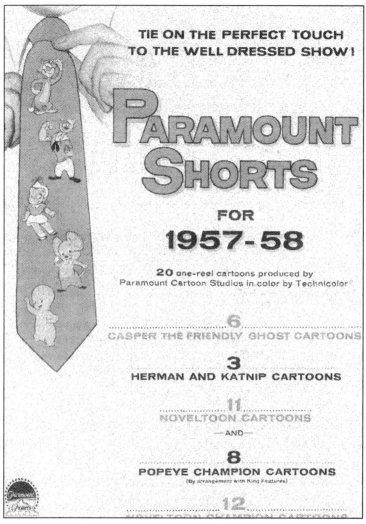

Trade ad announcing the completion of cartoon shorts for theatre distribution from Paramount Pictures for the 1957-58 season. Whether providing his vocal talents or writing skills, Jack Mercer was involved with the production of the films featuring the cartoon figures illustrated on the necktie: Katnip, Popeye, Lil' Audrey, Herman the Mouse, and Casper the Friendly Ghost.

series, which consisted of cliffhanger adventures, so they could be aired separately or as a two-part adventure. *Felix the Cat* was one of the earliest cartoon series made in color. Oriolo introduced new characters for Felix to become involved. These included the bookish but super intelligent Poindexter, who had an IQ of 222, Rock Bottom, a bumbling canine criminal and prankster, The Master Cylinder, King of the Moon and The Professor, who was after Felix's magic bag of tricks. The magic bag of tricks could shift into anything Felix needed. Production began during the very end of the 1950s through the early 1960s (one cartoon has Felix receiving a letter with a 1962 postmark). These cartoons turned out to be incredibly popular and widely syndicated. Many stations quickly renewed the films after their initial contract. In the November 4, 1964 edition of *Variety* an article read:

WFAA-TV Likes 'Felix' At Least Till 1971

Trans-Lux Television reports WFAA-TV, Dallas has renewed its pact for 260 "Felix the Cat" cartoons through 1971 and will telecasting the kidvid skein in tint.

In 1993, Donald Oriolo, editor and publisher of *The New Adventures of Felix and Friends* comic book, noted the similarities between the *Felix the Cat* and *Popeye* cartoon series. "First of all the voice of Popeye and Bluto and many other Popeye characters were performed by super-dooper voice-over artist, Jack Mercer. Jack also did all the voices in the *Felix the Cat* series, i.e., Felix, The Professor, Rock Bottom, Poindexter, Va-voom, Martian the Martian and The Master Cylinder. The scripts for both series were also written by many of the same writers. The incredible Popeye music was written, arranged and conducted by my personal hero, Winston ('Win') Sharples! And...yeah, you guessed it, he also wrote, arranged and conducted all of the Felix music. This explains the very similar pacings of the two series. The most interesting reason as to why there is something similar between Popeye and the Felix cartoons, animators! That's right, most of the animators that worked on the Felix series, also worked together at the Max Fleischer Studios in Florida and that's where the Popeye cartoons were produced with animators like Dave Tendler, Frank Endes, Steve Maffati, Rube Grossman, Grim Natwick and Joe Oriolo! What a team! I guess you could say that Popeye is actually a distant relative of our favorite feline, Felix the Cat!"

Don Oriolo recalled in an April 2006 interview, "My father went through tons of actors before selecting Jack; however, I think he always had him in mind as his first choice. They worked together at Fleischer Studios." When asked if it was Joe Oriolo's idea to have Mercer record all the voices in the series (which was unusual at this time), Don Oriolo recalled, "Yes, he asked Jack to try a Professor, which he liked. Rock Bottom was kind of like Bluto. Poindexter was recorded at 7 ½ ips and played back at 15. I ran the recorder (I was 12); we recorded all voices in the hallway of my father's studio." Though Mercer stated much later he found it difficult to voice one character and go right to the next without a break, Don Oriolo stated, "Jack switched back and forth seamlessly."

The popularity of the *Felix the Cat* cartoon series inspired a lot of merchandise, including Lido's cartoon character-inking stamp sets featuring both the Popeye and Felix the Cat characters. The *Felix the Cat* cartoons aired on local stations into the mid-1970s.

Mercer also began a writing stint on the *Deputy Dawg* cartoon series for Terrytoons. The character of Deputy Dawg was a deputy sheriff in the Mississippi bayous of the United States. Much of the comedy was based around comical accents and stereotypical southern characteristics. The half-hour cartoon series enjoyed a long run, including local syndication beginning in 1960, theatrical showings and a Saturday morning half-hour during the 1971-72 season on NBC.

Mercer worked again for producer Joe Oriolo in the early 1960s, providing voices in the initial television cartoons for *The Mighty Hercules* series, which began their syndicated run in 1963. Mercer voiced Hercules' half-human, half-horse pal, Newton, the evil wizard Deadalus and incidental characters. Mercer left the series after a little more than a half-dozen episodes. While no reason has been given for his short-stint on the series, one could guess, after providing multiple voices on the *Felix the Cat* series, he may possibly had wanted to get away from a constant shift of his vocal inflections.

Throughout the 1960s, Mercer's writing skills were being aired on television and movie screens via *Deputy Dawg* and *Popeye*. The muscle-bound sailor man's adventures were widely syndicated on television with a steady re-release of the

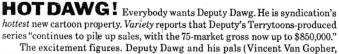

HOT DAWG! Everybody wants Deputy Dawg. He is syndication's *hottest* new cartoon property. *Variety* reports that Deputy's Terrytoons-produced series "continues to pile up sales, with the 75-market gross now up to $850,000."

The excitement figures. Deputy Dawg and his pals (Vincent Van Gopher, Li'l Whooper, Muskie and others) were created for the special delight of television audiences and advertisers (Lay's Potato Chips is sponsoring Deputy in dozens of Southern markets). Then there's a merchandising bonanza: Deputy Dawg apparel, comics, records, games, toys, books available from Grosset & Dunlap, RCA Victor, Dell Publishing, Ideal Toy Corporation and other licensees.

Better order your 26 Deputy Dawg half-hours today. Because, take it from us, he's *hot!* For details, call or write to the nearest office of... © **CBS FILMS**

"...the best film programs for all stations."
Sales offices in New York, Los Angeles, Chicago,
San Francisco, St. Louis, Detroit, Atlanta,
Dallas, Boston. In Canada: S.W. Caldwell Ltd.

A trade ad published on October 19, 1960 promoting the success of Deputy Dawg. *Jack Mercer was involved with writing episodes of the series.*

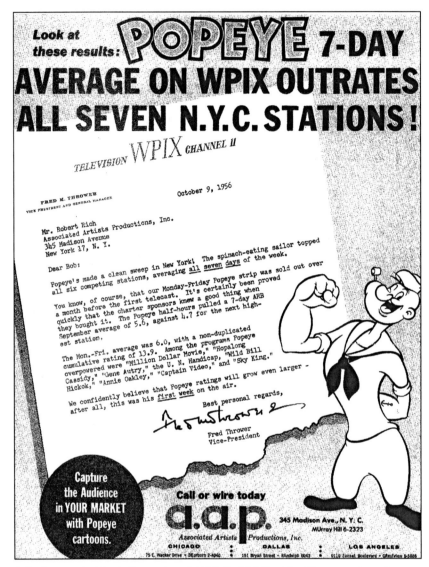

Debuting on television in September of 1956, the 234 theatrical Popeye cartoons became a smash hit on television. Local stations across the country ran the films either alone or with an adult-hosted format for several years. Associated Artists Productions, Inc. initially syndicated the Fleischer/Famous Studios films.

Famous Studios theatricals to movie theaters. In addition, Mercer's scripts for animated films, produced by Paramount Cartoon Studios, were screened in theaters and television via Mattel Toy's *Funday Funnies* on the ABC network beginning in 1959. The Paramount theatricals moved to the *New Casper Cartoon Show* on the ABC network in 1963 and settled in for a long run on Saturday mornings until 1969.

JACK MERCER'S POPEYE REUNION

While Mercer's was juggling his voice work for TV-cartoons and writing scripts for Paramount Cartoon Studios, he also recorded several children's albums and 45s as the voice of the Popeye characters. With the smashing success the 234 theatrical *Popeye* films were having on television since September of 1956, the sailor and his crew were found everywhere and on anything. Store shelves were lined with Popeye items and virtually every local television market aired the theatrical films, alone or with a host. King Features Syndicate, while owing the rights to the Popeye characters, did not have any financial involvement with syndication of the animated cartoons. King Features Syndicate decided to cash in on the Popeye hysteria by hiring executive producer Al Brodax, who commissioned five animation studios to crank out 220 new *Popeye* cartoons which the Syndicate would control.

One would think with Jack Mercer, Mae Questel and Jackson Beck, still quite active, they would be hired immediately to reprise their old roles (though Bluto was now called Brutus). Jackson Beck recalled to animation historian Leonard Kohl that he, Questel and Mercer were not happy with the proposed contracts for them. According to Beck, King Features Syndicate went behind their backs to find replacement voices, but it didn't work. As Beck said, "So we went to war with them and they auditioned everybody in California to try and replace us, and they couldn't. Finally, after a heck of a lot of blood, sweat and tears, we got the money back to where it ought to be, not all the way, but close enough and we did the whole series."

Beck recalled how a recording session went for these Popeye TV-cartoons, produced from 1960 through 1961 (though a very few have a copyright date of 1962). "When we'd do the Popeye cartoons, I'd figure it's going to take a half an hour, an hour, an hour and fifteen minutes and then I'm out of here. We worked fast there. An East Coast producer hired a studio for two days to do seven little cartoons or six the next. So, I said, 'That's too darn long! It's a five-minute thing and we're gonna be through in eight minutes!' He said, 'Oh you can't do it that way!' I said, 'Why not? Try it!' So, he said, 'Well. I'm going to keep the first day, eleven to five o'clock,' and I said, 'I tell ya, we'll be out at one-thirty, and you'll have what you want.' So, we went in there and we were out at one-thirty, a little before one-thirty, we had seven of these things in the can. The producer said, 'We take days to do this!' I said, 'Look, how many lines have I got in this thing? How many lines has Jack got? How many lines has Mae got? We've got four or five lines, really, that's all you ever had in that thing. We'll take two days if you want to take two days and we'll do ten one day and eleven the next. You pick the ones you want to do and we'll do them.' And that's the way we did it. When the producer left, he said, 'I've got to bring this back to the Coast!

I don't know what the heck we're doing wrong out there but this is great stuff!' All the ad-libbing that we did, all the line changes, because they were funnier, you know we always do that. Jack was a writer on this stuff, so he knew what the heck he was doing. This isn't a work of art! We know the lines! We know the characters!"

Mercer, Questel and Beck provided all of the voices for the 220 *Popeye* TV-cartoons, which often led to funny moments in the recording sessions. Beck recalled, "The whole thing was funny! Jack would start to ad-lib and the other two of us would pick it up, you had another picture there. There was a lot of stuff we fell over laughing, you know, but you're doing it one line at a time, the brief exchange, and then out of sequence, and it didn't make any difference. Some of it was written in the studio. There isn't much dialogue in that. He'd say, 'add an 'Uh!' here and a grunt there, and a laugh there,' so you'd do it. Jack Mercer was ad-libbing all the time, so what he ad-libbed was perfect, because, really, he'd written it in the first place. We'd been doing this thing for twelve or fifteen years or however long it was. I knew what I was doing. I knew what Jack was doing. I

For years Jack Mercer worked alongside Mae Questel (who was the voice of Mrs. Portnoy on the album, Mrs. Portnoy's Retort — A Mother Strikes Back). She was a character actress in several films in addition to providing the voices of Betty Boop, Olive Oyl, Swee'pea, The Sea Hag, Winky Dink and Little Audrey for animated cartoons. Mae Questel passed away in 1998 at the age of 89.

Jackson Beck, who passed away in 2004 at the age of 92, voiced Brutus (along with other male characters) for the 1960-61 Popeye TV cartoon series. Of Jack Mercer, Beck said, "Mercer was the most versatile voice man that I knew. If you were short of a sound effect, he'd do it with his voice." Beck said Mercer was "self-effacing and brilliant."

knew what Mae was doing and the same goes for them. They knew that we were doing! So, we'd go in, do our 'shtick' and that's it. You know what you're gonna do, yet, 'Let's go team!'" To this day, critics of these TV Popeyes feel that the best thing about them is the voice work of Jack Mercer, Jackson Beck and Mae Questel.

Virginia Mercer remembered that it was Jack who insisted Jackson Beck resume his role as Popeye's bearded nemesis in the new cartoons. She said, "I do remember that Gene Deitch (one of the suppliers of the new cartoons) had Jack doing Brutus' voice at the first recording [this would be for the 1960 cartoon, *Sea No Evil*]. He was doing two deep voices in addition to Wimpy and it was too much. He wanted Jackson Beck to do it as he usually did. Jack had the utmost respect for Jackson's talent and liked him as a person. So he rebelled and Jackson did the rest. In later years, the Screen Actors Guild permitted no more than three voices by more than one actor or they must receive double payment."

These five-minute cartoons would all be produced in color. This made them a very attractive package for local TV stations having continued success with the black-and-white Fleischer films and the color Famous Studios productions. The studios who worked on the series were Gerald Ray, Jack Kinney, Larry Harmon, Gene Deitch/William Snyder and Paramount Cartoon Studios. With so many different animators involved, the end results of the cartoons were mixed. Some cartoons have excellent animation, others abysmal. Children didn't care, however; they welcomed the new cartoons and ate them up

Virginia Mercer provided me with Jack Mercer's recording schedule for King Features Syndicate's television Popeye cartoons. It confirms Jackson Beck's comment, "Let's go team," as many episodes were recorded in one session:

Many local stations aired both the theatrical and TV Popeye cartoons together, but this trade ad from Variety (published on Popeye's birthday, January 17, 1963) promotes only the success the television episodes were having on WPIX-11. Despite animation ranging from poor to excellent, the TV cartoons were a huge success and children loved them. Critics, to this day, say the voice work of Jack Mercer, Mae Questel and Jackson Beck is the best thing about the films.

1960 POPEYE

Date Recorded	Total	Director
3/8	3	Gene Deitch
3/14	5	Charles Shows (Larry Harmon)
3/15	5	Charles Shows (Larry Harmon)
3/21	7	Jack Kinney
3/22	9	Jack Kinney
3/24	7	Jack Kinney
4/18	5	Ganon/TV Spots (Gerald Ray)
4/19	4	Fennell (Larry Harmon)
4/21	4	Seymour Kneitel (Paramount)
5/5	8	Jack Kinney
5/6	8	Jack Kinney
5/13	4	Gene Deitch
5/16	5	Charles Shows (Larry Harmon)
5/17	5	TV Spots (Gerald Ray)
6/6	2	Seymour Kneitel (Paramount)
6/27	3	Seymour Kneitel (Paramount)
7/11	6	Jack Kinney
7/12	7	Jack Kinney
7/13	7	Jack Kinney
7/14	11	Jack Kinney
7/18	5	Gene Deitch
7/18	4	Seymour Kneitel (Paramount)
8/25	5	Seymour Kneitel (Paramount)
8/31	3	Gene Deitch
9/19	5	Seymour Kneitel (Paramount)
10/17	7	Seymour Kneitel (Paramount)
11/7	7	Jack Kinney
11/8	8	Jack Kinney
11/9	6	Jack Kinney
11/9	6	Seymour Kneitel (Paramount)
12/12	3	Seymour Kneitel (Paramount)
12/13	5	Gene Deitch

1961 POPEYE

Date Recorded	Total	Director
1/12	4	Seymour Kneitel (Paramount)
1/23	6	Seymour Kneitel (Paramount)
2/14	8	Jack Kinney*
	1	Kinney (miscount)
	1	Paramount
3/7	9	Paramount
3/8	4	Rembrant**
4/24	5	Paramount
4/25	2	Rembrant
7/16	1	Rembrant

*According to the copyright date on the Jack Kinney-produced Popeye cartoons they were all produced in 1960. Perhaps, re-recordings needed to be done.

** There is no studio called Rembrant credited on the Popeye TV-cartoons. It is generally assumed Rembrant is associated with the Gene Deitch productions.

To document an example of Popeye's popularity during the 1960s and Mercer's ongoing exposure in the role is, in part, an article from June 10, 1964's *Variety*,

> Popeye's $20,000,000 Gross
> Champ Status as TV Grosser
>
> Popeye cartoons now occupy the Ft. Knox of video cartoon land. The gross of all Popeye cartoons to date is estimated at $20,000,000 with more dollars waiting in the wings as stations ride with renewals. The sailor man who made spinach famous has earned more than any individual cartoon character in television. King Features Syndicate, which has the made-for-TV Popeye version, has grossed some $6,000.000 in syndication. The theatrical version, which began its trek to TV in 1956, and is now, handled by United Artists Television has grossed about $14,000.000. Little did Paramount know in 1933 when it introduced Popeye in a Betty Boop cartoon on an experimental basis that when "boop-boop-a-doop" would become a tinsel echo in time, Popeye would remain as contemporary as the Beatles. Popeye is now being telecast in about 190 U.S. stations in about 170 markets. According to Irwin Ezzes, United Artists Television proxy, the renewal rate on Popeye is roughly 90%, a phenomenal renewal rate in a medium which buries its winners seasonally. King Features Syndicate, which filmed the made-for-TV Popeye version and put them in syndication three years ago, now is hitting the renewal trail. King's Popeyes have been sold to about 125 stations, most of the outlets playing both the theatrical and made-for-TV versions for kiddie viewing. King Features Syndicate, which introduced Popeye as newspaper cartoon series in 1929, and then sold the theatrical cartoon exploitation rights to Paramount, clung to Popeye when it came to making fresh cartoons for TV. As would be expected Popeye not only outgrosses any cartoon series in syndication but both series, theatrical and made-for-TV, account for 454 episodes, the largest number for any one cartoon star.

Virginia Mercer recalled it was the production of these TV Popeyes that made Paramount Pictures appreciate Jack's talent, which had been taken for granted by the studio. She recalled, "Someone asked Jack if Paramount ever showed any appreciation for his talent. He said not until King Features decided to do a whole batch of Popeyes and Paramount wanted to get in on

A photo of Jack Mercer, possibly from the 1960s when both his voice work and writing skills were featured prominently on television.

doing some of the animation.

"Al Brodax had already decided that Jack would do the voice for all the studios. Jack went on to say that he didn't know if Paramount was aware of that but the studio knew he was their boy and that sort of helped them get the job [to animate several of the TV Popeyes]."

Jack Mercer was involved with writing scripts for The Milton the Monster Show, *a Hal Seeger Production which aired on ABC Saturday morning television. Several personnel from Paramount Pictures cartoon staff were involved in the production of this series.*

In addition to the TV-cartoons, Jack Mercer supplied Popeye's voice for a well-animated commercial for Soaky Toys. The clever ad had Popeye and Brutus, not fighting over Olive Oyl, but boasting that each is a Soaky Toy. Soaky Toys were made in the shape of popular cartoon characters of the period.

THE MID-1960S
AND THROUGH THE EARLY 1980S

Jack Mercer worked on scripts for the ABC Saturday morning cartoon series *Milton the Monster*, a Hal Seeger Production which employed several former Famous Studios/Paramount Cartoon Studios animators and writers. Mercer had worked with Hal Seeger before writing a few scripts for his *Out of the Inkwell* TV-cartoon series, which starred Koko the Clown. Milton was a Frankenstein-type creature but with a Gomer Pyle-sounding voice. During his creation, he was given too much "Tenderness" juice, which made him a kind-hearted monster. Milton shared his cartoons with his creator, Professor Weirdo, his henchman, Count Kook, a skeleton named Heebie and a hairy Cyclops called Jeebie. Mercer also was involved with writing scripts for other shorts on this half-hour color production. *Fearless Fly* was a humble insect named Hiram, who gained super powers after wearing atomic-powered eyeglasses. Fearless Fly had a girlfriend, Flora, and battled the oriental villains Dr. Goo Fee and his henchman,

Gung Ho. Other animated segments in the *Milton the Monster* series, which appeared on an alternating basis, were *Penny Penguin*, a somewhat bratty young female pachyderm, *Flukey Luke*, a diminutive cowboy, *Stuffy Durma*, a pint-sized hobo who inherited ten million dollars, and *Muggy Doo*, boy fox. *Milton the Monster*, along with *The New Casper Cartoon Show*, both series Jack Mercer was involved with, were two of the best animated and scripted programs on Saturday morning television during this time. Milton the Monster aired on ABC for two seasons (1965-1967) and was syndicated thereafter.

Bob McFadden, another talented vocal artist who was the voice of the bumbling spy, Cool McCool, worked with Jack Mercer on the Milton the Monster series and the animated special, The Man Who Hated Laughter.

Mercer would reunite with Hal Seeger Productions in 1972 when the studio produced *The Man Who Hated Laughter*, an hour-long segment for *The ABC Saturday Superstar Movie*. Hal Seeger, in association with Jack Zander Productions, gathered several comic strip characters from King Features Syndicate's newspaper comic strips. Amongst the cavalcade of characters featured (many making their animation debuts) were Flash Gordon; The Katzenjammer Kids; Maggie and Jiggs (from the strip *Bringing Up Father*); Blondie & Dagwood; Quincy; Lil' Iodine; The Phantom; Tim Tyler; Mandrake the Magician & Lothar, Mandrake's assistant; Steve Canyon; Beetle Bailey; The Sarge & Otto, Sarge's dog; Snuffy Smith & Snuffy's wife, Loweezy; The Little King; Hi and Lois; Henry; and, of course, Olive Oyl, Brutus, Swee'pea, Wimpy and Popeye. Jack Mercer provided the voices of Popeye and Wimpy, while Bob McFadden (who also was a voice-artist for Hal Seeger's *Milton the Monster* series and provided the voice for *Cool McCool*, an animated detective spoof) voiced other roles in the production. *The Man Who Hated Laughter* (also known as *Popeye Meets The Man Who Hated Laughter*) was rerun in 1973 on ABC. The plot focused on an evil Professor who wanted to rid the world of laughter and aims to accomplish his goal by capturing the comic strip characters. He holds them prisoner on a secret island with Brutus as his henchman. The adventure comic strip heroes find the captured characters. When their departing submarine gets trapped underwater, it's Popeye who saves the day with the help of his spinach!

Jack Mercer recorded Popeye's voice in the mid-1970s for a Dr. Pepper commercial singing, "I'm Popeye the Pepper Man," toot! toot!

It was around this time that Mercer supplied Popeye's voice for a series of educational filmstrips, distributed to schools, called the *People at Work* series. These were produced by King Features Educational Division and were distributed along with a series of comic books where the sailor discusses career options to children.   Mercer also provided Popeye's voice for television commercials, including a musical ad for Dr. Pepper (soda) and Burlington House's Popeye bedspreads and sheets. Mercer also supplied Popeye's voice for the 1972 16mm-color safety film, *Look Where You Are Going*, which featured excellent animation by Myron Waldman, a veteran of both Fleischer and Famous Studios. The safety film was distributed to school systems across the country.

In 1977 the networks were reviving several old cartoon properties for new Saturday morning children's series. Among the characters were *Mr. Magoo*, *Tom and Jerry* and *Mighty Mouse*. Hanna-Barbera, pioneers of cartoon series specially produced for television, signed a deal with King Features Entertainment to bring back Popeye and his crew for yet another series of animated cartoons. As the sailor was now going to appear on the CBS network, rather than in syndication, the violence used so heavily in the past had to be eliminated. To the amazement of many, Jack Mercer and Mae Questel had to audition to resume voicing Popeye and Olive Oyl. Virginia Mercer recalled, "Art Scott [Vice President of Special Projects at the time for Hanna-Barbera] told Jack he sent a script for him to record. Obviously to see that his voice was still up to par [Mercer was in his 70s at this time]. Scott called immediately after hearing the tape and discussed with Jack about writing some of the stories." Questel, however, was not hired to resume her role as Olive Oyl. At the time, Hanna-Barbera stated they wanted a voice similar to the "original" Olive, while Questel said, years later, that she didn't want to make the move to California to record the cartoons.

In June of 1978, it was announced that *The All-New Popeye Hour* would premiere in September. Art Scott stated that the budgets for the cartoons would be larger than the 1960s series and the films would reflect the Fleischer era despite the considerable cut back on the violence. The one-on-one battles between Popeye and Bluto (the bully's name going back to his original moniker) were altered into competitions between the two men. While Popeye could punch inanimate objects onto his foes, a physical blow was out of the question. Both Popeye and Olive used their wits to outfox Bluto. Virginia Mercer said of the violence, "Popeye could hit a tree and the tree could fall on Bluto, but Popeye could not hit him directly." Mrs. Mercer also recalled Jack wrote the first "women's lib story with Olive as the lead." Popeye could not have smoke billowing out of his pipe and Mercer had to tone down the sound of it. Many characters from Segar's *Thimble Theatre* comic strip returned for these new adventures which, despite the no violence clause, became one of the highest rated programs on the Saturday morning schedule for the 1978-79 season.

In order to record the cartoons, Mercer moved from his longtime New York

A publicity photo of Jack Mercer during the production of Hanna-Barbera's Popeye cartoons for broadcast on the CBS Saturday morning schedule from 1978 to 1983. In addition to writing many of the cartoons, Jack Mercer provided the voices of Popeye, Poopdeck Pappy, one of Popeye's nephews and incidental characters. By this time he had been providing Popeye's for over forty years.

residence to California while the series was in production. Virginia Mercer recalled the circumstances regarding the location change for Jack. "Art [Scott] said Jack could live with Larz Bourne and Cal Howard (who worked on the series) and I protested. I said that Jack needed his own space where I could visit. So he was put up in a nice, completely furnished apartment and given a car to get around. His one-year contract was completed in four or five months and no one knew if CBS would renew. Hanna-Barbera was very good about Jack taking off time to record other commercials."

Virginia Mercer remembered that Jack's previous method of writing scripts, while appreciated by the Hanna-Barbera executives, was not necessarily welcomed by West Coast writers. She stated, "Jack worked in his apartment and when they ok'd a script's premise, he would draw the storyboards, which didn't sit well with the storyboard people. The CBS Vice President liked Jack's work and he was more detailed, I think. One day he was at the studio and the CBS Vice President took the writers to lunch, but did not include Jack. He was a little hurt. However, when they returned, he got snide remarks like 'teacher's pet.' It seemed the Vice President took Jack's work along to the lunch with the writers and said, 'This is what I want.' There has always been this feeling that West

Coast writers are superior to East Coast writers and Jack's skills were a great change."

Jack gave a few interviews during the production of *All New Popeye Hour*, which was renewed for the 1979-80 season (later becoming the half-hour *The Popeye and Olive Comedy Show*, which aired on CBS until September of 1983). One was published in *The Churchills* column for a Beverly Hills newspaper on September 14, 1978.

> Popeye-that spinach-guzzling sailor, who entertained millions with his heroics, is being re-introduced to a new generation of youngsters. Jack Mercer, the cartoon character's grit n' graty voice for 44 years, is starring in the Hanna-Barbera teleseries. CBS-TV with one prime-time special already completed has another coming up in three months plus the spanking new series for the small fry every Saturday morning on the CBS-TV network.
>
> We couldn't help rib Mercer during his lunch when he passed-by a spinach salad for roast beef.
>
> "Now don't give me that yuzzle hazzle'em," smiled Jack reverting to that trademark voice that sounds like a VW starting up in a cold morning. "What'd you say...what'd you say?" we chorused. "That's Popeyeze for don't give me the razzle-dazzle," Jack replied.
>
> Mercer, as Popeye, is a riot. As himself he is a mild-mannered gentleman who never saw Hollywood until a few months ago when Hanna-Barbera brought him out for the series. "I've written seven of 64 episodes," he told us. "Even those I haven't scripted, the typists leave blank spaces so I can convert the dialogue into Popeyeze." Such words as Holywoogs, embaraskin, flabbergassed, horsk (for horse) and brawlgame (for ballgame) are all part of the cartoon character's language.
>
> The series has definitely been updated with girlfriend, "Olive Oyl," now a liberated woman and "Wimpy" and "Bluto," more pest than punisher. The accent is on fun not violence.
>
> Mercer knows the cartoon business from the brush up, since he has apprenticed in every department.

"I have a drawing board in our apartment in New York and here in my office studio." In addition to Popeye he has supplied every voice for the popular cartoon series, "Felix the Cat."

"I think the kids will love Popeye, he's still eating his spinach, even though he sometimes has to use his pipe as a torch to open the can!"

Reported by Reba and Bonnie

In 1979, Jack provided Popeye's voice for the CBS network special, *The Popeye Valentine Special: Sweethearts at Seas.* Jack Mercer received his first on-screen credit as the voice of the animated Popeye at the end of the 1980 live-action film, *Popeye*, starring Robin Williams. The film begins with an opening taken from a Max Fleischer *Popeye* cartoon. Popeye's head appears between the ship's doors and Mercer says, "What's this, one of Bluto's tricks! I'm in the wrong movie!" Mercer also provided the sailor's voice for a series of commercials for Nintendo's popular Popeye games, which aired during the early 1980s.

He was so valued by Hanna-Barbera, even after recent heart surgery, that the studio called upon his talent as a writer. Virginia Mercer recalled Hanna-Barbera said at the time, "It's time for Jack to come and to write. I told them that Jack just had surgery, in the hospital and would not be able to do it. They asked, 'How's his voice?' I said fine when he barely talks. They would be sending Jack four scripts and want to record in a few days. I relayed this to Jack who wanted the scripts sent to the hospital. We had to find a soundproof room in the hospital to record. The best was

A drawing of Popeye, with a spinach-fueled heart, by Jack Mercer to his heart surgeon, "Doc Wallsh." It's signed, "With Heartfelt thanks from the Voice of Popeye, Jack Mercer."

SPOT. POPEYE "MY TURN" 8114 :30 (SECS)		ANIM.= 31 02			
SCENE	SCENE DESCRIPTION	FOOTAGE ↓	ANIMATION	SPEC. EFFECTS	OTHER
1	"MY TURN. MY TOIN. THIS NEW POPEYE VIDEO GAME HAS THE BOYS FIGHTING-" ESTAB. SHOT: POPEYE, BRUTIS -OLIVE WALKS IN.	7 13	4 5 / 5½	PHOTO-STATS OF PRODUCT·OLIVE HOLDS 'EM	CAMERA PANS RIGHT →
2	"-WORSE THAN EVER (POW) OH POPEYE" POPEYE PUNCHES BRUTIS INTO CEILING. OLIVE ENTERS	5 04	2 / 3½	ANIM. PLASTER FALLS	CAMERA SHAKES
3 (4)	"IT'S MY GAME!" POPEYE ZIPS BACK TO (OLIVE T.V. SET ENTERS)	2 00	4 5 / 1 3		
4 (5)	"IT'S GOT THREE SCREENS-JUST LIKE THE ARCADE" C.U. POPEYE-CAM. MOVES PAST HIM — INTO T.V. SCREEN	4 02	2 5 / 2 3		CAMERA MOVES INTO C.U. OF T.V. SCREEN
5 (6)	"WATCH OUT!" OLIVE & POPEYE AT T.V. SET.	1 13	4 0 / 1½		
6 (7)	"YIKES"	3 09	2 5 / 2½	NONE — GAME INSERT	
7 (8)	"OH, OH!" REVERSE SHOT. OLIVE & POPEYE — HAT FLYS UP	1 09	1.0		
8 (9)	"FIGHT LIKE A MAN-WHERE'S MY SPINACH-WHOAHHHH"	4 03	3 5 / 2 3	NONE- GAME INSERT	
9 (10)	"HA HA. YOU CHOKED, YOU WHIMP." "I AINT WHIMPY-I'M MEN—" POPEYE, BRUTIS, OLIVE AT T.V. WHIMPY WALKS IN.	5 05	2 5 / 3½		
10 (11)	"-BETTER LOOKIN-YUK YUK!" C.U. WHIMPY, POPEYE, & BRUTIS ANNCR.: "-THIS NEW POP-"	3 04	2 1 / 2 6		
11	" "-----" THE VIDEO GAME FROM PARKER BROS.	.02	3 /		ANIMATED

Mark Kausler, who animated a series of early 1980s Popeye video game commercials (for Nintendo) supplied this rare storyboard nothing, "Fred, this is the director's Sam Cornell's scene breakdown sheet from the Popeye video game spot, My Turn produced by Pacific Motion Pictures." Jack Mercer voiced Popeye in this television advertisement and Mae Questel reprised her Olive Oyl voice, possibly one of the final times the pair would work together in their legendary roles.

the auditorium with a banging elevator. I also had to arrange for a private duty nurse because there were rules about going off the floor. However, on the day of recording, the nurse didn't show and I yelled and screamed that I needed the head nurse. Then, the director came; a few others, plus the sound crew and even a man from World Vision. Jack was in a wheelchair with an IV in his arm. I was very concerned with the banging elevator (which would require re-takes). I know that Jack's doctors and nurses were in the auditorium. Jack recorded the four stories (which aired as part of *The Popeye and Olive Comedy Show*) and no one could tell the difference from his recording when he was in the real recording studio. After that, Hanna-Barbera arranged for Jack to record in New York and finished out the series."

Ultimately, Jack Mercer passed on, at the age of 74, of cancer, reportedly on December 4, 1984. His obituary in most newspapers was brief, headlining he was the cartoon voice of both Popeye and Felix the Cat. His legacy is, of course, as the voice of Popeye the Sailor, but as an artist and human being he was so much more.

Fortunately, much of Jack Mercer's voice work can be found on video and DVD. During the 1980s, several of the *Felix the Cat* and *Popeye* cartoons (both the 1960-61 and 1978-83 Popeye series) were issued on video. Several Popeye theatrical cartoons, produced by both the Fleischer and Famous Studios, which fell into public domain, were issued on numerous video cassettes. *Gulliver's Travels, Mr. Bug Goes to Town, Betty Boop, Superman, Casper, Baby Huey, Herman and Katnip, Buzzy the Crow* and *The Mighty Hercules* have all seen one or more video releases.

During the 1990s to the present, *Popeye* (public domain theatricals and television versions), *Felix the Cat, Casper, Baby Huey, Little Audrey, Betty Boop, Superman,* and *Gulliver's Travels* have been issued on DVD. In 2006 it was announced that Warner Home video would begin releasing the entire *Popeye*

Jack Mercer provided the voices for all of the characters in the Felix the Cat *TV-cartoon series which, as evidenced by this trade advertisement, was "knocking 'em dead" in the ratings. Several of Felix's television adventures have been released on both home video and DVD.*

theatrical (and later television) cartoons on DVD beginning in the Summer of 2007. Fans once more will be able to enjoy the hysterical mumblings of there favorite sailor...and the talents of Jack Mercer.

An early trade ad from Variety *dated March 28, 1962, a year before* The Mighty Hercules *animated TV-cartoons made their debut on the small screen. Jack Mercer was involved with voicing characters for the initial cartoons in the series. Cartoons in this series, featuring Mercer's voice work, were released on home video in 1990.*

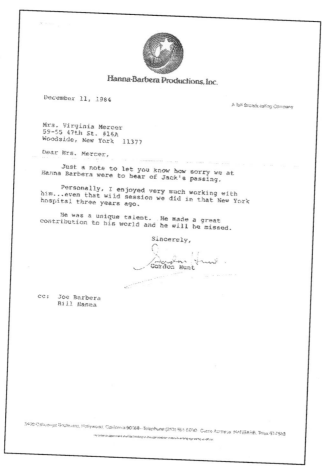

Hanna-Barbera Productions, Inc.

December 11, 1984

A Taft Broadcasting Company

Mrs. Virginia Mercer
59-55 47th St. #16A
Woodside, New York 11377

Dear Mrs. Mercer,

Just a note to let you know how sorry we at Hanna Barbera were to hear of Jack's passing.

Personally, I enjoyed very much working with him...even that wild session we did in that New York hospital three years ago.

He was a unique talent. He made a great contribution to his world and he will be missed.

Sincerely,

Gordon Hunt

cc: Joe Barbera
Bill Hanna

A letter from Gordon Hunt of Hanna-Barbera, dated December 11, 1984 to Mrs. Virginia Mercer regarding the passing of Jack Mercer. Note he mentions the "wild session" in the New York Hospital where Jack performed Popeye's voice (despite surgery) in order to complete the Hanna-Barbera Popeye cartoon series.

Left: The comic strip design of Brutus swings a punch at Popeye (voiced by Jack Mercer) from this rare pencil art used in the production of the video game television commercial called My Turn. Mark Kausler, who animated the ad, said, "I'm glad I could be a part of Popeye history. I guess Jack Mercer was doing a lot of recording for the 1980's Hanna-Barbera cartoons and just worked the spot in on the side. It was fun animating the characters, I tried to draw them more like the (E.C.) Segar version (Popeye's creator) but a bit of (Bud) Sagendorf crept in as well (Bud Sagendorf was one of Segar's successors on the comic strip and it is his version of Brutus which appears in the ad). Pencil art courtesy of Mark Kausler.

CITY OF LOS ANGELES

IN TRIBUTE

THE LOS ANGELES CITY COUNCIL EXTENDS ITS
DEEPEST SYMPATHY TO YOU IN THE PASSING OF
YOUR LOVED ONE

JACK MERCER

IN WHOSE MEMORY ALL MEMBERS STOOD IN TRIB-
UTE AND REVERENCE AS THE COUNCIL ADJOURNED
ITS MEETING OF DECEMBER 19, 1984.

SINCERELY,

Elias Martinez
ELIAS MARTINEZ, CITY CLERK

Presented by

Peggy Stevenson
COUNCIL OF PEGGY STEVENSON

The Council of the City of Los Angeles honored the talent of Jack Mercer on December 19,
1984.

VOICE CHARACTERIZATIONS FROM A TO Z

Though not a comprehensive listing (Mercer's voice work went largely uncredited during his career), this list gives the reader an idea of the variety of characters Jack Mercer voiced for both theatrical and television cartoons. I apologize for not having a complete character listing for the Felix the Cat *television cartoon series, but the films themselves did not have title listings.*

Admiral: Mercer had to jump back and forth to a voice with a commanding, military presence to one of immaturity for the Admiral in "The Hungry Goat" (Famous Studios, 1943). This entry in the *Popeye* series was a wild cartoon dealing with a ship-eating goat and Popeye's attempts to stop him. Befriending the goat, the Admiral says to seaman Popeye, "Swab these decks and see to it my little friend comes to no harm. As for myself [in a juvenile tone], I'm going to the movies, N-a-a-h-h!" The movie the Admiral ends up watching is "The Hungry Goat"!

Announcer: When a generic-looking character, such as an announcer, is needed for a cartoon, the visual design is often used again in different films. Such is the case of the announcer who tells Katnip that his friends from "cartoon land" have gathered to honor in him in the "Katnip's Big Day" (Paramount Cartoon Studios, 1959). This black-haired, thin man was seen again in the *Popeye* TV-cartoon, "Popeye's Double Trouble" (Paramount Cartoon Studios, 1961) doubling as a bandleader. In both films, Jack Mercer gave him the same voice.

The Admiral (Jack Mercer) enjoys a hearty laugh before immediately switching to a voice of authority in "The Hungry Goat" (Famous Studios, 1943). With this character, Jack Mercer's vocal range kept switching back and forth from a commanding voice to an immature buffoon. Filled with wild antics and characters from the film, actually watching it play on a movie screen shows it to be one unusual Popeye cartoon!

The Announcer (Jack Mercer) introduces one of Katnip's buddies to reminisce (via footage from previous theatrical cartoons) in "Katnip's Big Day" (Paramount Cartoon Studio, 1959), the final "Herman and Katnip" entry in the long-running series.

Antes (Jack Mercer) brags to Newton (also voiced by Mercer) he'll be as strong as Hercules when he puts on the ring which gives Hercules his strength on earth from "Hercules and the Stolen Ring," a Mighty Hercules TV-cartoon (Trans-Lux, 1963).

B Looney Baloney (Jack Mercer) arrives to draw funny pictures for Popeye's newspaper, "The Puddleburg Splash" in "What's News" (Paramount Cartoon Studios, 1960). He doesn't last too long on the job. B Looney Baloney and the plot of the cartoon has its roots in the "Thimble Theatre" comic strip by E.C. Segar.

Antes: A muscular, red-haired bully who gains Herculean strength after putting on The Mighty Hercules' magic ring. With the ring on his finger, the brute causes destruction until his actions cause a flood. Realizing he's not smart enough to stop the flood, he gives Hercules back his ring in "Hercules and the Stolen Ring" (Trans-Lux, 1963).

B Looney Baloney: He's a long-faced, depressing-looking "comic artist" who Popeye hires (and quickly fires) to draw funny pictures for his newspaper, *The Puddleburg Splash* in the *Popeye* TV-cartoon, "What's News" (Paramount, 1960). Jack Mercer gives him a befuddling-sounding voice.

Baggage Man: A man with a black mustache who encounters the ghost, Casper, and then leaps in the air, letting out a loud scream in "Zero the Hero" (Famous Studios, 1954), a Casper the Friendly Ghost animated theatrical cartoon. Jack Mercer was often called upon to provide the voice of the initial characters meeting Casper. His dialogue often would be "A Ghost!" followed by a blood-curdling scream.

Beatnik Mice: Jack Mercer provides the voices to mice (along with Bob McFadden) who are beatniks in "Miceniks" (Paramount Cartoon Studios, 1960).

Beaver: A beaver, wearing a blue cap and pants, who supervises the construction of a dam in "By the Old Mill Scream" (Famous Studios, 1953), an entry in the Casper the Friendly Ghost animated theatrical series. Jack Mercer gives the beaver an old man's voice much like that of Popeye's father, Poopdeck Pappy.

Blacksmith: Jack Mercer provided a confident voice for a white-bearded blacksmith. He spends a year forging a sword strong enough to slay the dreaded three-headed Hydra in "Hercules vs. the Hydra," an early entry in *The Mighty Hercules* TV-cartoon series produced by Trans-Lux in 1963.

A kindly blacksmith (Jack Mercer) explains to Hercules he has spent a year forging a sword strong enough to defeat the three-headed Hydra in "Hercules vs. the Hydra" (Trans-Lux, 1963). Unfortunately the sword breaks in battle and it's Hercules ingenuity which defeats the beast in this early entry in The Mighty Hercules series.

The Big Cheese: Literally, having a big round piece of cheese as a head and wearing a crown, he is the mean ruler of a planet Popeye, Olive and Wimpy crash land in "Hits and Missiles," the first *Popeye* TV-cartoon produced by Paramount Cartoon Studios in 1960. Jack Mercer uses a sinister, gruff-sounding voice, radiating pure meanness.

Bluto: Many an animation historian has tried to figure out which *Popeye* cartoons produced by the Fleischer Studios featured Jack Mercer performing Bluto's voice. His vocal characterization is so good that it's hard to identify which exact films he did. When the Fleischer Studios moved from New York to Florida, some of their voice personnel did not make the move. The Fleischers needed a new voice for Bluto and after unsatisfactory results in two cartoons, "Ghosks is the Bunk" and "Customers Wanted," both from 1939, a gruffer-sounding voice for the bully was heard in "Wotta Nitemare" and "It's the Natural Thing to Do," two additional 1939 entries. Based upon Mercer-voiced bullies of later vintage, it does sound like Jack Mercer's Bluto in "Wotta Nitemare" and "It's the Natural Thing to Do," though there has been no documentation stating this. For Bluto's next few appearances during Fleischers' tenure on the *Popeye* series, a Mercer-sounding Bluto was heard in

The Big Cheese (Jack Mercer) orders both Popeye and Olive Oyl to be locked up while he collects taxes (pieces of cheese) from the inhabitants of his planet in "Hits and Missiles" (Paramount Cartoon Studios, 1960). This was one of two pilot Popeye television cartoons shown to entice local stations on buying the entire series of 220 films. It took little persuasion to get television stations across the country to purchase the cartoons for broadcast.

Bluto is voiced by Jack Mercer in "Wotta Nitemare" (Fleischer, 1939). Exactly for what other cartoons Bluto's voice was provided by Jack Mercer has yet to be determined. He did state it for the record it was difficult for him to voice both characters while they were having a conversation, which led to the necessity of hiring other performers for Popeye's bearded rival.

"Me Feelings is Hurt"(1940), "Nurse Mates" (1940), "Onion Pacific" (1940) and "Fightin' Pals" (1940), which some have attributed to voice-over artist Pinto Colvig. Mercer has stated it was difficult for him to voice both Popeye and Bluto in the same cartoon, so perhaps, after "Wotta Nitemare" and "It's the Natural Thing to Do," other voice artists took over (a more sophisticated-sounding Bluto was heard in "Stealin' Ain't Honest" from 1940). Mercer's Bluto can be heard in a few lines, though another voice artist performed the role, in Fleischer Studio's "Olive Oyl and Water Don't Mix" (1942) saying "Why that one-eyed Casanova" and "Watch me play sick" in "Too Weak to Work" (Famous Studios, 1943). Both times this occurred, the character's mouth didn't move and it appears Mercer's Bluto voice was dubbed in.

Bob Hope: The famous film and television actor made a cameo, with a penguin's body and voiced by Jack Mercer, in "The Case of the Cockeyed Canary" (Famous Studios, 1952), featuring Little Audrey.

Boxing Referee: Jack Mercer often provided the voice when a referee appeared in a Paramount animated cartoon, as in "Punch and Judo" (Famous Studios, 1951). In the latter, he appeared as a pint-sized figure, physically demonstrating the moves not allowed in the ring. Mercer also voiced a well-dressed referee announcing, "And now for the star attraction, in this corner Battling Bluto and in this corner, his worthy opponent, Popeye the Sailor!" in "Out to Punch" (Famous Studios, 1956).

Boy in Movie Theater: Mercer often provided the voice for little children, but his most memorable line was heard in "The Hungry Goat"(Famous Studios, 1943). In silhouette, watching Popeye, in vain, trying to stop a ship-eating goat, the boy raises his fist and says, "Aw why don't Popeye eat his spinach and sock him one!" He is vocalizing out loud, what the audience is no doubt thinking watching the cartoon!

One of three bruiser boys (all voiced by Jack Mercer) confront Popeye (Mercer) who is disguised as an old lady who wants to enter the newly built school in "What's News" (Paramount Cartoon Studio, 1960).

Bruiser Boys: Three gruff-sounding, lookalike brutes that want to destroy the new schoolhouse Popeye has built so Olive can teach the citizens of Puddleburg how to read in "What's News" (Paramount Cartoon Studios, 1960). Preparing to bop Popeye disguised as an old lady, a bruiser boy bellows, "Listen, Grandma, you ol' hag, if you were a man, I'd bop ya one!" Popeye responds with his fist.

Brutus and Popeye carry on a conversation with themselves as they're both voiced by Jack Mercer in this TV-cartoon, "Sea No Evil" (Gene Deitch/William Snyder, 1960). Jack Mercer's wife, Virginia, stated it was planned her husband would voice both Popeye and Brutus for this new Popeye series made exclusively for television. Mercer found it difficult to switch from Popeye to Brutus to Wimpy and insisted Jackson Beck once again provide the voice for the sailor's bearded foe. Mercer's Brutus was a deep gruff sounding voice which he also performed on Popeye children's records.

Brutus: Originally, Popeye's bearded rival for Olive Oyl's affections was named, "Bluto." When King Features Syndicated decided to produce a series of *Popeye* TV-cartoons for television in 1960, Paramount Pictures, who produced the theatrical *Popeye* series, claimed they owned the name "Bluto." The studio was under the misconception that the bully appeared initially in the Fleischer Studios films. Not wanting to challenge Paramount's claim in court, King Features Syndicate slightly altered the look of the bearded bully, naming him "Brutus" (after Caesar's murderer). Jack Mercer provided a very gruff- and husky-sounding voice to the brute in "Sea No Evil" (Gene Deitch/William Snyder, 1960). For the record, Bluto first appeared in E.C. Segar's *Thimble Theatre* comic strip in 1932, thereby the strip's syndicator, King Features Syndicate, owned his moniker.

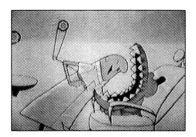

The dentist (Jack Mercer) asks Chew Chew the cannibal (with minimal dialogue by Mercer) to open "wider" and well, you can guess what happens next in "Chew, Chew Baby," a Noveltoon (Paramount Cartoon Studios, 1958). While this animated theatrical played on television during the 1960s and 1970s, it's doubtful it would get air time today.

Cole Oyl (Jack Mercer) informs his daughter Olive she must seek the help of Prince Popeye in "Olive Drab and the Seven Swea'peas" (Jack Kinney, 1960). The King Features Syndicate Popeye TV-cartoons featured many characters from the comic strip, unlike the theatrical series. This allowed Jack Mercer and Jackson Beck to create different male voices for a variety of characters.

Carp on the Beat: A fish, dressed up as a policeman, who handcuffs Little Audrey and takes her to "The Seapreme Court" (Famous Studios, 1954). Mercer uses his familiar Irish accent in bringing voice to the carp.

Cartoon Writer: A pudgy, red-haired man with a high-pitched voice (like Jack Mercer's rendition of Felix the Cat) who demonstrates a gag for an animated cartoon. He pulls out the tongue of his fellow writer and snaps it back in "Ghost of Honor" (Paramount Cartoon Studios, 1957), a *Casper the Friendly Ghost* cartoon.

Chew Chew: Jack Mercer supplied minimal dialogue (maniac laughter) to this tiny cannibal with a huge human appetite in "Chew Chew Baby," a Noveltoon produced by Paramount Cartoon Studios in 1958.

Cole Oyl: Olive Oyl's father, who first appeared in E.C. Segar's *Thimble Theatre* comic strip and made an appearance as a King, voiced by Jack Mercer, in the *Popeye* TV-cartoon, "Olive Drab and the Seven Swea'peas" (Jack Kinney, 1960).

Cop: Jack Mercer voiced dialogue for various men in blue in theatrical cartoons, including "Doing What's Fright" (Paramount Cartoon Studios, 1959), a *Casper the Friendly Ghost* entry, "Seeing Double" (Gene Deitch/William Snyder, 1960) and "Pop Goes the Whistle" (Paramount Cartoon Studios, 1961), two *Popeye* TV-cartoons. His more prominent role voicing a policeman with an Irish brogue was in "Moving Aweigh" (Famous Studios, 1944). Thanks to Popeye's pal (?), Shorty, the sailor ends up on the wrong side of the law and encounters a hefty policeman. He dishes out some physical punishment to Popeye, but gets squashed by a grand piano by cartoon's end.

Dadonis: This elderly gentleman with a long white beard is called the seer of Mt. Olympus, using a crystal rock to warn The Mighty Hercules of perils on earth. Mercer's brief dialogue was heard in "Hercules Saves the Kingdom" and "Daedelus Kidnaps Helena."

"I'm giving you a ticket fer speedin', dere ya are," announces a cop (Mercer). He then witnesses an invisible force tear up the ticket who appears as Spooky (Jack Mercer) shouting, "April Fool!" in "Doing What's Fright" (Paramount Cartoon Studios, 1958). Jack Mercer voiced various animated law enforcement figures as he did in this entry in the Casper the Friendly Ghost animated theatrical series.

Daedelus: Jack Mercer provided a sinister voice to the purple-cloaked evil wizard in the initial cartoons of *The Mighty Hercules* TV-cartoon series produced by Trans-Lux in 1963. Mercer's version of Daedelus was heard in "Hercules Saves the Kingdom," "Daedelus Kidnaps Helena," "Theft of the Magic Seal," "Double Trouble" and "The Chair of Forgetfulness."

In the initial cartoons of The Mighty Hercules series, Jack Mercer provided the voice of the hero's purple cloaked nemesis, Daedelus. The series aired in syndication into the 1970s and spawned merchandise which is highly collectible.

Devil: In the extremely patriotic *Popeye* entry by Famous Studios in 1943, "Seein' Red, White 'n' Blue," Bluto tries any means to avoid being drafted. He jumps out a window, with Popeye running to catch him below. Bluto smashes into Popeye on the sidewalk and the pair head straight down! All is quiet, and then you see a ladder emerge from the hole the pair made. Three figures emerge from the ladder, Bluto, Popeye and a Mercer-voiced Devil, who says, "Oh dear, oh dear, oh dear imagine one's own home being cluttered up with a lot of strange people dropping in all over the place when you least expect them and very uninvited I might add! By the way who did invite you, no never mind that I never been so humiliated in all my born days. Now get out; get out, twenty-three skid-oo, out, out,

Dr. Brainstorm (Jack Mercer) threatens a group of scientists to take his discoveries seriously and when they don't, he creates an anti-gravity machine creating havoc. Casper the Friendly Ghost flies to the rescue in "Down to Mirth" (Paramount Cartoon Studios, 1959).

A little Dutch boy (Jack Mercer with an accent to match the boy's origin of birth) causes mishaps when he and other children from different nationalities try to clean Santa Claus' home in "Santa's Surprise" (Famous Studios, 1947).

out, out! And I warn you if this incident occurs again, you'll have the Devil to pay, humph!" A totally bizarre, funny and unexpected moment in the cartoon!

Dr. Brainstorm: An evil scientist who Mercer gives a maniacal laugh. He creates an anti-gravity machine and turns it loose on the city. Casper the Ghost flies to the rescue in "Down to Mirth" (Paramount Cartoon Studios, 1959), an entry in the *Casper* theatrical cartoon series.

Dutch Boy: A blond-haired child dressed in traditional Dutch clothing who creates mishaps as he tries to help Little Audrey and her friends, from around the world, clean Santa Claus' house in "Santa's Surprise" (Famous Studios, 1947). Mercer also voiced the Chinese and Russian boys in this musical cartoon, which was the first appearance of Little Audrey.

Fairy Godfather: This magical man, who emerges from Popeye's pipe, gives "Cinderfella" (as Popeye is called in this cartoon), the chance to go to Princess Olive's ball. Mercer gives this dapper-looking fellow, with a magic wand, a voice similar to Poopdeck Pappy, and he certainly looks like Popeye's old man! Instead of using mice and a pumpkin, the white-bearded godfather says, "Fetches me a can of spinach or you'll be late fer the ball!" in "Ancient Fistory" (Famous Studios, 1953).

Felix the Cat: The internationally known and beloved feline made his silent film debut as a character known as "Master Tom" in a 1919 Paramount short, "Feline Follies," produced by an animation studio owned by Pat Sullivan. Paramount producer John

King suggested the cat be called "Felix" and his third film, released in 1919, was titled "The Adventures of Felix." In 1924, animator Bill Nolan redesigned the character, making him rounder in appearance. The silent cartoons have been called a wonderful example of surrealistic filmmaking. His famous pace -hands behind his back, head down, deep in thought: became his trademark. He is an all black cat, except for his huge white eyes and mouth. Just who created the character has caused much debate. American animator Otto Messmer and movie entrepreneur Pat Sullivan have both claimed they created Felix the Cat. Many animation historians argue it was Messmer who ghosted for Sullivan. What is known is that the character was a huge hit in silent films despite the fact his cartoon series had many distributors during the 1920s. Felix the Cat merchandise was everywhere and he also became the first image (a papier-mâché doll) ever broadcast by a television transmitter. Felix didn't translate well into sound theatrical cartoons and an attempt by the Van Buren Studios in 1936 to put him in three-color films failed to win back audiences. In 1953 Official Films added soundtracks to the silent films for release on television. By 1958, Felix was still being read in comic strips and comic books when Joe Oriolo, the new artist on the Felix strip, gained the rights to produce a new cartoon series for television. Felix now had a "magic bag of tricks," which could shift into myriad shapes based on his needs. Oriolo's plots revolved around the unsuccessful attempts by Felix's foes, mainly The Professor, to steal his magic bag. Other stories had Felix traveling in space with the Professor's nephew, Poindexter. Each episode was split into two-halves, with

Felix the Cat (Jack Mercer) hides his terror when meeting Dinah the Dinosaur (also voiced by Mercer) in "Do-It-Yourself Monster Book," a Felix the Cat TV-cartoon produced by Trans-Lux. Besides Popeye, Jack Mercer is remembered for voicing the cat who has survived long after his initial nine lives had been used up in theatrical animation, TV-cartoons, comic strips, comic books and a line of merchandise.

A pudgy florist (Jack Mercer) who rolls his tongue while speaking lists the different flowers he's brought for the King's consideration to be used for his daughter's wedding in the animated feature film, Gulliver's Travels (Fleischer, 1939).

A drawing of Swat the Fly from the animated feature film, Mr. Bug Goes to Town (Fleischer, 1941). Jack Mercer gave Swat a high-pitched voice, a precursor to what he developed for Felix the Cat's vocal sound.

the first having a cliffhanger ending with Jack Mercer's eerie-sounding voice saying, "What will happen to Felix in the next exciting chapter in the adventures of Felix the Cat?" The TV-cartoons were extremely successful on television, being one of the first productions filmed in color. Many local stations renewed their initial five-year contract with the series, some well into the early 1970s. The success of the TV-cartoons gave birth to new Felix the Cat products. Jack Mercer gave Felix a high-pitched, squeaky-clean-sounding voice in all of the television films, produced between 1958 through 1962. *(See the Appendix for a complete listing of titles where Jack Mercer voiced this character.)*

Florist: A rolly-polly man who presents a huge selection of flowers for King Little's approval in the 1939 animated feature film, *Gulliver's Travels*, produced by the Fleischer Studios. Jack Mercer rolled his tongue while having the Florist recite the different flowers on display.

Fly: When Paramount's animation studio needed a sound or brief dialogue for an animal or, in this case, insect, Jack Mercer supplied what was needed. In "Flies Ain't Human" (Fleischer, 1941) and the film's remake by Famous Studios, "The Fly's Last Flight" (1949), Mercer supplied the voice of the fly out to ruin Popeye's nap. The Fly's dialogue in both films mainly consisted of the "Hey" when it yells in the sailor's ear. In the 1949 version the cartoon ends with the fly playing a fiddle and singing, "Swing your partner." Mercer also gave voice to Swat the Fly, a cap-wearing fly with oversized glasses. He was the henchman to the villainous C. Bagley Beetle. Swat's slapstick antics provided much of the humor in an otherwise melodramatic animated feature film, *Mr. Bug Goes to Town* (Fleischer Studios, 1941).

Gang Boss: A criminal mastermind who creates a Popeye robot to commit a series of bank robberies in "Seeing Double" (Gene Deitch/William Snyder, 1960), a *Popeye* TV-cartoon. Mercer gives this criminal an Edward G. Robinson-sounding voice, slipping in "yeah-yeah" for emphasis. Mercer also provided the voices of the elderly security guard, bank manager and policemen in this cartoon.

A sophisticated sounding genie (Jack Mercer) is summoned by the evil Sea Hag (Mae Questel) to give her great treasures and turn Popeye into a mouse in "Aladdin's Lamp" (Paramount Cartoon Studios, 1961).

Geezil: Geezil was a memorable character in the *Thimble Theatre* comic strip, where Popeye made his debut in 1929. Created by E.C. Segar, Geezil was a shoe cobbler by trade who appeared, mainly in the Sunday page, from the early 1930s well into the late 1950s. With a long black bristle beard, Geezil was often tricked into providing J. Wellington Wimpy with free meals. Jack Mercer voiced the character when the Fleischer Studios gave him a prominent role in the cartoon "Olive's Boithday Presnik" (Fleischer, 1941). With a Russian accent, Geezil attempts to pass off a coat made of rabbit fur as bear skin. When Popeye succeeds in getting a bearskin coat from an actual bear, the label inside reveals itself to be from Geezil's shop!

Genie of the Lamp: A bald-headed genie, with a bow tie, pink in color, with an air of sophistication in his voice provided by Jack Mercer. The Sea Hag orders him to turn Popeye into a mouse in "Aladdin's Lamp," a *Popeye* TV-cartoon (Paramount Cartoon Studios, 1960).

Two evil Gremlins voiced by Jackson Beck (left) and Jack Mercer (right) cause havoc in "Goodie the Gremlin," a Noveltoon produced in 1961 by Paramount Cartoon Studios. This cartoon demonstrated the vocal versatility of Jackson Beck and Jack Mercer as they also voiced the friendly, then feuding, neighbors Fred and Jonesy in this cartoon.

Ghost: If a group of ghosts were seen in a Paramount theatrical or television cartoon, Jack Mercer voiced one or more of the spooky figures as he did in "Spooky Swabs" (Famous Studios, 1957), the last theatrical *Popeye* cartoon, "True Boo" (Famous Studios, 1951), an entry in the *Casper* theatrical series, or "The Ghost Host," a *Popeye* television cartoon produced by Paramount Cartoon Studios in 1960. One of his more prominent ghostly voices was featured when Casper the Friendly Ghost was put on trial in "Not Ghoulty" (Paramount Cartoon Studios, 1959), a *Casper* theatrical cartoon. Jack Mercer's ghost bellowed to a spook-filled jury; "Casper is on trial because he always breaks our ghostly laws! He will not shriek or boo or scare, he wants to make friends everywhere."

Ghost Exterminator: Casper the Friendly Ghost disguises himself as a ghost exterminator in order to scare someone to regain his ghostly powers in "Not Ghoulty" (Paramount Cartoon Studios, 1959), a *Casper* cartoon.

Giant: A giant who, in Popeye's dream, is hoarding valuable items needed for the war effort in "Ration For the Duration" (Famous Studios, 1943). Mercer gives the giant a wacky, offbeat voice.

Golfer: A tubby, bulb-nosed golfer who bothers a gopher collecting golf balls and ends up playing the sport on the moon in "It's for the Birdies" (Paramount Cartoon Studios, 1962).

Gremlins: Assorted nasty-minded gremlins were voiced by Jack Mercer for the *Goodie the Gremlin* series including, "Goodie the Gremlin" (Paramount Cartoon Studios, 1961) and "Tell Me a Badtime Story" (Paramount Cartoon Studios, 1963).

Groucho Marx: Popeye impersonated the famous movie star, with Jack Mercer's vocal characterization of the comedian, in "Puttin' on the Act" (Fleischer, 1940).

An Indian (Jack Mercer) spots the arrival of Betty Boop in "Rhythm on the Reservation" (Fleischer, 1939). Jack Mercer also voiced an Indian chief in the Popeye cartoon, "Pilgrim Popeye" (Famous Studios, 1952) and whenever needed during the production of an animated film for Paramount Pictures.

Gumshoe: An insurance agent sent to keep an eye on a million-dollar violin used by a maestro. Jack Mercer brings his Rock Bottom voice to the agent in "Fiddlin Around" (Paramount Cartoon Studios, 1962).

Humphrey Bogart: The famed film actor is heard briefly in the form of hard candy in the *Screen Song*, "Candy Cabaret" (Famous Studios, 1954).

Indian Chief: Jack Mercer's voice was used as an Indian Chief in the Betty Boop cartoon, "Rhythm on the Reservation" (Fleischer, 1939), which was Betty's last animated appearance, and "Pilgrim Popeye" (Famous Studios, 1951). Whenever Paramount's animation studios needed a gruff-sounding Indian voice for their theatrical cartoons either Jack Mercer or Jackson Beck was called upon.

Irving, the Practical Joker: This lanky-looking character appeared in a Betty Boop cartoon, "The Impractical Joker" (Fleischer, 1937). He plagues Betty with practical jokes. She must then call upon Grampy for help. Grampy, through his own inventiveness, treats Irving to some humiliating jokes.

Irving the Practical Joker (Jack Mercer) greets Betty Boop with a hand which shoots water in "The Impractical Joker" (Fleischer, 1937). Jack Mercer supplied the voices for incidental voices in the Betty Boop series and other theatrical cartoons produced by the Fleischer Studios.

J. Wellington Wimpy (Jack Mercer) is on the receiving end of Popeye's "lullaby punch" when the moocher attacks him while he's under the spell of the Sea Hag in "Hamburger's Aweigh" (Paramount Cartoon Studios, 1961). Wimpy was a prominent character in the made-for-television Popeye series produced by Al Brodax for King Features Syndicate.

J. Wellington Wimpy: E.C. Segar created this internationally known fat, hamburger-loving moocher for the *Thimble Theatre* comic strip. He first appeared in the early 1930s, and he is considered to be one of the greatest comic characters created for newspaper comic strips. In the comic strips, mainly in the Sunday page, Wimpy found ways to trick Popeye, Rough House, Geezil and many others in getting him food, free of charge. His catch phrases are legendary, most notable; "I'll gladly pay you Tuesday for a hamburger today." With a soft-pitched voice, Jack Mercer first gave voice to Wimpy in the color, two-reel classic, "Popeye the Sailor Meets Sindbad the Sailor" (Fleischer, 1936). Wimpy's main function in the cartoons was as comic relief as he pursues a duck on Sindbad's Island, with a duck dinner in mind. It wasn't until 1960 that Mercer began voicing the character full time for the 1960-61 *Popeye* cartoons series for television produced by King Features Syndicate. *(See the Appendix for a complete listing of titles where Jack Mercer voiced this character.)*

Japanese Commander: Jack Mercer voiced the Japanese Commander who, after Popeye defeats his crew and destroys his ship, decides he must lose face by drinking a huge bottle of gasoline and chewing on firecrackers. This pint-sized Japanese caricature was quite prevalent in animated cartoons at the time, and was seen in the first *Popeye* animated film produced by Famous Studios, "You're a Sap, Mr. Jap" in 1942.

Jeepers: When Paramount Pictures ended the theatrical *Popeye* cartoon series in 1957 and the films featuring Casper the Friendly Ghost, Herman and Katnip, Baby Huey and Little Audrey, the studio kept looking for a new character that could headline a long-running series. In 1960, the studio came up with a pair of dogs, Creepers, a small timid fellow, and paired him with Jeepers, a tall, overconfident dog. Jack Mercer voiced Jeepers in a striding, know-it-all voice that kept putting Creepers in situations he'd rather avoid. In "Busy Buddies" (Paramount Cartoon Studios, 1960), Jeepers helps Creepers pay off his income tax by entering him in a prizefight. Creepers, landing in the hospital by cartoon's finish, jumps out the window when Jeepers offers more help. These characters also appeared in the following theatrical cartoons produced by Paramount Cartoon Studios in 1960: "The Boss is Always Right," "Trouble Date" and "Scouting for Trouble."

Jeepers (Jack Mercer) was a slick-talking canine that caused problems for his pal, Creepers. Jeepers is pictured spouting more slick talk from "Busy Buddies" (Paramount Cartoon Studios, 1960).

Jimmy Durante: Popeye impersonated comic Jimmy Durante, complete with banana-sized nose and vocal characterization by Jack Mercer, in "Puttin' on the Act" (Fleischer, 1940). Mercer would voice the movie star again in "Popeye's Twentieth Anniversary" (Famous Studios, 1954) and "The Case of the Cockeyed Canary" (Famous Studios, 1952), with a bird's body!

"A fine friend you are…beat it!" yells Joe the Construction worker (Jack Mercer) when Casper, having lost his ghostly powers, fails to stop his fall into fresh cement in "Not Ghoulty" (Paramount Cartoon Studios, 1959). Oddly, Casper had many different voices throughout his theatrical cartoon career.

Joe the Construction Worker: A gravel-voiced constructor worker, who is a friend of Casper until the ghost, who has temporarily lost his powers, fails to save from falling into cement in "Not Ghoulty" (Paramount Cartoon Studios, 1959), a cartoon in the *Casper* series.

Goodie the Gremlin stops neighbors Fred (Jackson Beck) and Jonesy (Jack Mercer) from feuding (caused by evil Gremlins) by getting them intoxicated! From "Goodie the Gremlin" (Paramount Cartoon Studios, 1961). This was yet another attempt by Paramount Pictures to create a character who, they hoped, would star in a long-running animated series, following in the footsteps of Casper the Friendly Ghost and Popeye.

King Gulpo (Jack Mercer), ruler of a microscopic world, grows in sizes thanks to Poindexter's fast-grow formula in "Felix Baby-sits," a Felix the Cat TV-cartoon produced by Trans-Lux.

Joe the Nome: One of a group of Nomes who exclaims, "I just got back from a vaudeville show," and threatens to wake up Rip Van Winkle's slumber in "Popeye Meets Rip Van Winkle" (Fleischer, 1941).

Johnny: He is the skating, older brother to Billy (a name used often for the little boys Casper encountered) in "Ice Scream" (Famous Studios, 1957), an entry in the *Casper* theatrical series.

Jonesy: Jack Mercer was at odds again with Jackson Beck in this cartoon, "Goodie the Gremlin" (Paramount Cartoon Studios, 1961). While Mercer voiced Jonsey, Beck provided the voice for his neighbor, Fred. The two neighbors start out as friends, but a group of Gremlins cause them to battle each other. Goodie the Gremlin gets them drunk and they become pals again. Goodie was yet another attempt by Paramount to find a new star.

Katnip: The red-coated feline whose joy in life is to eat Herman the Mouse or his mice pals in Paramount Picture's *Herman and the Katnip* animated series. Syd Raymond provided Katnip's voice, but in "You Said a Mouseful" (Paramount Cartoon Studios, 1958), the cat owned his own pizza place and spoke in an Italian accent provided by Jack Mercer. Mercer also sang with an Italian accent in this clever cartoon where Herman must rescue his friend, Chubby, who is devouring Katnip's food.

King Gulpo: A big green blob, wearing a crown, who emerges from Poindexter's microscope after being splashed with an enlarging formula in "Felix Baby-sits," one of the *Felix the Cat* TV-cartoons.

King Little: The slightly, knuckle-headed regent of Lilliput, whose daughter, Princess Glory, was in love with Prince David in the animated feature, *Gulliver's Travels* (Fleischer, 1939).

Leprechaun: A red-haired little Leprechaun, given a cheery voice by Jack Mercer. He encounters trouble when he drinks The Sea Hag's tea laced with truth serum in her efforts to steal his pot of gold in the *Popeye* TV-cartoon, "The Leprechaun" (Paramount Cartoon Studios, 1961).

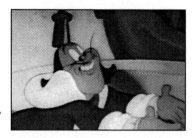

King Little (Jack Mercer) gives his approval to the arrangements being made for his daughter's wedding in the 1939 animated feature film, "Gulliver's Travels" produced by the Fleischer Studios.

Luigi: A character with Italian heritage who owns a glassware store and regrets renting the apartment above to a beatnik in "Drum Up a Tenant" (Paramount Cartoon Studios, 1963). Luigi also appears in "Sour Grapes" (Paramount Cartoon Studios, 1963). He has a vineyard of grapes which a fox wants to steal.

"C'mon, Betty, will help ya," exclaims Ma (Jack Mercer), one of the hillbillies Betty Boop encounters when she runs out of gas in "Musical Mountaineers" (Fleischer Studios, 1939). Jack Mercer provided the voices for both the male and female country folk in this musical cartoon.

Ma and her Hillbilly Brood: When Betty Boop's car runs out of gas she encounters a group of "Musical Mountaineers" (Fleischer, 1939). She performs some fine dancing along with the hillbillies. Jack Mercer provides the voice of some of the male hillbillies and most notably "Ma," one of the females who offers help to Betty's car.

Macintosh, the Worm: A worm with an Irish brogue that lives in an apple and frees Felix from his ropes after being captured by Rock Bottom in "Penelope the Elephant," an episode of the *Felix the Cat* TV-cartoon series.

Macintosh the worm (Jack Mercer using a Scottish accent) uses his choppers to bite through Felix the Cat's ropes when he's left bound by Rock Bottom who steals "Penelope the Elephant," a Felix the Cat TV-cartoon produced by Trans-Lux.

Major Mite (Jack Mercer) disguises himself as baby Swee'pea to gain entry into Popeye's house to search for the sailor's treasure map. From "A Mite of Trouble" (Paramount Cartoon Studios, 1961).

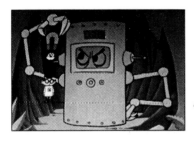

Top: *A menacing sounding Master Cylinder (Jack Mercer) uses a magnet to capture Felix the Cat and Poindexter (both voiced by Jack Mercer) in "Master Cylinder — King of the Moon," a Felix the Cat TV-cartoon produced by Trans-Lux. Bottom: Felix the Cat (Jack Mercer) greets a smiling and more jovial sounding Master Cylinder (also Mercer) when the space creature attends the feline's birthday celebration in "Public Enemies Number One and Two," a Felix the Cat TV-cartoon produced by Trans-Lux.*

Mad Scientist: Jack Mercer voiced the first madman to appear in an animated *Superman* cartoon. The Mad Scientist threatens to destroy the city with a new super ray gun. It's up to Superman to stop him! This film is known as "Superman" (Fleischer, 1941) and also referred to as "The Mad Scientist." The *Superman* theatrical cartoons were extremely expensive to produce, costing $90,000, according to the Fleischer Studios historian, Leslie Cabarga, but became very successful which encouraged the Fleischers to produce additional cartoons.

Major Mite: A black-mustached little fellow, who disguises himself as Swee'pea to search Popeye's house for a treasure map The Sea Hag wants to get her hands on in "A Mite of Trouble," a *Popeye* TV-cartoon (Paramount Cartoon Studios, 1961).

Master Cylinder: This enemy of Felix the Cat was a menacing figure that Jack Mercer gave a sinister voice. He once was a student of the Professor who kept blowing himself up so he put his great brain in a huge silver container. With his long arms, claws and piercing eyes he claimed to be the King of the Moon. His appearances in the *Felix the Cat* TV-cartoons, produced by Trans-Lux, include, though not limited to: "Master Cylinder-King of the Moon," "Master Cylinder Captures Poindexter," "Master Cylinder's Spacegram," "Venus and the Master Cylinder," "Martin the Martian Meets Felix the Cat" and "Public Enemies Number One and Two."

Martin the Martian: This small alien creature, who had big eyes and one antenna, became friends with Felix the Cat, yet only after a pact, in which Martin agreed to assist the Master Cylinder in capturing Poindexter, fell through. Mercer gave Martin a slight nasally voice in "Martin the Martin Meets Felix the Cat" and "The Martian Rescue." Martin also popped in, without dialogue, in "Public Enemies Number One and Two."

Mr. Bumble, the Bee: The kindly, elderly bee who operates the Honey shop, where his daughter Honey Bee works and who loves Hoppity, the grasshopper, in the animated feature film, *Mr. Bug Goes to Town* (Fleischer, 1941).

Mr. Tutor: "Mr. Tutor," is what Baby Huey called this well-dressed, diminutive duck with a German dialect who attempts to teach him after he is thrown out of Kindergarten in "Pest Pupil" (Paramount Cartoon Studios, 1957). The tutor suffers much physical abuse but after Baby Huey saves him from a shark, he gives the dim-witted duck a diploma, which he promptly tears into paper dolls!

Newton: The half-boy, half-horse creature who accompanied The Mighty Hercules in nearly all of his TV-cartoon adventures produced by Trans-Lux in 1963. Newton would speak his words twice. For example, he would say, "Gotta find Herc, gotta find Herc!" Jack Mercer initially provided the voice for Newton in "Hercules Saves the Kingdom," "Kidnapped by Wilamene," "Hercules vs. Teron the Evil Spirit," "Hercules vs. the Hydra," "Hercules and the Stolen Ring" and "Double Trouble."

The Princess Alona's parrot (Jack Mercer) uses his beak to open a spinach can so the sailor can recover and save his owner from the clutches of Bluto in "Alona on the Sarong Seas" (Famous Studios, 1942). Jack Mercer also provided the voice of a parrot in two other Fleischer Studio's Popeye entries, "Fowl Play" (1937) and "Leave Well Enough Alone" (1939).

Jack Mercer's voice was electronically sped-up to provide the voices Popeye's sound-a-like and look-a-like nephews, Poop-eye, Pip-eye, Pup-eye and Peep-eye.

Outer Space Professor: Mercer supplied the voice for this short mustached professor, who winds up pulling a "space boy" to earth with his giant magnet. The space boy calls upon his biker gang, which causes trouble in "From Way Out." This was a *Popeye* TV-cartoon produced by Gene Deitch/William Snyder in 1960.

Pet Store Parrot: Soft hearted Popeye frees all of the caged pets in Olive Oyl's pet store in "Leave Well Enough Alone" (Fleischer, 1939). A parrot, however, refuses to leave and sings a song called "Leave Well Enough Alone." Popeye has to rescue several dogs from the dogcatcher and returns the pets to the store. Jack Mercer provided a high-pitched voice to the parrot who councils Popeye and sings the title song. Jack Mercer also provided a parrot's voice in "Fowl Play" (Fleischer, 1937) and "Alona on the Sarong Seas" (Famous Studios, 1942).

Pip-eye, Pup-eye, Poop-eye and Peep-eye: Jack Mercer provide the voices for Popeye's lookalike and sound-alike nephews. Mercer's Popeye voice was used, but sped up to create a juvenile sound. The lads made their film debut in "Wimmen Is a Myskery" (Fleischer, 1940). In this cartoon, they appear as Olive Oyl's children in a dream she is having, prior to her wedding to Popeye. The abuse her children bring upon her ends any thoughts of wedding bells. The nephews appeared next in "Pip-eye, Pup-eye, Poop-eye and Peep-eye" (Fleischer, 1941). These lads had two primary functions in the series; to give Popeye someone to lecture to about the value of eating spinach and causing physical mishaps for the sailor. By the final theatrical cartoon, the four nephews had dwindled to two. These lads were created by the Fleischer Studios and not copyrighted by King Features Syndicate. Consequently, they didn't appear in the 1960-61 *Popeye* television cartoons produced by King. When Hanna-Barbera, in association with King Features, began production on a new series of Popeye television films, the four nephews returned, but Jack Mercer voiced only one. *(See the Appendix for a complete listing of titles where Jack Mercer voiced these characters.)*

Poindexter (Jack Mercer) is kissed by an affectionate alien in "Master Cylinder, King of the Moon," a Felix the Cat TV-cartoon produced by Trans-Lux.

Poindexter: The Professor's bald nephew, who wore big glasses and a graduation cap. He was a genius whose inventions occasionally backfired on Felix. Yet, the cat was quite forgiving and often accompanied the lad in his adventures to help keep him out of trouble. Felix and Poindexter also frequently traveled to space in the ship Poindexter invented. The pair often clashed with the evil Master Cylinder. On occasion, Poindexter would help Felix in stopping The Professor's evil plans. His appearances in the *Felix the Cat* TV-cartoon series include, though not limited to: "The Flying Saucer," "Felix Baby-sits," "Master Cylinder: King of the Moon," "Master Cylinder Captures Poindexter," "Felix and Poindexter Out West," "Martin the Martian Meets Felix the Cat" and "Public Enemies Number One and Two." Mercer's voice was mechanically raised and sped-up when performing Poindexter.

Poopdeck Pappy: Popeye's father, who loves the nightlife, booze and ladies, made his debut in E.C. Segar's "Thimble Theatre" comic strip in 1936. The executives at King Features Syndicate who distributed

Poopdeck Pappy (Jack Mercer) doesn't like being told he's too old to build a boat in "My Pop, My Pop" (Fleischer Studios, 1940).]

the comic strip, ordered Segar to clean up Popeye as his popularity among children was growing. To counter Popeye's goodness, Segar created his father, whose behavior was just the opposite of his kindhearted son. Segar's version of Poopdeck Pappy wasn't afraid to bop women as both Olive Oyl and The Sea Hag were often on the receiving end of his fist! Poopdeck Pappy made his debut in the classic cartoon, "Goonland" (Fleischer, 1938). Pappy later returned to animation in 1940 with Jack Mercer voicing the ninety-nine year old sailor. Mercer gave Pappy, a fun loving, without a care in the world vocal, while Popeye took the punishment for his father's actions. Several of the Fleischer cartoons featuring Poopdeck Pappy had the bearded sailor trying to convince his son he still had the stamina of a young swab. Poopdeck Pappy appeared in the theatrical films produced by Fleischer and Famous Studios and the television cartoons produced by King Features Syndicate and Hanna-Barbera. *(See the Appendix for a complete listing of titles where Jack Mercer voiced this character.)*

Popeye the Sailor: One of the world's famous and best-loved comic strip and cartoon characters, Popeye first appeared in E.C. Segar's *Thimble Theatre* comic strip on January 17, 1929. He soon became the star of the comic strip and appeared in a line of merchandise beginning in the early 1930s. The Fleischer Studios decided to use the pipe-smoking, fat-forearmed sailor in one of their *Betty Boop* cartoons titled, "Popeye the Sailor" (1933). The film was a huge success and the spinach-eater's own series began production. William Costello, who initially provided the rough-sounding voice for Popeye, was fired after demanding a vacation in the middle of production. Jack Mercer, then working in the Fleischer's art department, stepped in and provided a lighter-sounding tone to Popeye's voice. Mercer's rendition provided the character with more range, personality and the hilarious under-the-breath mumblings, which became a trademark of the Fleischer *Popeye* films. Much of Popeye's dialogue was heard despite his on-screen closed lips. Mercer delighted in ad-libbing though the mouth movements had already been completed. The *Popeye* series not only was the biggest success to come out of the Fleischer Studios, but it would go on to become the longest-running animated short subject series in motion picture history.

Popeye (Jack Mercer) becomes a conductor at the conclusion of "The Spinach Overture" (Fleischer Studios, 1935). This was the second cartoon Jack Mercer performed the sailor's voice, which he initially did with a soft muttering characterization.

Paramount Pictures took over Fleischer Studios, renaming it Famous Studios in 1942. Production on the *Popeye* series continued. Initially, the cartoons were in black and white, but they switched to full color with the last entry in 1943. Jack Mercer's trademark ad-libs and mutterings were much less frequent; the Famous Studios' shorts were now pre-recorded (prior to the animation being completed). Jack Mercer supplied Popeye's voice through mid-1957.

When the Fleischer/Famous Studios *Popeye* films made their television debut in September of 1956, they were a huge success. Local television markets across the country were scoring big ratings and Popeye became the most popular animated character on the small screen. King Features Syndicate, though owning the rights to the character, did not have any

A publicity photo from The All-New Popeye Hour which aired on CBS Saturday morning television from 1978 to 1980. While Jack Mercer continued to voice Popeye (and Poopdeck Pappy), Marilyn Schreffer provided the voice for Olive Oyl and Allan Melvin (prominent character actor) voiced bearded Bluto.

ownership of the theatrical cartoons. The Syndicate decided to cash in on the Popeye hysteria and hired five animation studios to crank out 220 TV-cartoons starring the spinach-eating sailor in color. These new films King Features Syndicate would own and distribute. This was a smart move as stations, already having success with the theatrical films, quickly bought the new additions.

Mercer voiced Popeye for the hour-long special "The Man Who Hated Laughter" (also known as "Popeye Meets The Man Who Hated Laughter") for *The ABC Saturday Superstar Movie*, which aired in 1972 and 1973. In 1972, Mercer supplied Popeye's voice for an animated safety film, distributed to school systems across the country, *Look Where You Are Going*.

Both the theatrical and TV *Popeye* cartoons continued to have success airing in syndication during the 1960s throughout the mid-1970s. It became fashionable in the late 1970s to give old cartoon characters new life as Saturday morning series on ABC, NBC or CBS. Popeye followed suit in September of 1978, with the debut of The *All New Popeye Hour*, which ran on CBS until 1980. Though lacking in violence, the program became one of the highest rated Saturday morning cartoon series during its initial season. The new cartoons were previewed with a special primetime half-hour episode in 1978, and aired from 1978 to 1980. Also featured on *The All New Popeye Hour* were longer cartoon segments where Mercer voiced the spinach-eating sailor called *Popeye's Treasure Hunt*.

Popeye returned to the CBS Saturday morning schedule in a half-hour series called *The Popeye and Olive Comedy Show* in September of 1980. In addition to new cartoons featuring Olive Oyl and Alice the Goon in the army, Jack Mercer voiced Popeye as a caveman in "Prehistoric Popeye." This half-hour series aired on CBS, Saturday mornings until September of 1983. *(See the Appendix for a complete listing of titles where Jack Mercer voiced this character.)*

Popeye's Mother: Since Jack Mercer voiced Popeye and his father, Poopdeck Pappy, why not step into the role as the female head of the family? Mercer could be heard voicing Popeye's mother in the opening scene of "Popeye's Pappy" (Famous Studios, 1952). She explains to her son, "And son when you were a young infink your Pappy went to buy you some spinach, he ain't never returned." Popeye's mother could also be heard in "Let's Stalk Spinach" (Famous Studios, 1951), and "Lunch with a Punch" (Famous Studios, 1952), saying to baby Popeye, "Here ya are, son, eat yer spinach and you'll be healthy and strong," and the 1960 *Popeye* TV-cartoon, "Mirror Magic" (Paramount Cartoon Studios).

Preacher: A kind-hearted, tender voice is given by Jack Mercer to the pastor who marries Popeye and Olive Oyl in her dream in "Bride and Gloom" (Famous Studios, 1954). Popeye, disguised as a preacher, uses an elderly voice in his plan to prevent Bluto from marrying Olive in "Nearlyweds" (Famous Studios, 1957).

The versatile voice of Jack Mercer. From facing page: The menacing, hungry fly from "The Cobweb Hotel," the gentle mother of Popeye from "Popeye's Pappy," the angry Irish cop from "Moving Aweigh," the lecturing older brother Johnny from "Ice Scream," the not so easily scared ghost exterminator from "Not Ghoulty." This page: the sophisticated diminutive butler Jeevie from "From Rags to Riches to Rags," the German-accented tutor from "Pest Pupil," the elderly seer of Mt. Olympus, Dadonis, from "Hercules Saves the Kingdom" and the happy-go-lucky leprechaun from "The Leprechaun."

Professor I. Stare (Jack Mercer) picks Olive Oyl's name out of the phonebook and uses her as a "human subject" in "Nix on Hypnotricks" (Fleischer, 1941).

The Professor (Jack Mercer) has Felix the Cat's magic bag (of course he won't keep it for long) in "Into Outer Space," a Felix the Cat TV-cartoon produced by Trans-Lux.

Prof. I. Stare: A short, lanky man, wearing a turban that needs a human subject to hypnotize. Flipping in the phone book, his finger lands on the name "Ms. Olive Oyl." For the remainder of the cartoon, "Nix on Hypnotricks" (Fleischer, 1941), Popeye saves Olive from impending disaster as she walks in a trance toward Prof. I. Stare's lair. Voiced by Jack Mercer, Prof. I. Stare sounds chilling when seeing Olive approach him. "I knew you would come, ha, ha, ha!" Of course, with the help of his spinach, Popeye trounces the hypnotist.

Professor: Felix the Cat's main adversary in the television cartoons was this short, balding man with white hair trimmed from ear to ear. He also sported a bushy white mustache that covered his mouth and usually wore a white lab shirt. His main objective was to steal Felix's magic bag of tricks and learn its secret. Even with the aid of Rock Bottom, the Professor always failed in his attempt to steal the magic bag. He was also the uncle of Poindexter, Felix's friend, and would ask the cat to baby-sit his nephew. Mercer gave the Professor a raspy-sounding voice. The Professor's TV-cartoon appearances included, though not limited to: "The Magic Bag," "Into Outer Space," "Abominable Snowman," "Do It Yourself Monster Book," "Blubberino the Whale," "Captain No-Kiddin," "Balloon Blower Machine," "The Money Tree," "Sheriff Felix vs. The Gas Cloud," "The Gold Fruit Tree," "Felix Baby-sits," "The Invisible Professor," "Finally, The Magic Bag Is Mine," "The Jewel Bird," "The Hairy Berry Bush," "The Professor's Committed No Crime," "A Museum, The Professor and Rock Bottom," "The Professor's Instant Changer," "Gold Digger Vavoom,"

"The Wizard and Sir Rock," "Mechanical Felix," "The Professor's Ancestor-The Wizard," "The North Pole and A Walrus Hunt," "The Trip Back from the North Pole," "North Pole Jail Hole" and "Public Enemies Number One and Two."

Professor O.G. WottaSnozzle: Jack Mercer and Jackson Beck were the only males supplying voices for the 220 *Popeye* television cartoons produced by King Features Syndicate in 1960-61. Occasionally, they would voice the same character, as in the case of Professor O.G. WottaSnozzle, who first appeared in the companion comic strip with *Thimble Theatre*, titled *Sappo* by E.C. Segar. In "Swee'pea Soup" (Gene Deitch/William Snyder, 1960), Mercer gave the Professor with the long white beard and graduation cap a voice. The frantic Professor tries to make Swee'pea soup by using the real Swee'pea as the main ingredient! Jackson Beck took over the voice for the rest of the TV-cartoon series.

Professor Schumltz: Another attempt by Paramount Cartoon Studios to find a character who could sustain a long-running animated series was this top-hatted, dapper, white mustached, know-it-all professor who Jack Mercer gave a confident-sounding voice with a German accent. Professor Schumltz appeared in two theatrical films in 1960, "Fiddle Faddle" and "Terry the Terror." In "Terry the Terror," after failing to change a bratty boy's personality by scientific methods, he resorts to paddling his behind! In 1961's "The Mighty Termite," his scientific look at a termite has him running in terror, to be consumed by the creature by the film's finish. His last appearance was in 1962's "Giddy Gadget." All

Professor O.G. WottaSnozzle (Jack Mercer) is concerned of having to learn what makes Swee'pea so sweet in "Swee'pea Soup" (Gene Dietch/William Snyder, 1960).

Professor Schumltz (Jack Mercer) tries to discipline "Terry the Terror" (Paramount Cartoon Studios, 1960). Mercer gave this big-nosed, top-hatted know-it-all professor a German accent.

Rock Bottom (Jack Mercer) and The Professor (also Mercer) marvel at the television demonstration of "The Gold Fruit Tree," a Felix the Cat TV-cartoon produced by Trans-Lux. While the cigar-smoking bulldog often teamed with the Professor, he tried on his own to outwit Felix.

four of his appearances were produced by Paramount Cartoon Studios.

Rip Van Winkle: Popeye takes the snoring Rip Van Winkle to his own bed after he's tossed out of his home for unpaid rent. After succeeding in keeping the neighborhood quiet so the old man can sleep, a coin falls to the floor. Rip Van Winkle, voiced by Jack Mercer, awakens and seeing Popeye says, "Oh, a pick pocket huh!" Winkle fires his rifle at Popeye, ending the cartoon, "Popeye Meets Rip Van Winkle" (Fleischer, 1941).

Rock Bottom: He was the muscular gruff bulldog that bullied Felix and often teamed with The Professor in his evil plots. He was often dressed in a dapper suit and tie, topped by a small cap, and frequently smoked cigars. Unlike The Professor, who was kind to Felix on occasion, Rock Bottom was seldom friendly and proved to be an irascible neighbor. Mercer gave a gruff deep voice to the character, whose TV-cartoon appearances included, though not limited to: "Balloon Blower Machine," "Penelope the Elephant," "The Money Tree," "Sheriff Felix vs. the Gas Cloud," "The Gold Fruit Tree," The Jewel Bird," "The Hairy Berry Bush," "A Museum, the Professor, and Rock Bottom," "Gold Dipper Vavoom," "The Wizard and Sir Rock," "The Invisible Professor," ""The North Pole and a Walrus Hunt," "The Trip Back From the North Pole," "North Pole Jail Hole" and "Public Enemies Number One and Two."

Roger Black Lay: Wearing a black top hat, with a long mustache, he is a evil-looking man, in the tradition of silent movies, who menaces Olive Oyl in the animated cartoon Popeye creates in "Cartoon's Ain't Human" (Famous Studios, 1943), the last black-and-white *Popeye* film. Mercer provides a sinister, yet humorous husky voice for the villain.

Rough House: The whiskered hamburger cook who is constantly tricked by Wimpy into getting free hamburgers first appeared in E.C. Segar's comic strip, *Thimble Theatre*, in the early 1930s. While Jackson Beck originated the voice in the *Popeye* TV-cartoons, produced by King Features Syndicate, Mercer voiced the rotund character in "Boing Boing Gone" and "The Whiffle Bird's Revenge," both produced by Paramount Cartoon Studios in 1961.

Villainous Roger Black Lay (Jack Mercer) and his horse (also Mercer) hiss at Popeye's nephews who are watching the sailor's homemade animated cartoon, "Wages of Sin" in the last black and white Popeye theatrical, "Cartoons Ain't Human" (Famous Studios, 1943).

Rube: Jack Mercer provided the voice of various elderly males, an example being the white-bearded "Rube," who needs to hail a taxi, which begins another competition between Popeye and Bluto, both driving one, in "Taxi Turvy" (Famous Studios, 1954). Mercer gives this gentleman a voice creating the impression of wealth when he says, "I said the Rich Hotel, dag-na-bit!"

Rueben, Dueben and Louie: These are three mice, Herman the Mouse's nephews in previous cartoons, who remind Katnip of the time they outwitted him in a drugstore in the final Herman and Katnip theatrical cartoon, "Katnip's Big Day" (Paramount Cartoon Studios, 1959). Jack Mercer's voice could be heard as some of Herman's nephews in previous entries of the series. In their final appearance, three mice were given names.

"Happy Christmas to all and to all a good night. Ho! Ho! Ho! Ho!" exclaims Santa Claus (Jack Mercer) at the conclusion of "Spinach Greetings" (Paramount Cartoon Studios, 1961).

Oh, Popeye! If only you hadn't grabbed the gun when Shorty wanted to blow his brains out, you could have saved yourself a lot of ensuing headaches! Shorty (Jack Mercer) is a pain in the neck and Popeye ends up shooting the troublemaker himself (in the dark, but Shorty survives and appears in two other cartoons) in "Happy Birthdaze" (Famous Studios, 1943).

Santa Claus: The Sea Hag kidnaps Santa and Popeye rescues him so he can wish the sailor, Olive, Swee'pea and Wimpy "Merry Christmas to all and to all a good night, ho! ho! ho! ho!" in "Spinach Greetings," a *Popeye* TV-cartoon (Paramount Cartoon Studios, 1960). Mercer gives a husky-sounding voice to ol' Saint Nick, who flies a plane rather than using Reindeer.

Shoe Salesman: A frustrated salesman trying to fit a size 3 shoe on Olive's huge foot. "But, Madame, it just can't be done," he exclaims in the TV-cartoon, "Popeye Goes Sale-ing" (Paramount Cartoon Studios, 1960).

Shorty: Popeye's pint-sized sailor companion, who, "trying to help," caused physical abuse to his pipe-smoking buddy. He first appeared in "Happy Birthdaze" (Famous Studio, 1943), causing Popeye to get pummeled attempting to celebrate the sailor's birthday. Popeye ends up shooting Shorty by the cartoon's finish. The scene is dark; a gun shot goes off, followed by "The Bitter End" appearing on the screen. Shorty survived and returned in "The Marry-Go-Round" (Famous Studios, 1943), trying to get Popeye to propose marriage to Olive. Olive ends up falling in love with Shorty, but the sailor gets revenge. Popeye tosses Olive in a washing machine and Shorty ends up tied to his bunk, with photos of Olive at every turn. Jack Mercer originated Shorty's voice in his first two appearances, while Arnold Stang took over for his final film, "Moving Aweigh" (Famous Studios, 1944).

Sideshow Barker: Jack Mercer voiced this character in the same scene twice. Initially the character was heard in "Quick on the Vigor" (Famous Studios, 1950) and later in "The Crystal Brawl" (Famous Studios, 1957), when the footage from "Quick on the Vigor" was reused. In both films, he is the man with the long nose who tells Popeye, "Ring the bell and win a box of sweets for your sweetie!" Mercer also provided the voice for a sideshow barker in the *Superman* short, "Terror on the Midway" (Fleischer Studios, 1942).

Sir Percival Prunepit (Jack Mercer) is The Phantom Moutacher (Paramount Cartoon Studios, 1961) who gets the crazy urge to draw mustaches on everyone he encounters!

Sir Percival Prunepit: A diminutive man with a white mustache who, it turns out, is "The Phantom Moustacher" (Paramount Cartoon Studios, 1961). He creates mishap in the streets of London by drawing mustaches on anything! Once captured, the jury finds him not guilty despite the fact they all have mustaches drawn on their faces!

A skating attendant (Jack Mercer) tries to find skates long enough for Olive Oyl's elongated feet when Popeye (also Mercer) teaches his girlfriend the sport in "A Date to Skate" (Fleischer, 1938).

Sir Reginald Tweedledum IV: An English aristocrat who must bring honor to his family by shooting a lion in "The Lion's Busy" (Paramount Cartoon Studios, 1961). Mercer voiced this character with a pronounced usage of the letter "P."

Skating Attendant: Popeye wants Olive Oyl to learn how to skate in "A Date to Skate" (Fleischer, 1938). The sailor must purchase skates for his long-footed girlfriend. When the skating attendant, voiced by Jack Mercer, asks the size of Olive's foot, the sailor man blushes and asks Olive to make a fist. The skating attendant wraps a skate around Olive's foot and comments, "She's got a hand like a foot and a half."

Spooky (Jack Mercer), Casper's troublemaking cousin, drinks a bottle of ink to scare Wendy the Witch in "Which is Witch" (Paramount Cartoon Studios, 1958). For every ounce of goodness Casper had, his cousin had the opposite. Mercer gave the ghost with the derby hat a wise guy voice who would address his cousin as "Hey, Casp!"

Jack Mercer often provided voices for characters with different occupations. In "The Spinach Scholar" (Paramount Cartoon Studios, 1960), he provides the voice for a woman teacher who, after Popeye accidentally puts his hand up, says, "I see your hand is up, Mister Popeye." Popeye tries counting both his hands and toes to answer a simple math problem while the teacher says, "I'm waiting for the answer."

Slippery Sam: He's a criminal on the run from the law who ends up at the home of muscle-bound Possum Pearl, who goes after any male with marriage on her mind! Jack Mercer also provided the voice of the handsome policeman who offers Possum Pearl a reward for Slippery Sam's capture. It is the policeman, himself, who is Possum Pearl's reward in "Possum Pearl" (Paramount Cartoon Studios, 1957).

Spider: A sinister-looking spider, whose creepy voice was supplied by Jack Mercer, ran "The Cobweb Hotel" (1936), a Max Fleischer color classic. He runs a cobweb hotel in an abandoned writing desk, trapping his fly victims. When Mr. and Mrs. Fly arrive, on their honeymoon, a rousing battle ensues. Mr. Spider is outmatched by Mr. Fly, a champion fighter, and the hotel's "guests" are freed.

Spooky: Casper's trouble-making cousin, wearing a derby hat and talking like a wise guy, which Jack Mercer voiced in the theatrical and TV-produced *Casper* cartoons produced by Paramount Pictures. Mercer voiced the ghost with a penchant for practical jokes in "Hooky Spooky" (Famous Studios, 1957), "Which is Witch" (Paramount Cartoon Studios, 1958), "Doing What's Fright" (Paramount Cartoon Studios, 1959) and "City Snicker" (Paramount Cartoon Studios, 1963), a TV-cartoon. Spooky would become better known for his long-running self-titled comic books published by Harvey Comics.

Stunt Movie Director: When Popeye applies for a job as a stunt man, he has to win the approval of a gruff-sounding movie director in "Doing Impossikible Stunts" (Fleischer, 1940).

Teacher: Whether it be male or female, Jack Mercer provided the voice for teachers seen in Paramount theatrical or television cartoons. Near the end of "Dawg Gone" (Paramount Cartoon Studios, 1958), the final *Little Audrey* theatrical film, Mercer voices the female school marm. In the 1960 *Popeye* TV-cartoon, "The Spinach Scholar," Mercer lends his voice to the female math teacher who asks the class, "How much is ten and fifteen?" which has Popeye counting both his hands and toes, struggling to give the correct answer.

The Stunt Movie Director in the Popeye cartoon, "Doing Impossikible Stunts" (Fleischer, 1940) is a good example of why voice credits would have been appreciated in the animated theatrical films produced by Paramount Pictures. This gruff-sounding, enthusiastic man sounds very much like Jack Mercer. However, as in the case of Bluto during this period, could also have been voiced by Pinto Colvig. The fact that Jack Mercer supplied Popeye's voice in this cartoon and the only other adult male was the Stunt Movie Director leads me to think this was not Colvig. "My little brain-child, you will be the sensation of sensations!" exclaims the Stunt Movie Director (carrying off Swee'pea after viewing his heroics from "Lost and Foundry" (Fleischer, 1937), when he chooses the baby over Popeye as his new stunt man!

Teron: An evil and terrifying blue genie-like creature who Jack Mercer gave a hearty sinister voice. It is unwittingly released by The Mighty Hercules' girlfriend, Helena, in "Hercules vs. Teron the Evil Spirit," an early entry in *The Mighty Hercules* TV-cartoon series produced by Trans-Lux in 1963.

Turtle: A turtle, with a skip in his step, who is a reporter trying to get a photo of a missile launching in "Turtle Scoop" (Paramount Cartoon Studios, 1961).

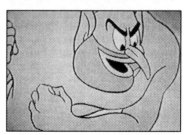

Uncle Angus: Popeye's white-bearded Uncle, who needs help from Popeye and his little nephews to stop Bluto from taking over his farm in "Old McPopeye Had a Farm" (Hanna-Barbera, 1978).

Teron (Jack Mercer), an evil blue genie-like creature with a hearty, menacing voice terrorizes Newton and Helena. It's up to Hercules to encase him in a whirlpool in "Hercules vs. Teron the Evil Spirit," a Mighty Hercules TV-cartoon produced in 1963 by Trans-Lux.

Jack Mercer didn't have to task his voice very much for supplying the voice for Vavoom, who spoke only one word, a rather loud, earth-shattering "VAVOOM!" Here, he demonstrates his vocal range in "Vavoom Learns How to Fish," a Felix the Cat TV-cartoon produced by Trans-Lux.

The Whiffle Bird (Jack Mercer) casts a spell on Wimpy (also Mercer) when the moocher tries to eat him. Whenever Wimpy says the word "hamburger" he turns into a wolf in "The Whiffle Bird's Revenge" (Paramount Cartoon Studios, 1961). Mercer gave the bird a nasal-sounding, timid voice.

Vavoom: A pint-sized friend of Felix the Cat who dressed in a parka and only spoke one word: VAVOOM!: that he yelled at the top of his lungs and often resulted in a group of people being knocked over or an avalanche being sparked. Jack Mercer's one-word vocal for Vavoom was heard in "Felix and Vavoom," "Gold Dipper Vavoom" and "Vavoom Learns How to Fish," all produced by Trans-Lux for the *Felix the Cat* TV series.

Vice Missile: A bow-tied-wearing missile, who gives Popeye, Olive Oyl and King Blozo a tour of Missile City in "Incident at Missile City," a *Popeye* TV-cartoon produced by Paramount Cartoon Studios in 1961

Villager: A concerned citizen who wails about the capture of Olive Oyl by a green-skinned Bluto-looking monster in Hanna-Barbera's "Popeye Meets the Blutostein Monster" (1978). Jack Mercer's primary roles in these new Popeye cartoons were to voice the sailor and write scripts. On occasion, he would voice incidental characters like this one.

Whiffle Bird: It first appeared in E.C. Segar's *Thimble Theatre* comic strip and by rubbing its feathers, Popeye gained super human strength in the sailor's initial 1929 appearance. When the Whiffle Bird was dropped from the comic strip, spinach was credited as the source of Popeye's strength. The yellow creature returned, with a whiny voice by Jack Mercer, in these King Features Syndicate-produced *Popeye* TV-cartoons: "Quick Change Ollie" (Paramount Cartoon Studios, 1960), sending Popeye and Wimpy traveling to

"Ye Olden Days," "Hamburgers Aweigh" (Paramount Cartoon Studios 1961), using his magic to make Wimpy hate hamburgers, "Giddy Gold" (Paramount Cartoon Studios, 1961), warning Olive of "three dangerous dangers" for seeking a treasure, and "The Whiffle Bird's Revenge" (Paramount Cartoon Studios, 1961), turning Wimpy into a werewolf as punishment because the moocher tried to eat him. In print, the character is also known as "The Whiffle Hen."

Whiffle Piffle (Jack Mercer) was yet another new character introduced in a "Betty Boop" cartoon in an attempt to breathe new life into the series. The diminutive little fellow with the nasal-sounding voice wrecks Betty Boop's home demonstrating cleaning equipment in "The Hot Air Salesman" (Fleischer, 1937).

Whiffle Piffle: This short little fellow, with a thin neck, round head and circular eyes, was another attempt by the Fleischer Studios to breathe new life in their *Betty Boop* animated series. When Paramount cautioned the studio to tone down Betty's sexual appeal, she often played second fiddle to new characters. Whiffle Piffle, supplied with a nasally voice by Jack Mercer, debuted in "Whoops I'm a Cowboy" (Fleischer, 1937), where he tries to become a bronco-busting cowboy to win Ms. Boop's affections. He returned in "The Hot Air Salesman" (Fleischer, 1937) to try and sell Betty one of his appliances. Poor Betty's house is nearly ruined by Whiffle Piffle and she throws him out! Apparently, movie audiences, too, threw out Whiffle Piffle, for he vanished after his second cartoon.

Wolf: Snoozer the sheep dog must stay awake to protect his charges from the Jack Mercer-voiced wolf in "Good Snooze Tonight" (Paramount Cartoon Studios, 1963).

Woodpecker: Popeye needs a tree for a mast, unfortunately he chooses one, which is the home of an Edward G. Robinson-

A zookeeper (Jack Mercer) keeps in touch with Felix the Cat when the feline goes in search of Wally the Walrus, which began a multi-part story arc (as many of Felix's television adventures were). Jack Mercer gave each incidental character (as in the case of this zookeeper) a distinctive voice.

sounding woodpecker in "Woodpeckin'" (Famous Studios, 1943). Popeye's tender heart wins out and the woodpecker's new home becomes part of the sailor's boat.

Zookeeper: A zookeeper with an excitable voice, who reports on Felix the Cat's progress when the feline goes in search of Wally the Walrus in "The North Pole and A Walrus Hunt," "The Trip Back From the North Pole" and "North Pole Jail Hole," a multi-part story (as many were) in the *Felix the Cat* TV-cartoon series.

JACK MERCER'S WRITING CAREER

Jack Mercer's writing career began while he was employed with the Fleischer Studios. Being an artist he also drew many of his own storyboards. A storyboard is a series of cartoon drawings, depicting what scenes will be used in the production of an animated cartoon. This is not a comprehensive list because writers were not always credited during Mercer's time. This section demonstrates the various situations and characters that Mercer wrote during his lifetime. A thank you must be given to animation historian Ken Layton, for his research of the Paramount Cartoon library used in this chapter.

BABY HUEY

Baby Huey, the enormous, dense duck dressed like an infant, lived in the town of Duckville with his Mama and Papa Duck. He first appeared in *Casper the Friendly Ghost* #1 in 1949, published by St. John, created by Martin Taras. The character would have a lengthy run in comic books published by Harvey Comics. His first animated appearance was in *Quack-A-Doodle Doo*, a Famous Studios production released by Paramount Pictures in 1950. Huey often matched what little wit he had with the sly fox who would wear a number of disguises in his quest to have Huey for dinner! Other cartoons had Huey's father receive unintentional physical abuse from his overgrown son. Baby Huey would return in new animated cartoons for *The Baby Huey Show*, which aired from 1994 to 1996. The series also aired films from his theatrical career. Throughout most of his animated career, Syd Raymond provided Huey's voice.

Huey starred in a total of 12 cartoons from Paramount, produced from 1950-1959, with Mercer's writing involved in the following Noveltoon theatrical cartoons:

Quack-A-Doodle-Doo (Famous Studios, 1950). Mrs. Duck, who longs to have a baby, swallows an entire bottle of vitamins and she lays a huge egg. Out pops a naked Baby Huey and, once dressed, attracts the attention of a hungry fox (with minimal dialogue by Jack Mercer). Co-written by Carl Meyer. Direction: Isadore Sparber. Animation: Dave Tendlar and Thomas Golden.

One Quack Mind (Famous Studios, 1951). The Fox, disguised as a babysitter, has a hunger for Baby Huey. Co-written by Carl Meyer. Direction: Isadore Sparber. Animation: Steve Muffatti and George Germanetti.

Party Smarty (Famous Studios, 1951). The Fox gives Baby Huey a birthday party but his wish is to eat the overgrown duck! Co-written by Carl Meyer. Direction: Seymour Kneitel. Animation: Dave Tendlar and Morey Reden.

Scout Fellow (Famous Studios, 1951). Baby Huey wants to be a Cub Scout and the Fox wants to lead Huey right into his mouth! Co-written by Carl Meyer. Direction: Seymour Kneitel. Animation: Dave Tendlar and Martin Taras.

Clown on the Farm (Famous Studios, 1952). Baby Huey wants to play circus! Co-written by Carl Meyer. Direction: Seymour Kneitel. Animation: Dave Tendlar and Martin Taras.

Starting from Hatch (Famous Studios, 1953). Baby Huey hatches from his egg, thinking the hungry fox is his mother! Co-written by Carl Meyer. Direction: Seymour Kneitel. Animation: Dave Tendlar and Tom Moore.

Jumping with Toy (Paramount Cartoon Studios, 1957). The Fox pretends he's Santa to have Huey as his Christmas dinner. His fur-coat ends up as Huey's gift to his Mama. Solely written by Jack Mercer. Direction: Dave Tendlar. Animation: William B. Pattengill.

Baby Huey hangs stockings on the chimney anticipating Santa's arrival but the fox shows up dressed up as Saint Nick in "Jumping with Toy" (Paramount Cartoon Studios, 1957), written by Jack Mercer.

Huey's Father's Day (Paramount Cartoon Studios, 1959). The final *Baby Huey* theatrical cartoon has Huey's father unable to rest on Father's Day, thanks to his dim-witted son. Co-written by Carl Meyer. Direction: Seymour Kneitel. Animation: Tom Johnson and William B. Pattengill.

Papa is angry at his son, Baby Huey, for creating headaches for him in "Huey's Father's Day" (Paramount Cartoon Studios, 1959) written by Carl Meyer and Jack Mercer. This was the last theatrical cartoon featuring "Baby Huey." Baby Huey, along with many other Paramount Pictures animated characters would be featured in hundreds of comic books published by Harvey Comics.

BUZZY THE CROW

Buzzy the Crow, the black bird with the straw hat, never had his own comic book series but appeared in issues of *Harvey Comics Hits* as well as *Famous TV Funday Funnies, Paramount Animated Comics* and *TV Casper and Company*. He is best remembered for his appearances in eight animated cartoons produced by Famous Studios. Buzzy was usually paired with dim-bubbled Katnip, who wanted to make a meal out of the crow. Buzzy's quick wit always got the best of Katnip. Jackson Beck gave him a Rochester-sounding voice (from The Jack Benny Show), which was not considered politically correct by the 1990s. When Buzzy's cartoons were aired during the 1990s, his voice was re-dubbed or the cartoons were simply not shown any longer. Buzzy's theme song was "Listen to the Mocking Bird."

Jack Mercer's writing was involved with the following Noveltoons, featuring Buzzy the Crow:

Sock-A-Bye Kitty (Famous Studios, 1950). Katnip has insomnia and Buzzy wants to make sure he sleeps-permanently before he ends up as bird food! Co-written by Carl Meyer. Direction: Seymour Kneitel. Animation: Dave Tendlar and Tom Golden.

As the Crow Lies (Famous Studios, 1951). Katnip has the hiccups and Buzzy pretends to cure him while inflicting physical abuse to the feline. Co-written by Carl Meyer. Direction: Seymour Kneitel. Animation: Dave Tendlar and Morey Reden.

Cat-Choo (Famous Studios, 1951). Katnip's bad head cold is mild compared to the abuse he gets when Buzzy attempts to cure his stuffed noggin! Co-written by Carl Meyer. Direction: Seymour Kneitel. Animation: Dave Tendlar and Martin Taras.

Buzzy the Crow reacts in shock to what his cold cure for Katnip does to a spoon in "Cat-Choo" (Famous Studios, 1951), a Noveltoon written by Jack Mercer and Carl Meyer.

The Awful Tooth (Famous Studios, 1952). Buzzy tries to get rid of Katnip's toothache before he ends up in the cat's stomach! Co-written by Carl Meyer. Direction: Seymour Kneitel. Animation: George Rufle and Al Eugster

CASPER THE FRIENDLY GHOST

Casper was created in the early 1940s by Seymour Reit and Joe Oriolo, the former creating the idea for the character and the latter providing the illustrations. *The Friendly Ghost* (Famous Studios, 1945) was the first *Noveltoon* to feature Casper. He appeared in two more *Noveltoon* shorts before Paramount launched his own series in 1950. In nearly every cartoon, Casper would search for a friend, whether it be a human or animal. In later cartoons his Cousin Spooky, voiced by Jack Mercer, would provide a little variety to the plots. Casper found himself with other ghosts who wanted him to be just as mean as they were. Casper went on to become Paramount Picture's second biggest animated star (the first being *Popeye*). From 1940 until 1959, Paramount released theatrical cartoons starring Casper the Friendly Ghost. Casper went on to become a huge success in several comic book titles (*Casper, Casper and Nightmare, Casper and Spooky, Casper and the Ghostly Trio,* etc.) published by Harvey Comics. He has also been used in all kinds of merchandise. There have been several revivals of Casper in made-for-TV-cartoons and feature films. Throughout his theatrical career, Casper had several different voices.

Jack Mercer's writing was involved with the following Casper the Friendly Ghost cartoons:

Fright Day the 13th (Famous Studios, 1953). Casper makes friends with Lucky, a little black cat. Casper tries to help Lucky find his good luck charm. Co-written by Carl Meyer. Direction: Isadore Sparber. Animation: Myron Waldman and Larry Silverman.

By the Old Mill Scream (Famous Studios, 1953). Shortail the Beaver gets Casper's help in building a dam. Co-written by Carl Meyer. Direction: Seymour Kneitel. Animation: Myron Waldman and Nick Tafuri.

An angry beaver (Jack Mercer) in charge of building a new dam is disgusted over the bungling of Shortail the beaver in "By the Old Mill Scream" (Famous Studios, 1953), an entry in the Casper the Friendly Ghost animated theatrical series. Written by Jack Mercer and Carl Meyer.

Zero the Hero (Famous Studios, 1954). Casper helps Zero the Dog become a good watchdog. Co-written by Carl Meyer. Direction: Seymour Kneitel. Animation: Myron Waldman and Larry Silverman.

Casper the Friendly Ghost tries to make friends with a black-mustached baggage carrier (Jack Mercer) who will soon scream, "A ghost!" in this entry from the Casper series, "Zero the Hero" (Famous Studios, 1954). Written by Jack Mercer and Carl Meyer.

Line of Screamage (Famous Studios, 1956). Little Billy gets football lessons from Casper. Solely written by Jack Mercer. Direction: Seymour Kneitel. Animation: Myron Waldman and Nick Tafuri.

Little Billy and his brother watch the football Billy kicked take on a life of its own when Casper the Friendly Ghost, while invisible, takes control of it in "Line of Screamage" (Famous Studios, 1956), an entry in the Casper series. Written solely by Jack Mercer.

Spooking About Africa (Paramount Cartoon Studios, 1957). Wheezy the Elephant's sneezing is a handicap to him until Casper finds the cause of the problem (a feather) and puts it to good use! Solely written by Jack Mercer. Direction: Seymour Kneitel. Animation: Myron Waldman and Nick Tafuri.

Casper befriends Sneezy the Elephant in "Spooking About Africa," an entry in the Casper the Friendly Ghost series produced by Paramount Cartoon Studios in 1957. Sneezy's voice was supplied by Syd Raymond, heard in many theatrical cartoons for Paramount Pictures. Raymond's memorial vocal characterizations include Baby Huey and Katnip the Cat.

Ice Scream (Paramount Cartoon Studios, 1957). Casper pretends he's a snowman to teach little Billy how to skate. Jack Mercer provides the voice for Billy's older brother. Solely written by Jack Mercer. Direction: Seymour Kneitel. Animation: Myron Waldman and Nick Tafuri.

Ghost Writers (Paramount Cartoon Studios, 1958). Two writers at Paramount Cartoon Studios look at footage from prior Casper cartoons to get an idea for a new one. Solely written by Jack Mercer. Direction: Seymour Kneitel. Animation: Tom Johnson and Frank Endres.

Good Scream Fun (Paramount Cartoon Studios, 1958). Casper tries to find a home for Ozzie the Ostrich, who eats everything, en route. Ozzie's destination turns out to be a taxidermist, but Casper saves his feathered friend. Solely written by Jack Mercer. Direction: Seymour Kneitel. Animation: William B. Pattengill and Nick Tafuri.

Down to Mirth (Paramount Cartoon Studios, 1959). Casper stops a mad professor who has created an anti-gravity machine to destroy the city after fellow scientists mock him. At first the professor says he doesn't believe in ghosts until he keeps clobbering Casper and finds him "indestructible." Jack Mercer gives a menacing voice to the mad professor. Co-written by Carl Meyer. Direction: Seymour Kneitel. Animation: Nick Tafuri and William B. Pattengill.

Not Ghoulty (Paramount Cartoon Studios, 1959). Casper loses his ghostly powers and won't get them back until he scares someone! Jack Mercer voices Joe the Construction Worker and the Ghost Exterminator, actually Casper in disguise. Casper's disguise scares a bunch of nasty ghosts and his powers are restored. Co-written by Carl Meyer. Direction: Seymour Kneitel. Animation: Frank Endres and Nick Tafuri.

DEPUTY DAWG

Deputy Dawg was the first star from the Terrytoons Studio (best known for Mighty Mouse) to debut in his own half-hour TV show in syndication. *The Deputy Dawg Show* started its syndicated run in October of 1960. The show quickly caught on and became popular in practically every TV market in America. Merchandise featuring the Deputy Dawg characters soon followed. These characters included: Ty Coon, Muskie the Muskrat (who shared a rather odd television commercial with Dick Tracy for Soaky toys), Vincent Van Gopher and the white-mustached humanoid toon, the sheriff. The NBC television network aired *The Deputy Dawg Show* on Saturday mornings for the 1971-72 season.

Deputy Dawg spoke in a southern drawl and was often badgered by his supporting cast. There were 102 TV-cartoons produced, with some making their way to the theaters. Aside from dolls, hand puppets, books and the usual array of merchandise, Deputy Dawg also appeared in comic books.

As there were no writing credits given to the *Deputy Dawg* series, cartoons with Jack Mercer's involvement are not available for listing.

HERMAN AND KATNIP

Herman the mouse and Katnip the cat both appeared in Paramount's *Noveltoons*, during the late 1940s, prior to teaming up in their own cartoon series. Their scrapes were more brutal versions of MGM's animated *Tom and Jerry* series. In the majority of the cartoons, Katnip would attack a group of mice (one or more voiced by Jack Mercer). The mice's savior, Herman, would arrive and, through his wit, would beat the tar out of Katnip. Herman first appeared in 1944 as a foil to Henry the Rooster while Katnip was considered an all-purpose foil. While no one is credited for creating the characters, Dave Tendlar was the main director for the *Herman and Katnip* series. Tendlar also drew their appearances in Harvey Comics. Arnold Stang voiced Herman while Katnip's vocal was supplied by Syd Raymond. Herman and Katnip's theatrical cartoon series ended in 1959, but they continued to appear as supporting players in Harvey Comics and showed up on merchandise.

Jack Mercer's writing was involved with the following theatrical cartoons featuring the characters independently or together:

The Henpecked Rooster (Famous Studios, 1944). A *Noveltoon* featuring Henry the Rooster, who is a henpecked husband whose wife wants him to get rid of Herman the Mouse. Co-written by Jack Ward. Direction: Seymour Kneitel. Animation: Orestes Calpini and Reuben Grossman.

Campus Capers (Famous Studios, 1949). A *Noveltoon* where mice from Harvard are having dinner. When a huge cat crashes the party, Herman sends him flying down a bowling alley. Co-written by Carl Meyer. Direction: Bill Tytla. Animation: George Germanetti and Steve Muffatti.

Mice Paradise (Famous Studios, 1951). A *Noveltoon* with Herman and Katnip. Herman and his cousins travel to an island to get far away from Katnip, but guess who shows up! Co-written by Carl Meyer. Direction: Isadore Sparber. Animation: Dave Tendlar and Tom Golden.

Cat Carson Rides Again (Famous Studios, 1952). A *Noveltoon*, with Herman and Katnip. Out west, Herman matches wits with Katnip and tries to throw him out of town. Co-written by Carl Meyer. Direction: Seymour Kneitel. Animation: Dave Tendlar and Martin Taras.

Northwest Mousie (Famous Studios, 1953). Pierre Katnip is on the prowl and it's up to Captain Herman of the Northwest Mousies to capture him. Co-written by Carl Meyer. Direction: Seymour Kneitel. Animation: Al Eugster and William P. Pattengill.

Rail-Rodents (Famous Studios, 1954). Herman and Katnip continue their feud on a moving train. Solely written by Jack Mercer. Direction: Dave Tendlar. Animation: Martin Taras and Tom Moore.

Mouseum (Famous Studios, 1956). Herman takes his three nephews to a museum, where Katnip is on the prowl. Solely written by Jack Mercer. Direction: Seymour Kneitel. Animation: Al Eugster and William B. Pattengill.

Mousetro Herman (Famous Studios, 1956). Herman and his mice friends want to have a jam session, but first they have to get rid of Katnip. By cartoon's finish, Katnip becomes one of the instruments! Solely written by Jack Mercer. Direction: Isadore Sparber. Animation: Al Eugster and William B. Pattengill.

Cat in the Act (Paramount Cartoon Studios, 1957). Katnip is the night watchman at Paramount Cartoon Studios, where Herman visits along with his three nephews. Solely written by Jack Mercer. Direction: Dave Tendlar. Animation: Morey Reden.

One Funny Knight (Paramount Cartoon Studios, 1957). Herman wins the love of a mouse Princess after he saves her from baron-robber Katnip. This cartoon features exciting chase scenes and excellent musical score by Winston Sharples. Solely written by Jack Mercer. Direction: Dave Tendlar. Animation: William B. Pattengill and Chuck Harriton.

Herman the Mouse reacts to a kiss from the Princess after saving her from Katnip at the conclusion of "One Funny Knight" (Paramount Cartoon Studios, 1957). Written solely by Jack Mercer.

You Said a Mouseful (Paramount Cartoon Studios, 1958). Herman tries to get his friend, Chubby, into shape, but Katnip's pizzas are just too tempting. Jack Mercer provides the voice of Katnip with an Italian accent. Solely written by Jack Mercer. Direction: Seymour Kneitel. Animation: Tom Johnson and Frank Endres.

Jack Mercer supplied both the speaking and singing voice for Katnip (with an Italian accent) in "You Said a Mouseful" (Paramount Cartoon Studios, 1958), solely written by Jack Mercer. The red-haired feline gets angry when he discovers Chubby the mouse is eating his pizza!

JEEPERS AND CREEPERS

This short-lived theatrical series from Paramount Cartoon Studios featured two dog characters. One was short and whined (Creepers), the other tall and a slick talker (Jeepers). Jeepers' schemes would cause problems for Creepers. The cartoons were seen, titled *Modern Madcaps*, on the *New Casper Cartoon Show*. Jack Mercer provided the voice for Jeepers and was involved with the writing of the following cartoons:

Trouble Date (Paramount Cartoon Studios, 1960). Jeepers (voiced by Jack Mercer) helps Creepers look up an old girlfriend. Co-written by Carl Meyer. Direction: Seymour Kneitel. Animation: Nick Tafuri and William B. Pattengill.

The Boss is Always Right (Paramount Cartoon Studios, 1960). Creepers, with Jeeper's help, tries to ask his boss for a raise. Co-written by Carl Meyer. Direction: Seymour Kneitel. Animation: Nick Tafuri and Irving Dressler.

Busy Buddies (Paramount Cartoon Studios, 1960). Jeepers enters Creepers into a prizefight to help pay his back taxes. Co-written by Carl Meyer. Direction: Seymour Kneitel. Animation: Nick Tafuri and Irving Dressler.

Scouting for Trouble (Paramount Cartoon Studios, 1960). Creepers wants to be a hero to his nephew Frisky, so Jeepers helps. Co-written by Carl Meyer. Direction: Seymour Kneitel. Animation: Nick Tafuri and Izzy Klien.

LITTLE LULU

Little Lulu was created by Marjorie Henderson Buell (known as "Marge"), who used her in a series of single-panel cartoons for *The Saturday Evening Post* starting in 1935.

Little Lulu made her animation debut with the Famous Studios cartoon, *Eggs Don't Bounce* (1943). It was in comic books that the mischievous

Print announcement from Paramount Pictures regarding the debut of Little Lulu's first theatrical cartoon, "Eggs Don't Bounce" (Famous Studios, 1943), written by Jack Mercer, Jack Ward and Carl Meyer. Little Lulu's series was a success for Famous Studios and would remain in production for five years.

Lulu achieved her greatest success and visibility. She made regular comic book appearances in her own self-titled comic book as well as others until 1984.

Although Little Lulu's animated cartoons were very popular, Paramount Pictures didn't renew their licensing agreement with Marge. The studio felt they could do just as well with their own character, Little Audrey, who never became the star Lulu was. Paramount revived the character briefly for animation in the early 1960s.

Jack Mercer's writing was involved with the following *Little Lulu* cartoons:

Eggs Don't Bounce (Famous Studios, 1943). Little Lulu breaks eggs she was supposed to be delivering, so she "borrows" some from Henrietta the Hen. Co-written by Jack Ward. Direction: Isadore Sparber

The Dog Show-Off (Famous Studios, 1948). Lulu tries to enter her dog in the dog show, but she keeps getting kicked out. She tries to make the dog bigger by dressing as the back end of the dog, wagging her tail. However, she is discovered. Finally, Lulu causes all of the other dogs to be disqualified, so her dog wins first prize. Co-written by I. Klein. Direction: Seymour Kneitel. Animation: Myron Waldman, Gordon Whittier, Nick Tafuri, Irving Dressler and William B. Pattengill.

MILTON THE MONSTER

The Milton the Monster Show was part of a trend in the mid-1960s to build television programs around likeable monsters. Audiences had already enjoyed *The Munsters* (1964-66) and *The Addams Family* (1964-66) during the evening hours, so Milton was created for ABC Saturday morning television.

The Milton the Monster Show premiered on October 9, 1965 and was the only network offering from The Hal Seeger Studios, who employed several writers and artists from Paramount Pictures' animation studio. Among the animators on the series were two veterans from the Fleischer Studios, Shamus Culhane and Myron Waldman. Jack Mercer, Kin Platt and Woody King served as the show's writers, which produced 34 episodes and aired on the network until 1967.

Jack Mercer, Kin Platt and Woody King served as writers on the ABC Saturday morning cartoon series, The Milton the Monster Show (1965-67). Bob McFadden, who was a prolific voice actor, provided the voice for the lovable Milton.

Bob McFadden, who also voiced the animated cartoon detective *Cool McCool* for King Features Syndicate, gave Milton a southern accent. The loveable monster became so sweet because his creator, Professor Weirdo, put too much "tincture of tenderness" in his mixture for making Milton.

Other segments on the series were *Fearless Fly, Flukey Luke, Stuffy Durma, Muggy Doo, Boy Cat* and *Penny the Penguin.*

Milton also appeared on a board game and one issue of a comic book published by Gold Key. *The Milton the Monster Show* was syndicated throughout the 1970s and 1980s.

Unfortunately, writing credits were not given on each individual cartoon to determine which episodes Jack Mercer was involved with.

MODERN MADCAPS

Modern Madcaps was the umbrella title for a series of theatrical cartoons produced by Paramount Cartoon Studios from 1958 to 1967 as a replacement for *Popeye*. Paramount hoped that several featured characters would provide the launching pad for individual series. The films were interesting as they featured many humanoid characters, though none became successful to launch their own series. *Modern Madcaps* were aired as part of the Saturday morning series, *The New Casper Cartoon Show* from 1963 through 1969. *Modern Madcaps*, like *Noveltoons*, featured excellent animation and wonderful musical scores by Winston Sharples. Title mix-ups have caused some cartoons to be called *Noveltoons*. Jack Mercer was involved with the writing of the following theatrical cartoons:

Right Off the Bat (Paramount Cartoon Studios, 1958). The manager of a baseball team sends his scout out to search for new players and ends up with a horse! The horse, named Rube Clodhopper, hits but won't run. He's already done that in the Kentucky Derby. Co-written by Carl Meyer. Direction: Seymour Kneitel. Animation: Tom Johnson and Frank Endres.

Audience's exposure to the animated theatrical cartoons Jack Mercer wrote for Paramount Pictures received a tremendous boost when several of the films went into syndication in 1969.

Talking Horse Sense (Paramount Cartoon Studios, 1959). Oscar Gullible meets Gabby, a horse who talks! Co-written by Sam Dann and Carl Meyer. Direction: Seymour Kneitel. Animation: Frank Endres and William P. Pattengill.

T.V. Fuddlehead (Paramount Cartoon Studios, 1959). Fuddlehead is a real TV addict and can't pry himself away from the set! Co-written by Carl Meyer. Direction: Seymour Kneitel. Animation: Tom Johnson and William Henning.

Mike the Masquerader (Paramount Cartoon Studios, 1960). After witnessing a robbery, by Mike the Masquerader, an elephant is put into protective custody. In various disguises, Mike, tries to silence the elephant. This elephant *does* forget, which is why he carries a tape recorder. Co-written by Carl Meyer. Direction: Seymour Kneitel. Animation: William B. Pattengill and Nick Tafuri.

Fiddle Faddle (Paramount Cartoon Studios, 1960). Professor Schmultz (voiced by Jack Mercer) sets out to prove that music soothes the savage beast. Co-written by Carl Meyer. Direction: Seymour Kneitel. Animation: Tom Johnson and Irving Dressler.

From Dime to Dime (Paramount Cartoon Studios, 1960). A downtrodden man finds a dime and gets hooked on gambling! Co-written by Carl Meyer. Direction: Seymour Kneitel. Animation: Tom Johnson and Irving Dressler.

The Shoe Must Go On (Paramount Cartoon Studios, 1960). Luigi the Blacksmith's constant pounding interrupts a concert. Luigi is voiced by Jack Mercer. Co-written by Carl Meyer. Direction: Seymour Kneitel. Animation: Irving Spector and Morey Reden.

Shootin' Stars (Paramount Cartoon Studios, 1960). Two rival TV Cowboy stars compete to sign a little boy's autograph book. Co-written by Carl Meyer. This same idea would be used for a *Popeye* TV-cartoon also produced by Paramount Cartoon Studios, *Autographically Yours*. Direction: Seymour Kneitel. Animation: Tom Johnson and Morey Reden.

Disguise the Limit (Paramount Cartoon Studios, 1960). Mike the Masquerader is on the loose again in this sequel to *Mike the Masquerader*. In this cartoon he dons various disguises to steal a jeweled dog collar. Co-written by Carl Meyer. Direction: Seymour Kneitel. Animation: Tom Johnson and Morey Reden.

Bouncing Benny (Paramount Cartoon Studios, 1960). A cartoon following a boy's life beginning with his life as a (literally) bouncing baby boy. Co-written by Carl Meyer. Direction: Seymour Kneitel. Graham Place and Otto Feuer.

Terry the Terror (Paramount Cartoon Studios, 1960). Professor Schmultz is called in to stop little Terry from being such a brat. After trying several different ways to become friends with the boy, Professor Schmultz's solution is to turn his behind red! Co-written by Carl Meyer. Direction: Seymour Kneitel. Animation: Tom Johnson and Tom Golden.

The Kid from Mars (Paramount Cartoon Studios, 1961). A kid from Mars arrives on earth, causing chaos with his ray gun which leads him to the Big Top! Turns out he is a hit at the circus and is offered a contract. He flies away on the contract. Co-written by Carl Meyer. Direction: Seymour Kneitel. Animation: Nick Tafuri and William Henning.

In the Nicotine (Paramount Cartoon Studios, 1961). Charlie Butt's chain smoking is threatening his marriage, so his wife sends him to Smokers Anonymous.   Co-written by Carl Meyer. Direction: Seymour Kneitel. Animation: Irving Spector and Sam Stimson.

Bopin' Hood (Paramount Cartoon Studios, 1961). Featuring The Cat, another character Paramount hoped would become as successful as Popeye or Casper. In Squaresville, jazz has been outlawed until the hip Bopin' Hood band comes to town. The town's sign reads, "No jazz, Rock and Roll, Blues & Rhythm by order of the King." Co-written by Carl Meyer. Direction: Seymour Kneitel. Animation: Irving Spector, Jack Ehret and John Gentilella. Mercer and Meyer also scripted *Cane and Able,* a 1961 Paramount theatrical billed as *The Cat,* rather than a *Modern Madcap* or *Noveltoon.* In this film, The Cat goes west to clean out a crooked gambling operation.

Popcorn and Politics (Paramount Cartoon Studios, 1962). Specs dreams what it would be like if he were President. Co-written by Carl Meyer. Direction: Seymour Kneitel. Animation: Martin Taras, John Gentilella and Larry Silverman.

Jack Mercer, possibly dreaming up another cartoon script during his tenure at Paramount Pictures.

Giddy Gadgets (Paramount Cartoon Studios, 1962). Professor Schmultz's inventions drive his wife crazy! Co-written by Carl Meyer. Direction: Seymour Kneitel. Animation: Nick Tafuri, Jack Ehret and Larry Silverman.

Hi-Fi Jinx (Paramount Cartoon Studios, 1962). Ralph thinks he's helping his neighbor Percy build a hi-fi kit, but destruction soon follows. Co-written by Burton Goodman. Direction: Seymour Kneitel. Animation: Martin Taras, Jack Ehret and William B. Pattengill.

Percy gets his wires crossed while getting instructions to hook up his hi-fi in "Hi-Fi Jinx" (Paramount Cartoon Studios, 1962), a Modern Madcap. Written by Jack Mercer and Burton Goodman. Though originally released to theatres, the Modern Madcap series received wider exposure when aired on The New Casper Cartoon Show on the ABC network's Saturday morning schedule from 1963 to 1969.

Funderful Suburbia (Paramount Cartoon Studios, 1962). A cartoon revolving around a modern suburb family, who can't take traffic jams, household and shopping problems. They end up moving into space. Co-written by Burton Goodman. Direction: Seymour Kneitel. Animation: Nick Tafuri, William B. Pattengill and Larry Silverman.

One of the Family (Paramount Cartoon Studios, 1962). Bobo the Dog seeks help from a psychiatrist. Co-written by Burton Goodman. Direction: Seymour Kneitel. Animation: Martin Taras and William B.Pattengill.

One Weak Vacation (Paramount Cartoon Studios, 1963). Morty takes his wife on a European vacation. Solely written by Jack Mercer. Direction: Seymour Kneitel. Animation: Martin Taras ,John Gentilella and Izzy Klein.

The Pig's Feat (Paramount Cartoon Studios, 1963). Kids listen to a story from Mr. Harmonica, who explains why pigs wallow in mud. They're searching for "beauty mud" which will wash away blemishes. Co-written by Irving Dressler. Direction: Seymour Kneitel. Animation: Martin Taras.

Goodie's Good Deed (Paramount Cartoon Studios, 1963). Goodie the Gremlin was another character Paramount hoped would become a long-running animated series. The Gremlins go out on Boy Scout Day, performing bad deeds. Goodie tries to correct the damage. Co-written by Irving Dressler. Direction: Seymour Kneitel. Animation: William B. Pattengill.

NOVELTOONS

Famous Studios had cancelled the *Superman* animated series, started by the Fleischer Studios, which left them with only *Popeye* and *Little Lulu*. *Noveltoons* were created with the hopes popular cartoon series could be launched. (Herman and Katnip were successfully launched from *Noveltoons* into their own series.) *Noveltoons* featured an array of characters and situations. The series was a fixture in theaters through the late 1960s. Jack Mercer's writing was involved with the following *Noveltoons*, excluding the cartoons featuring Herman the Mouse, Katnip the Cat, Buzzy the Crow and Baby Huey, all of whom have separate listings:

Yankee Doodle Donkey (Famous Studios, 1944). Spunky the Donkey, previously featured in color Max Fleischer animated shorts, disguises himself as a dog with the intention of joining the army. Co-written by Jack Ward. Direction: Isadore Sparber. Animation: Nick Tafuri and Tom Golden.

We're in the Honey (Famous Studios, 1948). When a bear attack destroys a hive, the Queen of another offers her hive's aid. Co-written by Izzy Klein. Direction: Bill Tytla. Animation: George Germanetti and Steve Muffatti.

Hep Cat Symphony (Famous Studios, 1949). Mice practice classical music while cats are practicing jazz. Co-Written by Carl Meyer. Direction: Seymour Kneitel. Animation: Dave Tendlar and Martin Taras.

Little Red School Mouse (Famous Studios, 1949). A mouse, who doesn't know what a cat is, brings one to school where the cat gets very hungry! Co-written by Carl Meyer. Direction: Isadore Sparber. Animation: Tom Johnson and John Gentiella.

A Mutt in a Rut (Famous Studios, 1949). Dogface isn't very friendly to a black kitten who suddenly shares his home. He dreams of going to Dog Hell! Co-written by Carl Meyer. Direction: Isadore Sparber. Animation: Dave Tendlar and Tom Golden.

Ups and Downs Derby (Famous Studios, 1950). A jockey tries all sorts of things to get his horse, Lighting, to stay awake for the big race. Co-written by Carl Meyer. Direction: Seymour Kneitel. Animation: Dave Tendlar and Tom Golden.

NewsHound (Famous Studios, 1955). Unless he gets a sensational picture for the newspaper, Snapper will get fired! Solely written by Jack Mercer. Direction: Isadore Sparber. Animation: Al Eugster and George Germanetti.

Poop Goes the Weasel (Famous Studios, 1955). Wishbone the Chicken is the meal target for Waxey Weasel! Co-written by Carl Meyer. Direction: Dave Tendlar. Animation: Martin Taras and Tom Moore.

Possum Pearl (Paramount Cartoon Studios, 1957). Muscle-bound female hillbilly, Possum Pearl, is on the prowl for a man! She ends up capturing a desperate criminal and carries off a policeman with marriage on her mind! *Possum Pearl* is a sequel to the Popeye theatrical cartoon, *Hill-billing and Cooing* (Famous Studios, 1956), where Popeye was her intended husband. Solely written by Jack Mercer. Direction: Seymour Kneitel. Animation: Tom Johnson and Frank Endres.

Possum Pearl keeps a firm grip on Slippery Sam (Jack Mercer) with marriage on her mind in "Possum Pearl" (Paramount Cartoon Studios, 1957), written solely by Jack Mercer who also scripted the first animated film she appeared in, "Hill-billing and Coo-in," an entry in the Popeye theatrical series produced by Famous Studios in 1956.

Dante Dreamer (Paramount Cartoon Studios, 1958). Dante is always dreaming and when he's asked to burn some rubbish, he dreams he's a knight fighting a fire-snorting dragon. Solely written by Jack Mercer. Direction: Isadore Sparber. Animation: Al Eugster and Dante Barbetta.

Okey Dokey Donkey (Paramount Cartoon Studios, 1958). Spunky the Donkey returns, looking for a girlfriend. Solely written by Jack Mercer. Direction: Isadore Sparber. Animation: Al Eugster and Dante Barbetta.

Houndabout (Paramount Cartoon Studios, 1959). Julius the dog decides he wants to try life as a human. Co-written by Carl Meyer. Direction: Seymour Kneitel. Animation: Tom Johnson and Frank Endres.

Out of this Whirl (Paramount Cartoon Studios, 1959). The occupant of a flying saucer takes the place of a woman's son, after the craft lands in her backyard. Co-written by Carl Meyer. Direction: Seymour Kneitel. Animation: Tom Johnson and William B. Pattengill.

Counter Attack (Paramount Cartoon Studios, 1960). A novelty store is the setting, where Scat the Cat is chasing a mouse. Co-written by Carl Meyer. Direction: Seymour Kneitel. Animation: William B. Pattengill and Jack Ehret.

Turning the Tables (Paramount Cartoon Studios, 1960). Tommy Tortoise and Moe Hare (who appeared in other Paramount theatrical cartoons) are uranium hunters trying to beat each other to the claims office. Co-written by Carl Meyer. Direction: Seymour Kneitel. Animation: Irving Spector and William B. Pattengill.

Fine Feathered Fiend (Paramount Cartoon Studios, 1960). So he can become a brave warrior, a little Indian boy goes after a feather for his bonnet. Co-written by Carl Meyer. Direction: Seymour Kneitel. Animation: Tom Johnson.

Northern Mites (Paramount Cartoon Studios, 1960). Two mischievous Penguins discover some Antarctic supplies and fool around. Co-written by Carl Meyer. Direction: Seymour Kneitel. Animation: Nick Tafuri and William B. Pattengill.

Miceniks (Paramount Cartoon Studios, 1960). Beatnik Mice are being menaced by a cat. Jack Mercer supplies some of the voices to the mice. Co-written by Carl Meyer. Direction: Seymour Kneitel. Animation: Tom Johnson and William Henning.

Silly Science (Paramount Cartoon Studios, 1960). Gags about modern science fill this animated cartoon. Co-written by Carl Meyer. Direction: Seymour Kneitel. Animation: Izzy Klein and Irving Dressler.

Be Mice to Cats (Paramount Cartoon Studios, 1960). Scat the Cat wants a Texas Grandfather-type mouse for his next meal! Co-written by Carl Meyer. Direction: Seymour Kneitel. Animation: Nick Tafuri and William B. Pattengill.

The Lion's Busy (Paramount Cartoon Studios, 1961). Sir Reginald Tweedledum IV (voiced by Jack Mercer) has to kill a lion to uphold the family tradition. He captures a lion and uses him as a live trophy. Co-written by Carl Meyer. Direction: Seymour Kneitel. Animation: Martin Taras and Al Pross.

Sir Reginald Tweedledum (Jack Mercer) is on the hunt for a lion to please his disgruntled father in "The Lion's Busy," a Noveltoon produced by Paramount Cartoon Studios in 1961 and co-written by Carl Meyer.

Cape Kidnaveral (Paramount Cartoon Studios, 1961). Specs and his two friends decide to build a moon rocket. Co-written by Carl Meyer. Direction: Seymour Kneitel. Animation: Myron Waldman.

Turtle Scoop (Paramount Cartoon Studios, 1961). Two reporters, a turtle and a rabbit, have to get a picture of a missile launching or be fired. Jack Mercer provides the turtle's voice. Co-written by Carl Meyer. Direction: Seymour Kneitel. Animation: Nick Tafuri and George Germanetti.

Kozmo Goes to School (Paramount Cartoon Studios, 1961). The space kid from *The Kid from Mars* returns and goes to school. Co-written by Carl Meyer. Direction: Seymour Kneitel. Animation: Nick Tafuri, Jack Ehret and Sam Stimson.

Mouse Blanche (Paramount Cartoon Studios, 1962). Released to theaters, along with Paramount's *Noveltoons* and *Modern Madcaps*. This was billed as a *Comic King* and featured Krazy Kat, who starred in a comic strip, distributed by King Features Syndicate. A credit card causes chaos for Ignatz the Mouse in the only Paramount-produced *Krazy Kat* TV-cartoon. Co-written by Burton Goodman. Direction: Seymour Kneitel. Animation: Morey Reden, William B. Pattengill and Jack Ehret.

Perry Popgun (Paramount Cartoon Studios, 1962). A soda-drinking private eye and his girl, Goldie, pursue criminals. Co-written by Carl Meyer. Direction: Seymour Kneitel. Animation: Morey Reden, George Germanetti and William B. Pattengill.

Gramps to the Rescue (Paramount Cartoon Studios, 1963). Scat the Cat tries to get rid of that troublesome grandfatherly Texas mouse from *Be Mice to Cats* by using a phony telegram as bait. Co-written by Izzy Klein. Direction: Seymour Kneitel. Animation: Morey Reden.

Hiccup Hound (Paramount Cartoon Studios, 1963). Goodie the Gremlin tries to cure a hunting dog's case of hiccups. Co-written by Irving Dressler. Direction: Seymour Kneitel. Animation: William B. Pattengill.

Whiz Quiz Kid (Paramount Cartoon Studios, 1964). WGAB-TV executives come up with an idea for a kid's quiz show. The answers are too hard for anyone to guess until they find Ollie Owl. The executives think Ollie is dumb but he's actually a genius! Co-written by Irving Dressler. Direction: Seymour Kneitel. Animation: Martin Taras

OUT OF THE INKWELL

In 1962, Hal Seeger's Studios was called upon to produce a series of TV-cartoons based upon Max Fleischer's early Koko the Clown animated theatrical series. In Koko's TV world he was joined by his girlfriend Kokette and mean-spirited archrival Mean Moe. Koko also had a dog named Koko-nut. Actor Larry Storch provided the male voices and Norma MacMillan did the voice of Kokette and most of the other female voices. One hundred five-minute cartoons, of which Jack Mercer stated he was involved in some of the writing, were syndicated to local cartoon programs. Information on the cartoons Jack Mercer was directly involved with is not available.

POPEYE

Jack Mercer is best remembered as the voice of Popeye the Sailor. However, during his tenure with the animation studios at Paramount Pictures, he was involved with the writing of several of the sailor's cartoons as well. He first received a writing credit on *Popeye* near the conclusion of the Fleischer Studios' production of the series. Mercer's writing was involved in many of the Famous Studios films and the TV-cartoons, produced for King Features Syndicate by Paramount Cartoon Studios. Many animation fans consider the batch of TV Popeyes produced by Paramount the best in the series of 220 cartoons. Mercer was also a writer for the Popeye TV-cartoons for *The All New Popeye Hour* and *The Popeye and Olive Comedy Show*, which aired on CBS Saturday morning television. As Art Scott, in charge of special projects at Hanna-Barbera (the studio which produced the cartoons), said at the time of production, "There are other problems with updating Popeye too. The original series was born in a violent era when prizefighting was a national craze. Popeye and Bluto would go toe-to-toe and really slug it out. We can't have people punching each other, so we have to find other ways of showing competition." Mercer felt, at the time, the decrease in violence was unnecessary as the old violent cartoons were still running on television, though he adhered to network standards. Mercer said, "I thought of the old gags and cleaned up the violence."

Storyboards by Jack Mercer for Hanna-Barbera used in the production of a "Prehistoric Popeye" cartoon, aired on the Popeye and Olive Comedy Show in 1980.

Jack Mercer's writing was involved with the following Popeye the Sailor cartoons:

Fleets of Stren'th (Fleischer Studios, 1942). Popeye leaps into action to battle the enemy in the sky and the ocean. He has a bit of trouble opening his can of spinach in this wartime cartoon. Co-written by Dan Gordon, Director: Dave Fleischer. Animation: Al Eugster and Tom Golden.

Olive Oyl and Water Don't Mix (Fleischer Studios, 1942). Popeye and Bluto both decide they're "Off women for life" until Olive Oyl boards their ship on visitors' day. Jack Mercer dubs a few lines for Bluto ("Why that one-eyed Casanova," and "Go save yourself!"). Co-written by Jack Ward. Director: Dave Fleischer. Animation: Dave Tendlar and Abner Kneitel.

Baby Wants a Bottleship (Fleischer Studios, 1942). Olive Oyl asks Popeye to mind Swee'pea while she goes shopping. The lad crawls aboard Popeye's huge ship and the sailor gets pummeled trying to save him. The last Popeye cartoon produced by Fleischer Studios. Co-written by Jack Ward. Director: Dave Fleischer. Animation: Al Eugster and Joe Oriolo.

Alona on the Sarong Seas (Famous Studios, 1942). Popeye and Bluto compete for the attention of Princess Alona, who looks like Olive Oyl. Jack Mercer provides the voice of the Princess' parrot. Direction: Isadore Sparber. Animation: Dave Tendlar and Abner Kneitel.

A Hull of a Mess (Famous Studios, 1942). Popeye and Bluto compete for a ship building contract. Bluto is extra nasty in this cartoon when he attempts to blow up both Popeye *and* his ship! Co-written by Jack Ward. Direction: Isadore Sparber. Animation: Al Eugster and Joe Oriolo.

Me Musical Nephews (Famous Studios, 1942). Returning home from a tour of duty, all Popeye wants to do is sleep but his musical nephews have other ideas. Jack Mercer provides the voices for Popeye's lookalike and sound-alike nephews. Co-written by Jack Ward. Direction: Seymour Kneitel. Animation: Tom Johnson and George Germanetti.

Ration for the Duration (Famous Studios, 1943). Popeye dreams he's battling a giant who is hoarding supplies needed for the war effort. Jack Mercer provides the voice of the giant. Co-written by Jack Ward. Direction: Seymour Kneitel. Animation: Dave Tendlar and Tom Golden.

Cartoons Ain't Human (Famous Studios, 1943). In the last black-and-white *Popeye* cartoon, the sailor makes his own cartoon film called "Wages of Sin." Jack Mercer provides the voice of Roger Blacklay and his horse. Direction: Seymour Kneitel. Animation: Orestes Calpini and Otto Feuer.

Her Honor, the Mare (Famous Studios, 1943). In the first color Popeye short, the sailor's nephews attempt to keep a horse as a house pet. Co-written by Jack Ward. Direction: Isadore Sparber. Animation: Jim Tyler and Ben Solomon.

We're on Our Way to Rio (Famous Studios, 1944). An excellent musical and dancing cartoon, with Popeye and Bluto competing for the attention of entertainer Olive Oyl. Popeye attempts to learn how to Samba dance despite Bluto's interference. Co-written by Jack Ward. Director: Isadore Sparber. Animation: James Tyler and Ben Solomon.

Wigwam Whoopie (Famous Studios, 1948). Pilgrim Popeye meets Olive the Indian maiden but the big Indian chief wants to roast Popeye alive. Co-written by I.Klein. Direction: Isadore Sparber. Animation: Tom Johnson and William Henning.

A lobby card from Mexico for the Popeye cartoon, "Wigwam Whoopie" (Famous Studios, 1948) written by Jack Mercer and I. Klein. Popeye is a pilgrim who angers an Indian Chief when his squaw, Olive Oyl, falls for the one-eyed explorer.

Pre-Hysterical Man (Famous Studios, 1948). Popeye has to save Olive Oyl from the clutches of a caveman. Co-written by I. Klein. Direction: Seymour Kneitel. Animation: Dave Tendlar and Morey Reden.

Snow Place Like Home (Famous Studios, 1948). Popeye and Olive end up in Alaska where a Frenchman sets his sights (and lips) on Olive Oyl. Co-written by Carl Meyer. Direction: Seymour Kneitel. Animation: Dave Tendlar and Martin Taras.

Lumberjack and Jill (Famous Studios, 1948). Lumberjacks, Popeye and Bluto, compete for the attention of the new cook, Olive Oyl. This cartoon features a dramatic rescue sequence accompanied by an exciting musical score by Winston Sharples. Co-written by Carl Meyer. Direction: Seymour Kneitel. Animation: Tom Johnson and George Rufle.

A Balmy Swami (Famous Studios, 1949). Bluto (in a nasal-sounding voice) is a swami who hypnotizes Olive Oyl, who proceeds to walk on a construction site. This film features a dramatic musical score while Olive takes each dangerous step. Co-written by Carl Meyer. Direction: Isadore Sparber. Animation: Tom Johnson and George Rufle.

Tar with a Star (Famous Studios, 1949). Popeye becomes a sheriff and has to battle "Wild Bill Bluto," a gunslinger with romantic intentions on saloon singer Olive Oyl. Co-written by Carl Meyer. Direction: Bill Tytla. Animation: George Germanetti and Steve Muffatti.

Barking Dogs Don't Fite (Famous Studios, 1949). Popeye is forced into taking Olive's French poodle for a walk and once they're spotted by Bluto (and his bulldog) the battle begins! Co-written by Carl Meyer. Direction: Isadore Sparber. Animation: Tom Johnson and John Gentilella.

Gym Jam (Famous Studios, 1950). It's "Ladies Day" at Popeye's gymnasium, so Bluto disguises himself as a blonde-haired female to get close to Olive Oyl. Co-written by Carl Meyer. Direction: Isadore Sparber. Animation: Tom Johnson and John Gentilella.

Jitterbug Jive (Famous Studios, 1950). Another fun musical cartoon, where Popeye battles "Skate" for Olive's attention at her party. Oddly, Olive announces at the beginning of the cartoon, "Popeye and Bluto will soon arrive." But Bluto must have lost her address, as he doesn't appear in this film. Co-written by Carl Meyer. Direction: Bill Tytla. Animation: George Germanetti and Harvey Patterson.

Baby Wants Spinach (Famous Studios, 1950). Olive asks Popeye to mind "Cousin Swee'pea" while she goes shopping but the tyke leaves the house, with Popeye in pursuit. Swee'pea saves Popeye by eating his spinach in a most unusual manner. A huge gorilla squashes the spinach can, causing its contents to fly in the crying infant's mouth. Swee'pea is drawn like a generic-looking baby and not as he appeared in the Fleischer Studios cartoons nor the *Thimble Theatre* comic strip. Co-written by Carl Meyer. Direction: Seymour Kneitel. Animation: Al Eugster and William B. Pattengill.

Quick on the Vigor (Famous Studios, 1950). Olive is attracted to Bluto the Strongman until he gets her alone on the Ferris Wheel. Co-written by Carl Meyer. Direction: Seymour Kneitel. Animation: Tom Johnson and John Gentilella.

Vacation with Play (Famous Studios, 1951). All Popeye wants to do is sleep on his vacation with Olive Oyl, but when Instructor Bluto spots his girlfriend, the sailor intervenes. Co-written by Carl Meyer. Direction: Seymour Kneitel. Animation: Tom Johnson and John Gentilella.

Thrill of Fair (Famous Studios, 1951). While attending a fair, Swee'pea is on the trail of a balloon, which leads him into all sorts of trouble (of which Popeye takes the punishment). This cartoon features an exciting rescue scene with accompanying music. Co-written by Carl Meyer. Direction: Seymour Kneitel. Animation: Tom Johnson and John Gentilella.

Pilgrim Popeye (Famous Studios, 1951). Popeye's nephews want a turkey dinner, so the sailor dreams up a story how a turkey saved his life when he was a pilgrim. Jack Mercer provides the voice of the Indian chief. Co-written by Carl Meyer. Direction: Isadore Sparber. Animation: Al Eugster and George Germanetti.

Lunch with a Punch (Famous Studios, 1952). Popeye tells his nephews a story of himself, Olive Oyl and Bluto when they were classmates together. In a plot twist, Bluto grabs Popeye and says, "Now I've got you without your spinach!" It's up to Popeye's nephews to chomp on the vegetable and save their Uncle. Co-written by Carl Meyer. Direction: Isadore Sparber. Animation: Al Eugster and George Germanetti.

Swimmer Take All (Famous Studios, 1952). An excellent musical score by Winston Sharples highlights this cartoon of a swimming race between Popeye and Bluto. Jack Mercer provides the booming voice of the announcer over the speaker. Co-written by Carl Meyer. Direction: Seymour Kneitel. Animation: Tom Johnson and John Gentilella.

Popalong Popeye (Famous Studios, 1952). The plot of trying to coax his nephews to eat spinach is given a western flavor as Popeye explains how eating the vegetable turned him from a "tenderfoot" to "Popalong Popeye." Co-written by Carl Meyer. Direction: Seymour Kneitel. Animation: Tom Johnson and John Gentilella.

Child Sockology (Famous Studios, 1953). An exciting chase cartoon with an excellent accompanying musical score by Winston Sharples. Popeye and Bluto frantically try to rescue baby Swee'pea, who has crawled on to a construction site. Despite a brutal attack by Bluto, Popeye rescues the bully when he finds himself in peril. Co-written by Carl Meyer. Direction: I. Sparber. Animation: Tom Johnson and Frank Endres.

Popeye's facial expression says it all! Baby Swee'pea is in danger when he wanders on to a construction site in "Child Sockology" (Famous Studios, 1953). Written by Jack Mercer and Carl Meyer. This cartoon features an excellent music score by Winston Sharples. Sharple's musical scores were loaned out to be used in other cartoon series produced for TV including King Leonardo, Tennessee Tuxedo, and Rocket Robin Hood.

Popeye's Mirthday (Famous Studios, 1953). Olive has planned a surprise birthday party for Popeye so his nephews deploy traps to keep him out of her house until it's ready. Co-written by Carl Meyer. Direction: Seymour Kneitel. Animation: Tom Johnson and Frank Endres.

Toreadorable (Famous Studios, 1953). Olive and Popeye watch "Senior Bluto from Brooklyn," a bullfighter who puts jumping beans in the sailor's spinach can. This keeps Popeye out of the picture as he tries to kiss Olive. Co-written by Carl Meyer. Direction: Seymour Kneitel. Animation: Tom Johnson and John Gentilella.

Baby Wants a Battle (Famous Studios, 1953). Popeye tells Olive Oyl about one of his earliest encounters with Bluto, when they were both babies. Jack Mercer provides the Popeye voice to a young Poopdeck Pappy. Co-written by Carl Meyer. Direction: Seymour Kneitel. Animation: Al Eugster and George Germanetti.

Firemen's Brawl (Famous Studios, 1953). Olive Oyl's house is on fire and firemen Popeye and Bluto compete to save her. It's Olive who eats Popeye's spinach and ends up rescuing the competing firemen. She takes over their firehouse. Co-written by Carl Meyer. Direction: I. Sparber. Animation: Tom Johnson and Frank Endres.

Popeye, the Ace of Space (Famous Studios, 1953). By the early 1950s, 3-D was all the rage and this cartoon was shot with three-dimensional effects. Popeye is taken captive by aliens who think they have a "typical earthman specimen." Co-written by Carl Meyer. Direction: Seymour Kneitel. Animation: Al Eugster and George Germanetti.

Floor Flusher (Famous Studios, 1954). Jack Mercer gets to sing (as Popeye), "By a waterfall, I'm calling you-ooh-ooh-ooh" while Bluto wreaks havoc with Olive Oyl's plumbing! Co-written by Carl Meyer. Direction: Isadore Sparber. Animation: Tom Golden and Bill Hudson.

Fright to the Finish (Famous Studios, 1954). With no spinach in sight, Popeye is able to defeat Bluto who has designs on keeping Olive Oyl to himself on Halloween. Solely written by Jack Mercer. Direction: Seymour Kneitel. Animation: Al Eugster and William B. Pattengill.

Popeye uses vanishing cream, not a can of spinach, to get rid of Bluto's presence in Olive Oyl's house in "Fright to the Finish" (Famous Studios, 1954), written solely by Jack Mercer.

Nurse Ta Meet Ya (Famous Studios, 1955). Popeye and Bluto's arguing awakens the baby in Nurse Olive's care so the two sailors compete to make him laugh. Solely written by Jack Mercer. Direction: Isadore Sparber. Animation: Al Eugster and William B. Pattengill.

Mister and Mistletoe (Famous Studios, 1955). Bluto disguises himself as Santa Claus to get Popeye out of the picture. Once that's done, he says to Olive, "How about a kiss for Christmas!" Solely written by Jack Mercer. Direction: Isadore Sparber. Animation: Al Eugster and William B. Pattengill.

Hill-billing and Coo-ing (Famous Studios, 1956). Popeye and Olive encounter Possum Pearl, a muscle-bound female hillbilly who wants to marry the sailor. When Popeye loses his spinach can, Olive eats the contents and flings Possum Pearl into space. She lands on a star and goes after the man in the moon! Solely written by Jack Mercer, who a year later scripted the sequel, *Possum Pearl*, a *Modern Madcap*. Direction: Seymour Kneitel. Animation: Tom Johnson and John Gentilella.

Popeye for President (Famous Studios, 1956). Popeye and Bluto step up their competition as they're both running for President of the United States and each needing farm girl Olive's vote to decide the outcome of the election. Solely written by Jack Mercer. Direction: Seymour Kneitel. Animation: Tom Johnson and Frank Endres.

I Don't Scare (Famous Studios, 1956). Proving again he can defeat Bluto without eating spinach, Popeye gets even with the bully for ruining superstitious Olive Oyl's date with him. Solely written by Jack Mercer. Direction: Isadore Sparber. Animation: Tom Johnson and Frank Endres.

Spree Lunch (Famous Studios, 1957). Popeye and Bluto operate Diners across the street from each other, competing for one customer, J. Wellington Wimpy, who says his famous phrase, "I'll have a hamburger for which I will gladly pay you Tuesday." Solely written by Jack Mercer. Direction: Seymour Kneitel. Animation: Tom Johnson and Frank Endres.

Top: Jack Mercer's writing credit for "Spree Lunch" (Famous Studios, 1957). Bottom: Wimpy discovers what happens when you swallow Mexican Jumping Beans in "Spree Lunch." This cartoon had no spinach involved and the physical violence is saved for the last few moments but offered no fist fight! In this, the next to last theatrical Popeye film, Bluto and the sailor compete for Wimpy's business for their respective diners. The humor lies in the pair's attempts to lure Wimpy with a sign advertising beautiful waitresses, a magnetized steak and a long, long piece of spaghetti. With no spinach can or fist fight in site, Jack Mercer's script allowed for more inventiveness.

The Baby Contest (Paramount Cartoon Studios, 1960). Swee'pea is depressed so Popeye enters him in a baby contest to win a loving cup. Brutus enters a baby in the contest, tries to bribe Judge Wimpy with a plate of hamburgers and bops Popeye into a tree. Swee'pea, after eating Popeye's spinach, becomes the hero by not only winning the loving cup but punching Brutus! Co-written by Carl Meyer. Direction: Seymour Kneitel. Animation: Morey Reden, Irving Dressler, Jack Ehret, I. Klein and Al Pross.

Oil's Well That Ends Well (Paramount Cartoon Studios, 1960). Olive wins an oil well which Brutus, wearing a disguise, plans to swipe. Co-written by Carl Meyer. Direction: Seymour Kneitel. Animation: Martin Taras, Irving Dressler, Jack Ehret and Jim Logan.

County Fair (Paramount Cartoon Studios, 1961). Brutus and Popeye compete as farmers in a series of tests to see who will win the blue ribbon. Brutus speaks to the television audience, explaining why he wants to eat Popeye's spinach, rather than his own, "You didn't think I was gonna play fair with that runt and take a chance against his spinach!" Co-written by Carl Meyer. Direction: Seymour Kneitel. Animation: Martin Taras, Dante Barbetta, Dick Hall and Jim Logan.

The Cure (Paramount Cartoon Studios, 1961). Wimpy tries to give up Hamburgers, but this will ruin the Sea Hag's restaurant business! In a plot twist, it's Wimpy who eats spinach to fight off one of the Sea Hag's Goons! Co-written by Carl Meyer. Direction: Seymour Kneitel. Animation: Martin Taras, George Germanetti and Larry Silverman.

Aladdin's Lamp (Paramount Cartoon Studios, 1961). The Sea Hag learns that Olive bought the famed Aladdin's Lamp with a genie inside at an auction. The ol' witch steals it and has the sophisticated pink genie turn Popeye into a mouse! Co-written by Carl Meyer. Direction: Seymour Kneitel. Animation: Martin Taras, Gerry Dvorak, Jim Logan and Larry Silverman.

Autographically Yours (Paramount Cartoon Studios, 1961). A little boy wants an autograph from his favorite western hero, Popeye. Brutus tells the lad they write those movies to make Popeye win, "But in real life I always top him!" Popeye and Brutus compete for the honor to sign the autograph book. Popeye saves both the lad and Brutus from a fierce lion. Brutus decides he wants Popeye's autograph too! Co-written by Carl Meyer. Direction: Seymour Kneitel. Animation: Morey Reden, Jack Ehret, George Germanetti and Sam Stimson.

Love Birds (Paramount Cartoon Studios, 1961). Popeye buys a male bird as a companion for Olive's lonely female lovebird. Following an argument, the male bird runs away with Popeye in pursuit. Co-written by Carl Meyer. Direction: Seymour Kneitel. Animation: William B. Pattengill, Dick Hall, and Al Pross.

Boardering on Trouble (Paramount Cartoon Studios, 1961). Owners Popeye and Brutus split their hotel in half. Popeye feels fine food will draw in customers while Brutus thinks it's great entertainment. Olive Oyl arrives and the boys test their theories on her. Co-written by Carl Meyer. Direction: Seymour Kneitel. Animation: William B. Pattengill, Gerry Dvorak, Dick Hall and Jim Logan.

A Mite of Trouble (Paramount Cartoon Studios, 1961). The Sea Hag asks Major Mite, a circus midget (voiced by Jack Mercer), to masquerade as Swee'pea to find Popeye's treasure map. Co-written by Carl Meyer. Direction: Seymour Kneitel. Animation: Martin Taras, Gerry Dvorak, George Germanetti and Jim Logan.

The Leprechaun (Paramount Cartoon Studios, 1961). A Leprechaun (voiced by Jack Mercer) revives Popeye with Shamrock juice after he's knocked out by The Sea Hag's vulture. Popeye helps the Leprechaun get back his pot of gold, stolen by the Sea Hag. This cartoon features eerie instrumental music by Winston Sharples. Co-written by Carl Meyer. Direction: Seymour Kneitel. Animation: Morey Reden, William Henning, Al Pross and Larry Silverman.

Pop Goes the Whistle (Paramount Cartoon Studios, 1961). Swee'pea narrowly misses danger on the trail of anything that "toots"! Co-written by Carl Meyer, Direction: Seymour Kneitel. Animation: Irving Dressler, Gerry Dvorak, Jack Ehret and George Germanetti.

Jack Mercer is listed as one of the writers on the end credits for the *Popeye* television cartoons produced by Hanna-Barbera, which began production in 1978.

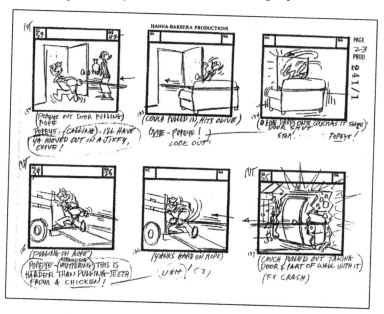

Storyboard by Jack Mercer for Hanna-Barbera used in the production of "Olive's Moving Experience," a Popeye cartoon cartoon aired on the Popeye and Olive Comedy Show in 1980.

INTERVIEWS WITH JACK MERCER

MICHAEL BARRIER

I have found in dealing with animation historians they are a generous and sharing group of individuals. One such person is Michael Barrier, author of Hollywood Cartoons: American Animation in its Golden Age, *published by Oxford University Press. He is also the proprietor of a website devoted to animation and comic art,* http://www.michaelbarrier.com. *He recorded an interview with Jack Mercer on February 5, 1976, which was sent to me by Virginia Mercer. Jack Mercer was concerned following his interviews that some of his remarks regarding former "associates" may have been on the "derisive side" and his wife shared his feeling. Out of respect for Jack and Virginia Mercer, I kept this in mind when transcribing this interview. During the interview, Jack Mercer called Carl Meyer (his co-writer on numerous animated films) "Mike," with "Carl" possibly being a nickname. To correspond with the name given on screen, I have referred to him as Carl Meyer. Here, courtesy of Mr. Barrier, is his interview.*

(As the interview opened we were talking about the various people who have fraudulently claimed to be Popeye's voice).

Barrier: Did Harry Welch have any basis at all for his claim to have been Popeye's voice?

Mercer: He had done that character in vaudeville; he was allowed to dress in the costume. He claimed that he did all of the characters in the cartoons.

Barrier: There was a fellow before you, though.

Mercer: Yes, Red Pepper Sam [William Costello]; he was the first one. I've never denied that.

Barrier: I want to go back to your beginnings, and go chronologically through your career. Gordon Sheehan [animator at Fleischer Studios] said you had an uncanny knack for imitating people. He said, "His folks were show people. His mother and his aunt had played the old Palace Theater on Broadway, and his father was a circus acrobat, actor and created the sets."

Mercer: That's right.

Barrier: I believe that I. Klein [animator with Paramount Pictures animation studios] said that you were on the stage right from the time you were an infant.

Mercer: That's right. My first appearance was as a baby, and there was a cue where I was supposed to cry. So they pinched me on the posterior. That was my first part.

Barrier: What kind of act was this?

Mercer: This was a repertoire company. My folks had a repertoire company.

(Virginia Mercer was also speaking during the interview)

Virginia Mercer: Someone wanted to sign him up for Hollywood when he was a child.

Mercer: Nothing really happened, but we visited New York one time. I think it was at the Palais Royale that I got up and directed the orchestra on a chair. I was that small and I had a Buster Brown haircut. Some people from Hollywood wanted to sign me up but my Uncle, who was managing the show at the time, wouldn't hear of it, because that would have broken up the family. It was sort of a family show.

Barrier: Was everybody in the traveling company part of your family?

Mercer: Most of them, yes; my aunt, my mother, my father, my grandmother. We had a pretty good hold on the whole company. There were a few added characters, like the ingénues, and the heavies, and a few people like that which they hired.

Barrier: Did they travel all over the country?

Mercer: Mostly in the Middle West.

Barrier: Where were you born?

Mercer: Worthington, Indiana, in between acts.

Barrier: Was that your family's home base then?

Mercer: My grandmother, my father's mother, had a home there, and I guess they used that as a headquarters. They had a tent show at one time.

Barrier: Your father's parents did?

Mercer: Yes.

Barrier: Did what you did later, your voices and so on, grow out of this family activity?

Mercer: No, that just came naturally. I never had any desire to do it. I just did.

Virginia Mercer: Jack's family thought he should get into something respectable.

Mercer: My family had been in it [show business] so long, and they figured it was a real hard profession. They touted me out of that, and wanted me to become an artist or something else. I could draw a little bit. My father could draw quite a bit; as a matter of fact, he did a lot of the scenery for the shows. He was very clever at doing all sorts of things. He made some stage effects on some of the shows, storm effects and things like that. He had a box lit up like it was a bolt of lighting that came down from the aisles and hit a tree and that fell over. I guess I got a little bit of that from him.

Barrier: What kind of plays did your family put on?

Mercer: Those old plays, *Rebecca of Sunnybrook Farm* type, *Tess of the Storm County*. Melodramatic shows were the thing at the time.

Barrier: Did they ever put on comedies of any kind?

Mercer: I imagine they did. I can't remember exactly, but they had a varied repertoire.

Virginia Mercer: Some of the family, like Jack's Aunt Winnie, went on to play with Lucille Ball and Zachary Scott.

Mercer: That was my mother. My aunt continued in the dramatic shows in Hartford, CT. She did stock there.

Barrier: But your mother was in —

Mercer: Vaudeville. Eventually my aunt and my mother had an act in vaudeville [after the family's repertoire company]. They played the Palace, Loew's and the Keith-Orpheum and all the big-time circuits.

Barrier: Where did your family eventually settle, when they stopped touring?

Mercer: In New York.

Barrier: Your mother and your aunt went into vaudeville after you settled down in New York City?

Mercer: Yes.

Virginia Mercer: And your mother did some radio, didn't she, and didn't she make a picture?

Mercer: Yes, she was in a short, but I can't remember exactly what it was. It was filmed on Long Island someplace.

Virginia Mercer: And actually, it was her agent who suggested you go to the Fleischer Studio.

Mercer: That's right.

Barrier: That was what…1933?

Mercer: No, it was before that; 1932 or something like that.

Barrier: Had you taken any art classes before you went to Fleischers'?

Mercer: I did go very briefly to an art school. The only thing that I did that was anything at all was, some of these curtain companies requested designs from various schools around; they could get them for two cents apiece, I guess. I made out pretty good designing lace curtains. I was knocking them out like crazy. I didn't last very long there.

Barrier: Sounds far removed from cartooning.

Mercer: Oh yeah, I never had any idea of doing cartooning at that time, as far as that goes.

Barrier: Before you went to Fleischers', were you at all aware of cartoons? Had you paid any attention to them?

Mercer: They were showing Betty Boops, I think, at that time, and I did think they were pretty good.

Barrier: But you hadn't thought seriously about a career.

Mercer: No, it never entered my head.

Barrier: Until your mother's agent suggested it.

Mercer: That's right. He had a connection there, and he knew there was some drawing required. He figured that might be an opportunity for me.

Barrier: Were you actively looking for a job at that time?

Mercer: No. There was a vaudeville act. I think I was fooling around with that. I rehearsed in it, and then they didn't use it. It was a bellboy part, with some dancing required. But as far as we got was the rehearsing, and then it was disbanded, for some reason.

Barrier: Would that have been on the same bill with your mother and your aunt?

Mercer: Oh, no.

Barrier: What kind of act did they have?

Mercer: It was a comedy act; my mother was a comedienne.

Barrier: So there was that comedy connection before you got into cartoons. Gordon Sheehan told me he started to work at Fleischers' in April 1933, and was seated next to you on his first day at work. He said you were opaquing cells, and you were given the job of teaching him how to put the brush in the paint and then paint the cells.

Mercer: (*Laughing*) I don't remember that.

Barrier: He said that shortly after that, both you and he were promoted to the tracing department, and worked several months on tracing, and then went into the in-betweening department. You were in-betweening, weren't you, at the time you were called on to do the Popeye voice?

Mercer: Yes.

Barrier: I have two versions of how that happened, one from Gordon and one from I. Klein, and I wanted to check with you and find out which one sounds closer to the truth. There isn't that much difference between them, but there's enough that I thought you might be able to pin down one or the other as the most accurate. Gordon said that you were constantly keeping the other in-betweeners entertained with imitations of radio personalities and varied sound effects. He said that one of your favorite imitations was of Popeye's voice, which you had down pat. Do you recall doing that sort of entertaining?

Mercer: Oh yes. That's how they noticed me, doing the voices. While I was in-betweening, I might be drawing a certain character, and I would supply the voice as I was working on it. Then everybody would laugh, and the boss would come down and tell me to shut up, so they could get some work done.

Barrier: So while you were in-betweening on Popeye, you'd be talking like Popeye?

Mercer: That's right.

Barrier: Gordon [Sheehan] said that one lunch hour, Dave Fleischer was showing some guests through the studio and he overheard you doing the Popeye

CAN MAX FLEI-? SCHER

By Jack Mercer

As I eagerly waited for the big plane to get started, I noticed that the Pillet, who was half asleep, was having trouble with the motor; I asked him if we would soon be ready to start. He was a Scotchman with Schwartz all over his face. He said, "Ut Fox o Lod of time to fix this uld rusty engine."

That sounded very encouraging. "Well", I said, "let's get Cohen, I've got to be in Florida by Tom Moore."

Sidney the plane Rose into the air with a loud report from the engine. Sophie started the David a bang.

It was A-bbott ten o'clock in the morning, and I was tired of looking Otto the window. I Van Der-ed-veer I put the Animated News. I had nothing to read, Sirota letter.

Al at once it became very Lindley, and the big ship shook from stem to Sturm. The pilot yawned, and yelled back to me, "Uts getten Vera Coleman, looks like we're caught in a Sturm".

"That's just Fine", I said, "anyway I hope that this crate Getz Aaron time." I thought I'd offer the pilot a Seeger just to be sociable, and found that he was asleep.

"Wake up, you Lager head, this storm will Rocker to pieces".

"Wot's the matter wi' ya, are ye a Friedman?"

"No, Miele careful and I don't relish the thought of holding a Lillian my hand. If it's all the Sam to you, I'd just as soon Turner 'round and go back. Besides, you've Shlepp most of the way, and now we're lost."

"Ut'll only tak' a minute ta get me Bearens". (Weldon my lad, Weldon) "Say, did you see that lightning? The storm has broken with all its Feury",

The lights went out, and it was so Doc I couldn't Seymour than an inch in front of me. We Werner awful spot.

The pilot found a Crandall and lit it with a spark of genius.

"How much longer Willis keep up? Can't you go any Pfister? Take a chance on landing this Bird."

"None o' your Lippman, I am the pilot and there's Nolan in sight. To be Frank wi' ye, we're lost over the ocean, Earl is leakin' in the motor and U'll hav' to Deneroff. I'm gonna jump Hoffman, wi' ma chute, Halse if I can find a spot t'land. Gud bye and gud luck.

I couldn't help ad-Myron a man with nerve enough to jump off into 'pace. The ship was falling Rabbitt-ly now. Kneitel you I was getting darned Izzy, and what I wouldn't have given for a big bottle of Gordon Sheehan. I felt very Fain. I guessed it was Saul over. I went Don, Don, Don. Hicks was Lockey for me that a steamer came in the Nick of time, or I would still be floating around in the ocean.

The next time I go any Place, Altura the country by train.

A big mystery to me is the fact that having only arrived home yesTeddy, this story was printed in the Animated News the day before.

Voak you dere, Charlie?

-12-

An article written by Jack Mercer for the Fleischer Animated News, *a publication for studio employees. It is called* Can Max Flei-?scher *and he worked studio employee's names into the story.* COURTESY OF JERRY ALVAREZ.

voice. Shortly after that, Dave invited you to make a recording test. The test turned out well, and you became the new Popeye voice, and later created other cartoon voices as well.

Mercer: That's right.

Barrier: Do you recall Dave coming through and overhearing you?

Mercer: It could have happened that way, I don't know exactly how it happened, but I know they were looking for somebody to do the voice, and I think Dave heard from somebody else that I was imitating it. I don't know whether it was Dave, himself, overhearing me doing the voice. I changed the character quite a bit. William Costello was very militant at times. I tried to change it so only when it was necessary did I appear to be rough. He's a nice guy until he's backed up against a wall, then he lets his opponent have it.

Barrier: Why were they getting rid of Costello? Were they dissatisfied with the voice, or was he asking for too much money?

Mercer: I really don't know, exactly. Just the same as you heard, that's about what I heard, several different reasons.

Barrier: When you began doing voices, did you remain in the in-between department? Were you called out of the in-between department to do voices?

A cartoon from the Fleischer's Animated News, a publication for studio employees, by Warren Foster. It depicts the reaction one would have discovering skinny Jack Mercer was the voice of the heroic Popeye the Sailor! COURTESY OF JERRY ALVAREZ.

Mercer: A short time after that, I transferred to the Fleischers' story department, because I was writing these little ad-libs in Popeye's dialogue. Then they had the *Animated News* and I wrote several articles for it. I guess that might have influenced them in thinking that I had some ability in that line. But, of course, writing cartoons at that time required a lot of sight gags, not so much dialogue. I seemed to be able to fall right in line with that, with the background that I had. I advanced very well in that department.

Barrier: I wanted to ask you several questions about the muttering and the ad-libs. What led to your doing that? Do you recall the circumstances? It's such a unique thing.

Mercer: I must say that Costello did a little bit of it, but it was to the point where you couldn't understand it. I think he forgot his lines, or something. So I used that, as a means of putting in funny lines.

Barrier: Did you actually ab-lib or was it written out?

Mercer: It would all depend. At this time with the Fleischer Studios, we used to record everything at once. There was no pre-recording of these things. They would show the picture and we had to do the lines as the picture ran. This was called post-recording. They used this system with the bouncing ball for our cues. In between where the actual lines were written, we would ad-lib lines to fill up.

Barrier: For quite a while, the other characters would be muttering too, without any mouth action.

Mercer: When we did the pre-recordings everything was timed, so we had some time to figure out better ad-libs. Sometimes we could change them, at will. I might have a line written out, as an ad-lib, and then when we did the recording, something else would strike me as funny. But they would only use what they thought was best. The other [scripted] recordings, they made several takes and used the best ones.

Barrier: Do you roughly recall how long it was after you started doing Popeye's voice they stopped post-recording and started pre-recording?

Mercer: I haven't any idea. It might have been at the time of the move to Miami that we made the change. We had our own sound studio down there.

Barrier: When you were in the story department, were they making storyboards of the kind that later became common?

Mercer: When I first went into the story department, I was working a lot with the story men, and I would be handed certain scenes to gag up. If I remember correctly, I sketched a lot of my gags and handed them to the head story man, Bill Turner. We used to hand in our material and I think he typed up a script. Then the script was handed in [to the heads of the studio] to see if they accepted it.

Barrier: There would be some sketches before the script was typed up, and a complete storyboard afterwards.

Mercer: I think the sketches were made so Bill Turner could mull them over, and select the gags he thought were permissible for the story.

Barrier: There weren't the elaborate Disney-type storyboards?

Mercer: Not until later. What we used to do was present a synopsis, and if they liked that - just the basic idea, they [the studio heads] would accept it and say, go ahead and make a storyboard on it. Then, we would. Then, we would make the typical Disney storyboard.

Barrier: Did the directors look in periodically?

Mercer: We'd have a meeting every once in a while and see how we were progressing, with the directors, and the animators. We'd have several story meetings.

Barrier: This was more at Famous Studios than at Fleischers', wasn't it?

Mercer: That's right.

Barrier: Gordon Sheehan said he had the impression Dave Fleischer was very much involved with the story department in New York. He paid much more attention to the story department than to the animation department. Was he involved frequently in the work you were doing?

Mercer: When I was first in the story department [at the Fleischer Studios], it seemed to me that Bill Turner was the one who conducted the whole thing. Dave came in on maybe the final story meeting. Everybody got in on it then. We'd throw the gags back and forth, and throw out what wasn't permissible. Dave took care of the recordings more than anything else did, it seemed.

Barrier: Would you see Dave Fleischer a lot at the recording sessions? What was he doing?

Mercer: Directing.

Barrier: So he'd be telling you how to deliver the lines?

Mercer: In a way.

Barrier: Since you had been working on the stories all along, it would seem that anyone telling you how to deliver the lines would be superfluous.

Mercer: They left you more or less on your own. Once in a while, Dave would make a suggestion or something like that. Sometimes it wouldn't be acceptable. It got to the point where I was directing the dialogue, at one time.

Barrier: So you were directing the other actors?

Mercer: That's what I did, many times. Many times, Izzy [Sparber] or Seymour [Kneitel] would become very confused as to how to get a certain actor to read a line. I would butt in and say, "Would you mind if I see if I can get them to say this line the way I think you would like it read?" I did an awful lot of that.

Barrier: When you were pre-recording the dialogue would you always have all of the actors there, and do the whole thing at once, or would you sometimes have to record different actors at different times?

Mercer: Doing the recording separately would be an unusual thing, I think.

We had the cast all together and, of course, a lot of the dialogue was asking and answering, so there was a sort of play back and forth, between the characters. It would be a rare occasion when someone was called in to do a separate recording.

Barrier: When you first started doing Popeye, did they [the Fleischer Studios] have an actual written script that you would read?

Mercer: Oh yes, as I said, they used the bouncing-ball system and that matched the animation of the mouth.

Barrier: The mouths had been animated to specific dialogue?

Mercer: Yes.

Barrier: Sometimes the animation doesn't look that specific.

Mercer: I don't think they figured that was quite as important. They had several charts of mouth openings and closings. I think they all just followed the vowels and the consonants.

Barrier: The animators didn't have your voice to listen to, to get facial expressions.

Mercer: That's right; they just read the line themselves and tried to animate it.

Barrier: On the early Popeyes [Fleischer Studios], it seemed the stories have more variety in them than was the case later [Famous Studios] when Seymour Kneitel and Izzy Sparber were directing.

Mercer: I guess it was because we wanted to improve them. We took a little more time in creating them. I don't know what else to say about that.

Barrier: In the '30s, the stories didn't always have the spinach and the climactic fight, which became standard later on.

Mercer: I think [Famous Studios] figured that was what was putting them over. The audiences expected the fight. When they first started, they probably didn't know exactly where to go with it.

Barrier: When you were working on the Popeye stories later on did you feel it was obligatory to include the spinach and the fight?

Mercer: No one ever questioned it. If somebody had said, "Look, we've got to get off this spinach bit," we would have all hustled, I suppose, and tried to figure out some other angles.

Barrier: There were characters from the comic strip [*Thimble Theatre*] that weren't used very much, like Eugene the Jeep and the Sea Hag.

Mercer: I think you might find there it was something to do with the copyrights.

Barrier: You just had the license for certain characters?

Mercer: That or they would have had to be paid for - something on that order.

Barrier: So you were restricted in the number of characters from the comic strip that you could use.

Mercer: Yes. As a matter of fact, I think the villain's name was changed [from Bluto to Brutus] for the same reason in the Popeye cartoons made for television. However, other characters from the comic strip, such as the Sea Hag, were used in the TV cartoons, even though they hadn't been used in the theatrical cartoons, which would suggest Bluto's name was changed for some other reason.

Barrier: Now, you did the voice for those TV cartoons. There were a remarkably large number of them.

Mercer: There were 220 for television.

Barrier: And those were turned out, I know, in almost no time at all.

Mercer: We did nine cartoons at one recording. They'd [King Features Syndicate] farmed them out to various companies [for the animation] and they all came in for the recording. The directors flew in from the coast.

Virginia Mercer: That last night, Jack Kinney [one of the producers of the TV Popeyes], his wife, Jack and I went to celebrate, after they did that one last big push. I would say his *Felix the Cat* was done in the same manner. He'd do four or five in one night, after working all day at Paramount. It's a wonder he didn't kill himself. He did every voice in *Felix the Cat*.

Barrier: Have you done other voices, besides those for Paramount and the Felix show?

Mercer: I did some stuff for Joe Oriolo later on; he was doing a few odd cartoons [Mercer possibly is speaking of his brief work on *The Mighty Hercules*].

Virginia Mercer: You did voices for *Gulliver's Travels* and *Mr. Bug Goes to Town*.

Mercer: But not for other studios.

Barrier: I guess *Mr. Bug Goes to Town* is one of the few times you got screen credit as a voice.

Virginia Mercer: He got screen credit for story at Paramount, but they just would not give screen credit for the voices.

Mercer: I don't know what it was; maybe they figured that if they wanted to change somebody, they wouldn't have any trouble.

Barrier: At the time you went to work in the story department at Fleischers', I guess there was just one story department, period?

Mercer: Yes, just one room, there were several men in there; each one was assigned to a different story. When I first started there, I was more or less an apprentice, being broken in. There was no previous way of knowing how to write a story, I don't believe there was any school you could go to. I had to start from scratch.

Barrier: They just gave you part of a script, to see how you did gagging it?

Mercer: Right. I would hand in ideas, of course, story synopses. I just did all sorts of things in that end of it, till I had advanced to the point that I was actually handed a story to do.

Barrier: When you were handed a story to do, you would be given a synopsis?

Mercer: At this point, yes, but later on, you had to hand in a synopsis or idea.

Barrier: The synopsis would come from Bill Turner. He would give you the idea?

Mercer: When I first started, yes.

Barrier: Did he originate these? You mentioned that you would hand in synopses.

Mercer: Somebody else might have handed him a synopsis; one of the story men who had been established there a while or other people outside could have. Every once in a while an animator might get an idea. They would submit synopses.

Barrier: So the ideas for stories could come from anyplace?

Mercer: Yes, but not too often.

Barrier: The bulk of these ideas originated in the story department?

Mercer: Yes.

Barrier: After a while, were you originating most of the synopses yourself, for the stories you worked on?

Mercer: I got to the point where I was working with someone; Jack Ward and Carl Meyer. I worked with Jack Ward for a while; then I worked with Carl Meyer. Then I worked by myself at the end [this was primarily at Famous Studios].

Virginia Mercer: In 1953, this is when I came into the picture, I think you and Carl were allowed six weeks for a picture, from beginning to end, and to try to come up with something new that would possibly make a series.

Mercer: Yes, any type of a new character.

Barrier: You were one of a group of story men [at Famous Studios] including I. Klein, Carl Meyer and Larz Bourne. Klein mentioned that it took a story team four to six weeks to complete a storyboard.

Mercer: Yes

Barrier: What were these guys like, Bill Turner, Jack Ward and Carl Meyer? Were they funny people to work with, practical jokers?

Mercer: Well, not too much, but we'd always have a pretty lively conversation going. We stuck pretty much trying to get ideas, and we got our kicks, you might say, by trying to top each other on gags, and the stories, and what not.

Barrier: Did you specialize in stories with certain characters?

Mercer: No, I think we all were just handed whatever was required. After we got through with a picture, if they had something that had to be put on schedule, they'd day, "Here, try this one." I don't know that you could say we were typed. We all took a crack at most anything they had.

Barrier: You weren't assigned to any particular director, either, were you?

Mercer: No, that worked the same way. Whatever director had a picture coming up, he handled that. No one was assigned to any particular series. Everybody had to pitch in and do whatever was handed to them.

Barrier: There was a strike at the Fleischer Studios in, I believe, 1937, before the move to Miami.

Mercer: I think that's what brought on the move, actually.

Barrier: Do you recall anything about the strike, what led up to it and what was involved with it?

Mercer: I guess it was a matter of money. I think it was the opaquers and the inkers who wanted to form a union. Of course, Max was against that. So they decided to go on strike and demonstrate. I wasn't involved at the time, because I was in the story department. I had just gone into the story department, as a matter of fact. They had asked us, on the side, if we would mind helping out in the in-between department in the meantime so they could continue their production. I remember one time, when I went home on the subway, there were two very strange-looking characters who sat down on either side of me. I just didn't know if that was something that had to do with me or not. They used to send balloons up to the windows, with signs on them, "scabs" and all sorts of signs like that, and we'd take paper clips and break the balloons. Sometimes we'd grab the balloons and fill them up with water and throw them out the window. Once or twice the paddy wagon came along and picked them up. I think they had a rule at that time no one was supposed to clutter up the sidewalk with all these signs. They took photographs of everybody that went in the studio.

Barrier: Gordon said that one reason the animator, and I guess the story men, too, didn't strike was that they had individual contracts at that time.

Mercer: I suppose that's true. But since I was just a newcomer at that time, I don't recall having a contract myself [Virginia Mercer sent the author correspondence between the Fleischer Studios and Jack Mercer, which appears to be contracts.]

Barrier: Did the strike ever end with an agreement, or did it just kind of peter out?

Mercer: I guess it just petered out. I never paid any attention to that stuff. I just went along and did my work.

Virginia Mercer: He still doesn't. He belongs to AFTRA, and the Screen Actors Guild. He hasn't the slightest idea of what he should be paid for a commercial. I do all of that. He absolutely cares nothing about business matters. Consequently, he doesn't involve himself, and he doesn't remember anything about it.

Mercer: Well, there's no gags in those things.

Barrier: When the move to Miami came up, were you ready to go, or did you hesitate?

Mercer: I was sort of hesitant, because I wasn't sure whether I wanted to leave the city, and what the future would be down there. I wasn't enthused about it, but I figured, that's where they're going, that's where I'll have to go.

Barrier: So you did go along at the same time the studio moved down there.

Mercer: Oh, yeah. Things were in production and, after all, I was doing Popeye's voice, so I thought it would be rather foolish to cut that off all together.

Barrier: Did they [the Fleischer Studios] ever show appreciation for the work you were doing as the voice, in salary or in other ways? Did they ever act like they really valued you, because you had contributed so much to Popeye's success?

Mercer: No, not really. I can't say that there was any great change until later on, almost at the end of the regime; all of a sudden they started to say I was the great Popeye, and all sorts of things. But it was too late then.

Virginia Mercer: Actually, this came about when King Features was going to do a whole new batch [of Popeye cartoons for TV], and they [Paramount] wanted to make sure they got in on doing some of the animation. Jack was a wedge there. Al Brodax, producer of the TV Popeye series, had already decided that Jack would do the voice for all the studios, not just Paramount. Brodax wouldn't permit anyone to change that voice; it had to be the same as the old one. I don't know whether Paramount was aware of that, but they knew that Jack was their boy and that sort of helped them.

Barrier: When you started doing the Popeye voice, was it very long after that before they started having you do other voices? Did you start doing other voices right away?

Mercer: Yes, right away. I worked on the Betty Boops, and any of the other cartoons they had at the time. I would pick up any odd voices that they had incidental voices throughout the pictures.

Barrier: It seems surprising, in a way, considering the number of voices that you did that you never wound up as the Mel Blanc [voice artist of Warner Bros.] of Paramount Studios. Mel, of course, wound up doing almost everything.

Mercer: Well, actually, there other characters were so incidental. I believe at other studios they made a thing out of creating more characters, which eventually developed into featured characters, in their own cartoons. They stuck mostly to a few favorite characters, and everything else was incidental. There was no big deal. You'd go to a recording session and they'd hand you a script and say, "You do this, you do that, you do this" and what not. There was no thought of character, or anything else; it was just a voice.

Barrier: They didn't realize the potential of developing the voices?

Mercer: I don't think so.

Barrier: To what extent was Max Fleischer involved in the production of the cartoons? Was he the front office, as opposed to being involved in the actual production?

Mercer: Yes, more or less. He was involved a lot in some of the innovations. He was working on inventions and things like the three-dimensional effects. But every once in a while he would come in and look at the finished cartoon. I don't think he had too much to do with it, later on.

Barrier: There were other Fleischers besides Max and Dave at the studio weren't there?

Mercer: Oh, yes. Lou was the music director and he rehearsed many of the cartoons, dialogue rehearsal. He took charge of that most of the time. Joe was another; he was more or less a mechanic of some kind.

Barrier: You mentioned that Dave would direct dialogue, Lou would rehearse it, and Dave would come in for the actual recording.

Mercer: Yes.

Barrier: When you were working up stories, under Bill Turner in the Fleischer story department, would you have much contact with the animation directors like William Bowsky and Dave Tendlar and the other people who were in charge of the animation units then?

Mercer: I think that was probably Bill Turner; if there were any questions on the story, I think he was involved with the animators at the time. Once in a while, as I said, they would have a final story meeting, and the animators would sometimes come in. Later on, when I was writing stories with Carl Meyer and Jack Ward, they would call in the animator when we had pretty much of a completed storyboard. They would come in on a final story meeting. Then, if there were a lot of changes to be made, the head animator might make suggestions, or the director himself might make suggestions, and changes would be made, and then they'd have another final meeting, which the animator would be called in on. Everyone would agree on the final storyboard.

Barrier: How did your ideas differ on comedy from the directors at Famous Studios?

Mercer: I guess everybody disagrees about what comedy is, and many times we would have arguments as to what is funny and what isn't. It was a matter of opinion, and the story men always felt that we had the better outlook on comedy

Barrier: You mean you would have your storyboard on the wall, and they [the directors] would come in and say, "Why don't you have Popeye doing this here, instead of that."

Mercer: That's right. There were always some little arguments about which gag is funny and Carl was very good about sticking up for the ideas on the board. It got pretty hot in that room; some of the drawings started to burn - and you couldn't touch the thumbtacks.

Barrier: I guess the directors at Famous had the final say, though, didn't they?

Mercer: Oh yeah. Many times, they would switch a story all around and say, "You can't do this; this is no good," blah, blah, blah. So we'd do it their way, and nine times out of then they'd come in and say, "Gee, we'd better do it the old way." We'd never throw the old drawings away; we'd put them in the basket, but when they'd walk out, we'd pull them out and put them in a drawer, figuring that they would be back soon, and we could use the old drawings again.

Barrier: Did you work much with Bill Tytla? [Tytla was one of Disney's original animators and is considered by many to be the best character animator working during the Golden Age of Hollywood animation. He later joined Famous Studios and directed several Paramount theatrical films. His directorial work on Popeye includes, *Service with a Guile* (1946), *Popeye Meets Hercules* (1948), *Tar with a Star* (1949) and *Jitterbug Jive* (1950).]

Mercer: Not too long, he was there only two years or so.

Barrier: He's a guy I've admired very much as an animator and wondered what he was like to work with as a director, especially compared to others at Famous.

Mercer: He was very knowledgeable, and easy to get along with.

Barrier: People who have worked with him describe him as a very ebullient guy, full of vitality.

Mercer: Yes, enthusiastic about his work. He acted like he was anxious to do a good job on it, which he did.

Barrier: Did his ideas about comedy fit with yours?

Mercer: I think so, yes. Carl knew him, too, very well, from Disney, so there was camaraderie there, probably.

Barrier: Gordon Sheehan indicated that when you went to Miami, there were a lot of changes in the way the [Fleischer] studio operated? Was that the impression you had? Was it a different ballgame when you got to Miami?

Mercer: When they [Fleischer Studios] got into the feature [*Gulliver's Travels*], of course, the studio started to employ people from the coast, which gave a different atmosphere to the place. They brought Disneyland to Florida.

Barrier: I wanted to ask you about Dan Gordon. He became a director there. [Dan Gordon was a storyboard artist and film director. He directed what are considered some of the zaniest *Popeye* cartoons produced at Famous Studios during the early 1940s.] Gordon Sheehan said Dan was one of four people running Famous Studios, along with director Isadore Sparber, Seymour Kneitel [Max Fleischer's son-in-law, who animated and directed] and Sam Buchwald, after the Fleischers left.

Mercer: He was a very clever and terrific model man. He was a very good friend of Carl's.

Barrier: Did you work with him in Miami?

Mercer: I wrote a couple of Popeye stories with him.

Barrier: Did you work on *Gulliver's Travels* as well as the shorts?

Mercer: Sure; everybody pitched in on that. A lot of the coast boys got in on the feature pictures; I think they were brought in for that reason.

Barrier: So you and other people would switch back and forth from *Gulliver's Travels* to the shorts, as the need arose?

Mercer: Right.

Barrier: Was there any resentment of these new people?

Mercer: I think it was hard for the old hands at the Fleischer Studios to accept these types, because they were a little wilder.

Barrier: Some studios, when they were upgrading, used story sketch men to re-draw the story men's sketches. Gordon Sheehan mentioned that the storyboards got much more elaborate for *Gulliver's Travels*.

Mercer: Yes, that was for the feature picture.

Barrier: You did have story sketch men for the feature?

Mercer: Yes, some of those coast boys. I guess you could say they were more artistic in their work. They took over the drawing of the feature sketches.

Barrier: Story sketch men usually take the story man's rough sketches and polish them up into something more elaborate; that's what these guys did?

Mercer: Yes, I believe that's the way it worked. There were so many variations on that, and it was quite a big studio at the time, so what they were doing in another section, I wouldn't know.

Barrier: The feature production was organized, wasn't it, with several different units working on different segments of the picture?

Mercer: Right.

Barrier: Did you stick with any one part of the picture?

Mercer: No, I would go in on various sequences, every once in a while, because, as I said, we were working on the shorts.

Barrier: I know you did the voice of the Lilliputian King in *Gulliver's Travels*; what other voices did you do in that picture?

Mercer: I did one of the spies; I forget which one and the chef.

Barrier: When you were working on a story, especially on shorts, did you have to keep the budget in the back of your mind, and think, "We can't do this idea because it would cost too much"?

Mercer: Right ... that was very much the thing.

Barrier: How did that affect you? What kinds of ideas did you have to avoid?

Mercer: Any type of thing that would require a lot of animation.

Barrier: So you couldn't let the director worry about that, you had to think about it too.

Mercer: Yes; sometimes the whole idea might depend on something like that. If it did, we'd be out of luck.

Barrier: Did this ever get frustrating? Did you ever get a great idea that you realized you couldn't carry through on?

Mercer: Oh, that was always apparent. Even when it wasn't anything to do with the budget type of thing, if we got an idea that we thought would be great, and they'd turn it down, you'd grit your teeth and tuck your tail between your legs, and slink out the door.

Barrier: Did you ever do any writing for comic books, for anything outside of animated cartoons?

Mercer: I did a few.

Virginia Mercer: I said forget it. It doesn't pay well enough to fit all these things in little squares.

Mercer: That was a limited thing, too, thinking in terms of straight pictures.

Virginia Mercer: Jack's particular personality would just not permit him to work on any comic book that was really violent. In other words, if he thought something might hurt a child, or its imagination, he would not do it.

Barrier: Do you recall any of the comic books you did work on?

Mercer: Harvey.

Barrier: When you were working on a story that called for a new character, how was character design handled? Would the story men actually be responsible for his design?

Mercer: We'd have a rough idea of a character, and that could be refined, or handed to someone else in that line of work. I think Myron Waldman [an animator at both Fleischer and Famous Studios] was one who handled characters. Carl Meyer wasn't bad himself at drawing characters, so lots of times he would work up a drawing. There wasn't a great amount of time spent on these things.

Barrier: Back in the '30s, what was the Fleischer Studio like, as a place to work? Was there a lot of pressure?

Mercer: Everything had to be done on time, and I guess you could say it was like a factory. You're turning out a product.

Barrier: Was it an enjoyable place to work, despite that?

Mercer: In my case, after I got into the story department, there would always be an interest in trying to create material. I can't very well speak for the rest of the artists there; whether the animators felt that way or not, I don't know. I assume that the opaquers and the tracers, those people, might have been bored with doing the same thing over and over again.

Barrier: But in your case, you had plenty of stimulation.

Mercer: I was always amusing myself.

Virginia Mercer: I went to his office only once, and I was horrified. It was like a barn! Who could work or be inspired in such an atmosphere? It was awful.

Mercer: That was like a conference room, and there weren't any decorations; it was just a room. It looked like there'd been a factory in there, and they'd moved out.

Barrier: Were things any better in Miami?

Mercer: It was more modern, yes; they tried to spruce it up a little bit.

Barrier: But you couldn't say that the Fleischers or Famous Studio ever had plush surroundings for you.

Mercer: Well, it was clean. The Miami Studio had been newly built, so everything was new—except the stories. In the '30s we were over at 1600 Broadway and if there had been sewing machines in there, you'd have figured we were in the garment business.

Barrier: Then when you came back [to New York, after the Miami Studio closed], you were in the same kind of place, just at a different location.

Mercer: That's right. A typical New York office building. Sing Sing had better accommodations. There were no bars on the windows, that's all.

Barrier: You were gone during World War II, weren't you?

Mercer: Yes, I was in the Army for two years.

Barrier: What did they do to replace you? Didn't they have Mae Questel do Popeye's voice once or twice?

Mercer: That's what they said; she might be able to do the ad-lib voice, but they said that Buckley, some guy, who did it on radio years and years ago, might have done one or two. I did a lot of them while I was still in Camp Edwards, on leave. I don't know who the heck, if anybody, did any of them or whether they used repeat dialogue from old pictures, or what.

Virginia Mercer: When Jack was in the Army, all of a sudden when they realized what he had done - and he had done all this training here, just prior to going over to the European Theater - they offered him a job at the USO, which would have been plush. And, you know, he turned it down. He wanted to be with his buddies because he trained with them. That's the kind of a person he is.

Mercer: We had a good gun crew; I didn't want to break it up.

Barrier: Where did you wind up overseas?

Mercer: In Germany, on the Rhine. We were defending a bridge that the Second Armored Division was crossing over at the time, to meet the Russians.

Barrier: What do you recall about the studio's move back to New York [when Fleischer Studios closed in Miami and was renamed Famous Studios]? Were you prepared for what happened?

Mercer: No, I think they had moved when I came back.

Barrier: You went in the Army before they moved back from Miami? So when you came back they were back in New York?

Mercer: Yes.

Barrier: When you came back to the studio after the war, did you notice any major changes from the way it had been under the Fleischers?

Mercer: It didn't seem the same. It was very unsettled, for one thing. There was that feeling of that possibility of not continuing; business wasn't too good.

Barrier: Something I forgot to ask you earlier, on the ad-lib muttering; that ended didn't it, about the time the Fleischers left? Was there a deliberate decision to stop the muttering, and go to the straight dialogue? Or did it happen because of your going in the service?

Mercer: Maybe so. I don't actually remember stopping it all together until the TV cartoons were made. They had all of these various people doing stories, and they were all timed, and we had to do nine of them, or eight, or seven, and there was no time, really to think of anything. The only thing I could do would be to take a line that had been written straight and do it in an ad-lib voice. An ad-lib line was supposed to be somebody thinking out loud; and since there was so much dialogue in these later pictures, there really wasn't much chance to put that type of thing in. The other pictures had a lot of action to them, so you felt like you had the opportunity just to add some thought to a gag, before it was done, or after it was done.

Barrier: But they did get away from the muttering where they didn't have the synchronization of the dialogue with Popeye's mouth movements; that lack of synchronization is not as evident in the Famous cartoons. But as far as your own recording of the dialogue?

Mercer: I tried to put it in, yes.

Barrier: The Famous cartoons of the '50s seem to be aimed more directly to children than the Fleischer cartoons of the '30s were.

Mercer: I know one thing, they were very conscious of being criticized for violence. There were a lot of these women's clubs writing in, and complaining about the treatment that Olive Oyl was getting. We began to be censored, more or less, so that might have had some effect. The directors, presumably, were afraid they might be censored on the big fights between Popeye and Bluto. They started to let up on these things. They got to the point where they found that children were emulating some of these characters. Kids were putting on sheets and jumping out of windows hoping to fly like Superman. They were afraid this might be the case with Popeye, with kids trying to show how strong they were.

Barrier: Did you get this kind of complaint in the '30s, too, or was this something that only came along later?

Mercer: We just went along, and nobody seemed to say anything about it. I'm sure somebody would have said something about it if there had been some complaint about it.

Barrier: Were you with Paramount until it closed?

Mercer: Yes. [Mercer's writing for the Paramount theatricals, based on the films' credits, ceased to appear by the beginning of 1964, while the studio remained active until late 1967.]

Virginia Mercer: Then you did some freelance, and you did stories for Terry's [Terrytoon's *Deputy Dawg*].

Mercer: I did some Kokos [*Koko the Clown*] for Hal Seeger, and I did a few stories for Joe Oriolo, as well as voices.

Virginia Mercer: As I say, Jack was the type not to go out and audition for commercials; he just didn't like "cattle calls," when he was used to just being called down to do a voice. He didn't want to be one of 30. I went along with it. Jack had a mild heart attack during this period and I was relieved that he was not undergoing any stress. If he is called, which he was, periodically, by King Features, he was there to do something with Popeye. Right now he's not working and he's sort of goofing off, except for Popeye.

THE POPEYE AND FRIENDS SHOW WITH TOM HATTEN

When the theatrical Popeye films were released to television in 1956, local stations often featured the films with live hosts. One of the best remembered associated with the sailor man was Tom Hatten.

In 1952 Tom launched his broadcasting career off the sunny shores of downtown Hollywood at KTLA studios. It was his first broadcasting job and, like a lot of people in the early days of television, he wore many hats at the station, from commercial spokesman, staff announcer and newsman to wearing a sailor's hat for the afternoon kid's show, The Popeye Show. *KTLA had just acquired the classic Paramount Popeye cartoons and Tom Hatten began his hitch on the show. He soon became popular and well liked while drawing his own renditions of the Popeye cast. Tom left KTLA for twelve years, but came back to the station in a new version called* Popeye and his Friends *in 1976 (these color telecasts aired until 1988). Hatten would explain to the children (and grown-ups) watching his program how the Fleischer cartoons came to life and invited people involved with the Popeye theatricals to appear on the show. On Easter morning, Tom Hatten's guest was Jack Mercer, who was in Hollywood to begin work on Hanna-Barbera's All New Popeye Hour series. Here are some highlights from Tom Hatten's conversation with Jack Mercer, courtesy of Mark Kausler and Jerry Beck:*

Tom Hatten: Jack Mercer from New York City, all the way to California just to be on our show on Easter Sunday morning.

Jack Mercer: That's right.

Hatten: Jack, I can't tell you we have had so many letters from so many kids and their parents wanting to know who does the voice of Popeye. Because there have been a lot of impostors around. People in supermarkets and shopping centers they say, "I'm the original voice."

Mercer: That's true.

Hatten: This is the gentleman, Mr. Jack Mercer!

Mercer: I thank you.

Top: *On Easter morning in 1977, Jack Mercer was Tom Hatten's special guest on his* Popeye and His Friends *show which aired locally in Los Angeles on KTLA.* Bottom: *Jack Mercer clucks like a chicken to demonstrate for Tom Hatten the various voices he performed in the Fleischer Studio's animated cartoons.*

Hatten: Jack, we're so pleased to have you with us.

Mercer: I'm very pleased to be here.

Hatten: We have told the boys and girls throughout the years, based on the Fleischer book, *The Fleischer Story*, the stories about how you were an artist yourself. You then became a voice man and I thought during the show, in between cartoons, we'll really find out the truth on how you go about being a cartoon star!

Mercer: Great!

Hatten: You've seen what he looks like. We're going to be putting him through his paces and really make him talk about the old days of cartooning and when the animation was a little bit wilder than it is now with Jack Mercer, the voice of Popeye, right after the next cartoon. This one is called *Olive Oyl and Water Don't Mix*.

(Back from the cartoon)

Hatten: You've had a chance to see our show so you know it's very loose. We say anything we like and worry about the lawsuits later. First off, I think the boys and girls would like to know just why you are in Southern California. I joked about you just coming for our show, but you've got other reasons. Tell us what's happening out at Hanna-Barbera. Sounds exciting to me.

Mercer: Well, we're making some Popeye cartoons, once again.

Hatten: Brand new ones.

Mercer: Forty-eight of them.

Hatten: When will they be on?

Mercer: Well, I don't really know that, I mean we just started so they're working on them. We just started to work on them.

Hatten: They hope to get them on maybe next year, next fall?

Top: *When Tom Hatten pulled out a child's letter to win a prize, Jack Mercer read the viewer's name in Popeye's voice.* Bottom: *Performing in Popeye's voice, Jack Mercer sings the sailor's famous theme song for Tom Hatten.*

Mercer: Probably, by that time ... yes.

Hatten: On one of the networks with the three names, CBS like that.

Mercer: CBS, right.

Hatten: Good. CBS has said they're going to try and get them on next fall on Saturday mornings. Let's just re-cap a little bit about Max Fleischer. He started with Betty Boop and Popeye was introduced in a Betty Boop cartoon. You weren't the voice at that time.

Mercer: No, no.

Hatten: Who was that?

Mercer: That was Red Pepper Sam; he did the voice at that time.

Hatten: He had been an actor on the old *Betty Boop Radio Show*.

Mercer: That's right, yes. He did a gorilla and they just used that voice for Popeye later on.

Hatten: I see, the story in the book says that he wanted more money or he got a little persnickety.

Mercer: So they say.

Hatten: How did you happen to get in the action then?

Mercer: Well, you know, I use to imitate the characters I was working on at the time.

Hatten: What were you doing?

Mercer: Inking Department.

Hatten: Inking Department of the Popeye cartoons.

Mercer: No, all sorts of cartoons. I would imitate some of the characters, you know. For instance, if I was working on a chicken character, I would make a chicken sound [Jack makes a chicken sound for Tom Hatten] ... Bbbbuccckkkk, you know everybody would laugh. Finally, I started to imitate the Popeye voice and somebody heard me and suggested I try out for it.

Hatten: In other words, the guy who created it was leaving and they needed someone in hurry to replace him.

Mercer: That's right. So I said at the time I didn't think I could really do it well enough. So I went home and practiced. About a week or so later my voice cracked and I got this peculiar sound and I thought, oh my gosh, something happened here. It was the actual tone that I wanted to get so I went back and I told him I think now I could really do the voice. So I gave an audition over the telephone to someone at Paramount.

Hatten: No kidding!

Mercer: That's right.

Hatten: So once you got the job did you continue your artist work as well?

Mercer: That's right, I stayed in the in-between department for a while, then I went into the story department after that.

Hatten: In-between department is something I've tried to explain to the kids, but I bet you can do it better than I can. What is an in-betweener; what does he do actually?

Mercer: Well, he puts drawings in-between the action drawings that the animator makes. For instance, the extreme drawings, if you want Popeye to hit a character he will draw this picture [Mercer raises his arm and fist to the left], then he will draw the final picture [Mercer raises his arm and fist to the right]. Now the person, who does the in-between drawings, puts drawings in between those two.

Hatten: So they go real fast. That's the action.

Mercer: That's an in-betweener.

Hatten: I tried to explain that to myself last week so I knew nobody else knew what I was talking about. Now there was Max Fleischer, Max, Dave and Lou.

Mercer: And Joe and Charlie.

Hatten: My gosh, there were Fleischers all over the place.

Mercer: The whole place was full of Fleischers.

(Cartoon break)

Hatten: The gentleman on my right is Mr. Jack Mercer, who is the voice of Popeye and has been that since 1930 ....

Mercer: Four

Hatten: 1934. [Mercer's first Popeye cartoon was released in 1935.] You're going to do it until you get it right.

Mercer: I'm going to try.

Hatten: I guess after a while they [Popeye cartoons] kind of melt one into another.

Mercer: That's right, they all kind of lookalike to me.

Hatten: Well, the ones that we have, we have the old black and whites and then the Jack Kinney ones [the 1960-61 *Popeye* TV-cartoon series], which they show at channel, am-hmm [Hatten muffles his voice by putting his hand across his mouth]. You did those too.

Mercer: I did those too.

Hatten: And you'll be doing the new series on CBS in the fall. Tell us a little bit about the other people you worked with. Who played Olive Oyl?

Mercer: Olive Oyl, Mae Questel.

Hatten: I've told the boys and girls that I believe she's the lady who does the Auntie Bluebell commercials.

Mercer: That's correct.

Hatten: What about Bluto?

Mercer: Well that was Jackson Beck and he does a lot of commercials in New York.

Hatten: And what about Wimpy?

Mercer: Well, I did Wimpy.

Hatten: You did Wimpy as well? Could I hear a little Wimpy voice?

Top: *Tom Hatten introduces the 1938 Popeye cartoon, "A Date to Skate" produced by the Fleischer Studios, one of his personal favorites. On both incarnations of his television series, only the theatrical Popeye series was shown. Tom Hatten preferred these over the later television-produced Popeye shorts.* Bottom: *Tom Hatten, a talented cartoonist and historian on the Fleischer Studios, draws a caricature of Jack Mercer.*

Mercer: [In Wimpy's voice from the 1960-61 TV-cartoons] *I'll gladly pay you Tuesday for a hamburger today.*

Hatten: That is definitely Wimpy. But I do have some news because Jack was telling me there's a new Wimpy. He decided he didn't want to press his luck, he's got forty-eight Popeyes to do, you better get some help and our friend Daws Butler is going to be Wimpy and we're very excited about that.

Mercer: That's right

Hatten: You had mentioned the other Fleischers. Lou Fleischer was in charge of the orchestra, right?

Mercer: That's right; he directed and wrote some of the music at one time. [Lou Fleischer has been credited as the one overhearing Mercer doing his

Popeye impression, which led to him getting the job.]

Hatten: We see Dave Fleischer's name as the director of a lot of them. Now what does a director in a cartoon do? There are no actors to direct. What does he do?

Mercer: Well, he actually does direct the actors.

Hatten: He does?

Mercer: He sits in on the recording and tells the actors how he wants the lines read. He would decide on the final dialogue.

Hatten: All right, does he also decide as far as the drawings are concerned? That drawing isn't good enough, that has to be done again, that sort of thing.

Mercer: Well, not necessarily. They'd have animation directors. But he [the director] would sit in on the final picture.

Hatten: In other words, the director is overall of everything and he would have some directors underneath.

Mercer: Underneath.

Hatten: Different cartoons are made in different ways. For instance, when you watch *Snow White and the Seven Dwarfs* or *Pinocchio*, the Disney cartoons, and probably some of Mr. Fleischers too, you notice that the mouth always moves with the word. In that cartoon we just saw [*A Date to Skate*, a Fleischer Studios' Popeye] and some cartoons we're going to be watching, the lines are funny and the jokes are there but they don't always match, there doesn't seem to be any talking going on. How does that work? When you were making the cartoons back in the '30s did they finish the cartoon first and then you put the voices in afterward?

Mercer: Yes, that's the way it was done. You see, we watched the finished cartoon, and remember the old bouncing ball that was used on the screen songs?

Hatten: Oh, gosh, I do, but the kids don't. Why don't you explain it to the kids?

Mercer: Anyway, there was a bouncing ball that went up and down on either side of the screen in rhythm. We had to follow the bouncing ball to read our lines. We cued in with the bouncing ball.

Hatten: Did each actor have his own bouncing ball to follow?

Mercer: Each actor had his bouncing ball, musicians had a bouncing ball and the soundman had a bouncing ball. It looked like a tennis match.

Hatten: I see. That's where the director comes in; he must have had to keep in charge of the whole thing.

Mercer: That's correct. Then in between that we would ad-lib lines. Just to add, throw something in there to fill up the empty spaces as it were. Whatever you would feel like saying at the time.

Hatten: We get so many notes from adults and kids, mind you, who say we like the old black-and-white cartoons so much better because they seem much more looser. Does the fellow who makes Popeye, his voice, does he make up those up as he goes along?   So the answer I guess is some he does and some he takes from the script.

Mercer: That's correct, yes.

Hatten: Tell us about your life away from the Popeye series, Jack. Do you do other things besides Popeye voices?

Mercer: Well, I do commercials every once and awhile. I've done some for Burlington and Coca-Cola, and then there was one I did for Popeye's Fried Chicken.

Hatten: Oh, I don't believe we get that out here.

Mercer: I think that's down South.

Hatten: What about writing, do you still write Popeye storylines?   I know you did a lot of those.

Mercer: Well, I am writing now.

Hatten: In addition to doing the voices for Hanna-Barbera, you're doing some of the storylines.

Mercer: But I did do some Kokos [Koko the Clown from the *Out of the Inkwell* TV-cartoon series produced by Hal Seeger] and I did a couple of *Deputy Dawg*.

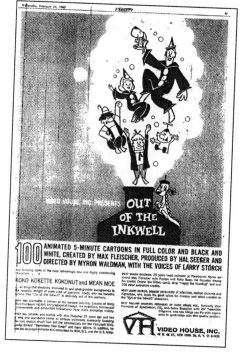

Jack Mercer wrote episodes of Hal Seeger's animated Out of the Inkwell *series starring Koko, a character from the silent film days of the Fleischer Studios. Pictured is an advertisement promoting the availability of the cartoons from Variety dated February 21, 1962.*

Hatten: What about your family? Do you have a wife and children?

Mercer: Well, I have a wife that's sitting over there.

Hatten: I knew that all the time. She's very pretty too. Are you going to let her stay out here all the time while you're here in California?

Mercer: Well, I'd like too but I'm afraid that won't be possible.

Hatten: Oh well, we'll take her as long as we can get. I've been talking so much I didn't get a chance to even ask you to do a "I Yam What I Yam" or "I eats me spinach," just anything you feel.

Mercer: Suppose I just sing the song.

Hatten: Why don't you - that would be terrific!

Mercer: [as Popeye]

Oh, I'm Popeye the Sailor Man, uck-uck-uck, uck.
I'm Popeye the Sailor Man, scibb-bidy-di-do
I'm strong to the finich
'Cause I eats me spinach,
I'm Popeye the Sailor Man...Woo! Woo! [Jack Mercer uses his voice rather than pipe to provide the toot! toot! Sound] *Dere' ya are.*

Hatten: You don't need an orchestra, you don't need a sound effects man, you don't need anything except Jack Mercer and you've got the whole ball of wax! You were an artist, did you take drawing lessons?

Mercer: I just sort of picked it up.

Hatten: Was your family theatrical?

Mercer: They were all in show business. As a matter of fact, they had tent shows, repertoire companies and whenever a kid part came up then I was chosen for that part. As a matter of fact, the first part I ever did was as a baby. They carried me on in one spot and there was a place where I was supposed to cry. So they pinched me on the derriere on cue and I would cry at that spot. That was my first speaking part.

Hatten: What part of the country did you come from, Jack?

Mercer: This was in Indiana.

Hatten: Ladies and Gentlemen, boys and girls, I hope you've had a good time as we had. Jack, I can't thank you enough for being such a good guy.

Mercer: Oh, and I certainly appreciate you having me on the show.

JACK MERCER SPEAKS FOR HIMSELF

Virginia Mercer sent me some notes Jack had jotted down which he called "Amuseing Incidenses," as Popeye would call Amusing Incidents. Here are his notations:

MAKING A FIRST IMPRESSION

"When I first started to do the Popeye voice I was young, only 5 foot 4 and as thin as a rail. I probably looked the model they used for the ad, 'send this boy to camp.' Well, one day at the studio, a newly hired writer arrived and when I was introduced as the voice of Popeye he made an awestruck take and said, "First, it was Santa Clause ... and now this!"

THE SPINACH SURPRISE

"After a Popeye recording session the director along with the other voice people and myself stopped in a restaurant to have a bite to eat. When the waiter asked me what I wanted I said in my regular speaking voice that all I wanted was a side order of spinach. He looked at me kind of funny and said, 'Who do you think you are - Popeye?' I answered in the Popeye voice, 'Who'd ya think I was Tom Thumb?' Well, his jaw dropped and he made an awkward exit backwards into the kitchen. When he finally returned, he brought me the largest plate of spinach I've ever seen."

OLIVER TWIST

"King Features asked me to record a 'Popeye's Birthday' record with the boys in the musical show, Oliver Twist, then playing on Broadway. After we were all introduced at the first rehearsal, the boys [in the musical show] became very enthusiastic about having met 'Popeye.' They started quizzing me as to how Popeye could do all of those feats of strength. Suddenly the cast of Oliver took an unexpected twist, they decided to test my strength by grabbing my legs and they dared me to escape their hold. Lucky for me their manager threatened to cancel their daily treat of double chocolate milkshakes if they didn't release me pronto. The excuse I gave for not being able to break away was that I didn't have my spinach with me, which I'm sure was not accepted by the boys but they were a good group otherwise. All returned to normalcy and no further demonstrations took place."

EXCITABLE ECHO!

"One time a few extra sound effects had to be added to a cartoon and were to be done vocally. A small studio in an office building was booked for the recording instead of the usual large soundstage. I was to supply the sounds for men yelling for help, mixed with the roaring of a monster that was chasing him. After a few takes it was decided that they wanted an echo effect. The studio had no echo chamber so they set up the microphone, to get the echo effect, out in the hallway of the studio. I started roaring and yelling, 'help, save me.' Through earphones I was directed to give more each time, making take after take. The reverberating yells and roars became more intense. Excited people started running out of their offices all up and down the hall. Suddenly a guy came scrambling out of the men's room trying to hold up his pants. People were screaming, 'What the hell is going on out there? Somebody call the police!' At this point I decided that enough takes had been recorded and I made an embarrassed exit back to the studio past a glowering, indignant group."

JACK MERCER'S RECORDING CAREER

Jack Mercer's recording career is primarily known for a series of Popeye recordings he did, from 1951 to the early 1980s. In 1951 he sang (as Popeye) the sailor's classic theme song for the Golden Records label. This version was later re-released as part of other 45s and albums well into the 1960s. It is on these records that Jack Mercer was credited for being the "voice of Popeye." While Mae Questel would join him as Olive Oyl for several recordings, Mercer also worked alone, providing voices for the entire cast of characters, which would include Wimpy, Brutus, Rough House and Olive Oyl!

Here is a listing of the recordings Jack Mercer was involved with:

It's Fun to Eat (Winant Productions, 1946, 78RPM) Jack Mercer sings "Sip-Sip-Supper." Instructs children on the importance of eating.

Jack Mercer sings on the song, Sip-Sip-Supper featured as part of the 78 RPM record, It's Fun to Eat produced by Winant Productions in 1946. Winston Sharples, who composed and directed the music for this record, scored countless animated theatrical and television shorts for Paramount Pictures.

Joey the Jeep (Willida Productions, 1949, 78RPM) Jack Mercer is the voice of Joey the Jeep. This is a sweet love story about an out-of-work Army jeep (Joey), who falls for a cute convertible (Suzy). Narrated by Gloria Swanson.

Popeye the Sailor Man and Blow the Man Down (Golden Records, 1951, 78RPM) Jack Mercer (as Popeye) sings the sailorman's theme song with a male chorus. This version was so well received, that it was reissued on several Popeye albums, 78s and 45s, through the 1960s. Record sleeve reads, "Voice of Popeye - Jack Mercer," The Sandpipers, Mitchell Miller and orchestra. Song by Sammy Lerner.

Popeye the Sailor Man and Scuffy the Tugboat (Golden Records, 1958, 78RPM) Popeye's classic theme song, heard in the 1951 record, is reissued here, along with Scuffy the Tugboat. The same talent is heard on this record as in the 1951 issue. Jack Mercer is billed as the "Voice of Popeye."

Never Pick a Fight with Popeye and Help! Help! Starring Olive Oyl. (Golden Records, 1959, 78RPM) Two original Popeye-related songs were recorded. This 78RPM was no doubt produced, as with the others which would follow, due to the popularity the theatrical Popeye films were having on television. Record sleeve reads, "Jack Mercer and Mae Questel and the Seaweed Singers." Jimmy Carroll Orchestra. Mercer sings a hearty rendition of "Never Pick a Fight with Popeye," which remains memorable to the sailor's fans.

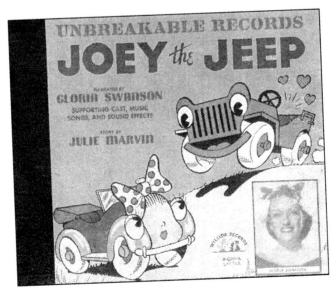

Jack Mercer provides sound to Joey the Jeep, a 78 RPM record narrated by Gloria Swanson, produced by Willida Records in 1949.

1951's Popeye the Sailor Man, Golden Record, is believed to be the first time Jack Mercer was credited as being the voice of the sailor man. This version of Popeye's theme, sung by Jack Mercer and backed by a male chorus, was heard on later records featuring the spinach-eating sailor man.

3 Complete Little Golden Records on one 45RPM, TV Favorites. Bugs Bunny, "What's Up Doc," Mighty Mouse Theme Song and Popeye, "I'm Popeye the Sailor Man!" Sleeve reads, "With the original voices of Bugs Bunny and Popeye, The Terrytooners, The SandPipers, Mitch Miller and orchestra." Also on this record was Farmer Alfalfa, a Terrytoons cartoon character. Jack Mercer's classic 1951 rendition of Popeye's theme song was heard on this record.

Original TV Sound Tracks, Pat Sullivan's Felix the Cat (Album released by Cricket, 1958) Recordings pulled from the Felix the Cat TV-cartoons. Written by Joe Sabo and Joe Stultz, Dialogue by Jack Mercer, Music and Lyrics by Win Sharples, Edited by Fred White, Special Effects, E. Pomponio, Direction, James Tyler, Stephen Muffatti, Reuben Grossman and Frank Endres, Executive Producer, Pat Sullivan and Directed and Produced by Joe Oriolo. Four stories, "The Thinking Hat," "The Money Tree," "The Great Rubber Racket" and "Hard Luck Rock!"

Popeye's Zoo (Album released by Noble Records, 1959) "I'm Popeye the Sailor Man," "Tiger! Tiger!," "The Camel Ride," "The Hippo Song," "The Tricky Monkey," "Funny Giraffe," "The Elephant's Nose," "Don't Pet the Alligator," "The Bouncy Kangaroo," "It's Time to Feed the Seal," "The Penguin Song" and

"Grumpy, Grizzly Bear." Jack Mercer provided the voices for all the characters heard on the album. The back of the album reads, "Starring Jack Mercer, who has played Popeye's voice in more than 200 Paramount Picture films released to the nation through its movie houses and on television. Jack Mercer will also play Popeye's voice in the brand-new series of 208 cartoon films produced especially for television by King Features Syndicate. The showing of this new series of Popeye films will coincide with the release of this album."

Popeye's Favorite Stories (Album released by RCA Camden 33 1/3 , 1960) "Baby Sitter Popeye," "Popeye, The Cowboy," "Popeye Flies a Rocket," "Popeye Goes to the Jungle," "Popeye the Skin Diver" and "Popeye and The Man From Mars." Stories written by Richard Kleiner, music by Bill Simon, Jack Mercer as Popeye, Wimpy, Brutus and narrator. Mae Questel as Olive Oyl and Swee'pea. The back of the album reads, "Playing the part of Popeye is Jack Mercer, the real Popeye voice. Since Jack began, there have been countless imitations, but no one quite conveys Popeye's benevolent belligerence as he does."

Popeye's Songs about... (Album released by Golden Records, 1961) "Shake Hands," "A Friend Is Someone You Like," "I Have a Little Friend," "A Friendly Town," "Red and Green," "When You Ride Your Bicycle," "Never Play With Matches," "Swimming," "Lonely Tooth," "Sleepy Head," "Scrub and Scrub," "AH-CHOO!," "Polite Ways Make Happy Days," "It Matters If You Have Good Manners" and "When You Go to A Show." "Voices by Jack Mercer and Mae Questel and Musical Direction by Jim Timmens." This album was released again in 1964 by Golden Records.

Popeye the Sailor Man and his Friends (Album released by Golden Records) "I'm Popeye the Sailor Man," "Popeye in Cartoon-Land," "Strolling Through the Park," "Help! Help!" and "I Had a Hamburger Dream," "Home on the Range," "Television Night," "Never Pick a Fight," "Every State is a Great State," "Take Me Out to the Ball Game," "The Emperor of Japan," "A Game for a Rainy Day" and "Why Do You Answer a Question with a Question." "Featuring the voices of Jack Mercer and Mae Questel, written by Bill Kaye, music and orchestra by Jimmy Carroll." This album was released again in 1974 and 1981 by Wonderland Records.

Popeye Songs of Health (Golden Records, 45RPM) Original songs relating to health and safety. While many of these records have no copyright date, the cover art depicting Popeye and Swee'pea as they looked in the 1960-61 TV-cartoon series suggests this was released around the same time period. Sleeve reads, "Voices of Jack Mercer and Mae Questel, musical direction by Jim Timmens." Songs featured are "Lonely Tooth" and "AH-CHOO!"

A 1960's Golden Record, featuring the TV Voices of Jack Mercer and Mae Questel *titled,*
Popeye — 5 Songs of Friendship, Safety, Health and Manners. *This record, as many
released during the 1960s, was produced based on the success of the theatrical and TV-
produced animated cartoons were having on television.*

Popeye's Songs of Safety (Little Golden Records, 45RPM) Sleeve gives credit
to Jack Mercer and Mae Questel. Original songs are "Red and Green" and
"Never Play with Matches."

**3 on 1 Golden Record, Popeye, 5 Songs of Friendship, Safety, Health and
Manners (45RPM)** Sleeve reads, "The TV voices of Jack Mercer and Mae
Questel." Original songs are "Scrub and Scrub," "It Matters if You Have Good
Manners," "A Friend is Someone You Like," "When You Ride Your Bicycle" and
"Swimming."

Popeye the Sailor Man (Golden Records, 45RPM, 1966) Jack Mercer's 1951
rendition of Popeye's theme is featured, along with a reissue of "A Friend is
Someone You Like," "When You Ride Your Bicycle" (imprinted on the record
as "When You Ride Your Bike to Town"), "Splish-Splash," "Scrub and Scrub"
and "It Matters if You Have Good Manners." This was later re-released by
Wonderland Records in a 45RPM format.

Popeye The Sailor Man 4 Exciting Stories (Album released by Peter Pan, 33 1/3) Four original stories: "Moon Struck," "Pollution Solution," "Oyle on Troubled Waters" and "A Child Shall Lead Them." Jack Mercer is the voice of Popeye.

Popeye the Sailor Man, Pollution Solution (Peter Pan, 45RPM) Jack Mercer is the voice of Popeye, along with the Peter Pan Players.

Popeye, A Whale of A Tale, Book and Record (Peter Pan, 45RPM, 1973) Jack Mercer is the voice of Popeye.

Popeye, Oyle on Troubled Waters, Book and Record (Peter Pan, 45RPM, 1976) Jack Mercer is the voice of Popeye.

While older Jack Mercer recordings continued to be re-issued, new ones were produced, as in the example of 1977's Four Exciting Christmas Stories with Popeye and Friends *by Peter Pan Records. Pictured is Jack Mercer's star billing as* The Original Popeye Voice. *Though William Costello originated the sailor's voice in the theatrical cartoons produced by Max Fleischer and Harry Welch recorded his own Popeye records, Jack Mercer's association with Popeye was cemented by 1977.*

Four Exciting Christmas Stories With Popeye and Friends (Album released by Peter Pan, 33 1/3 RPM, 1977) Four original stories: "Christmas Pie," "Pearl Burgers" (based on a *Thimble Theatre* Sunday strip), "Deck the Halls" and "Santa Popeye." On album cover: "Starring: Jack Mercer, The Original Popeye Voice."

Book and Recording, Popeye the Sailor Man (Album released by Peter Pan, 33 1/3 RPM) Two stories: "In the Movies" and "Spinach on the Spanish Main." On album cover: "Featuring the Popeye voice of Jack Mercer."

Popeye the Sailor Man (Album released by Peter Pan Picture Disks, 1986) Four original stories: "Popeye in the Movies," "Spinach on the Spanish Main," "Gold Fever" and "Who's Afraid of a U.F.O." Jack Mercer is the voice of Popeye. This album was later released by Peter Pan without the colorful picture disk, which served as the record for the 1986 edition.

Popeye the Sailor Man 4 Fun-Filled Stories (Album released by Peter Pan, 33 1/3 RPM) Four stories: "Popeye the Astronaut," "Popeye's Secret Formula," "Popeye & the River Queen" and "Sweet Pea's Disappearing Act." Jack Mercer is the voice of Popeye.

MUSICAL MERCER

Aside from providing dialogue for cartoon characters, Jack Mercer often found himself singing. This is especially true in the Popeye animated series when the sailor would conclude many of his films with lyrics, based on the plot of the cartoon, accompanied by the "I'm Popeye the Sailor Man" theme song. Many of the songs in the theatrical films were composed by Sammy Timberg and Sammy Lerner. Presented is a selected listing of song lyrics to cartoons where Jack Mercer sang, in character, in both theatrical and television films. Thank you to The Rough House, a Popeye-related website (http://www.theneitherworld.com/popeye) for providing many of the lyrics.

King of the Mardi Gras *(Fleischer, 1935) was the first Popeye cartoon where Jack Mercer supplied the voice of the spinach-eating sailor. Right from the beginning he not only voiced the sailor man but sang the title song in character.*

In Jack Mercer's first cartoon as the voice of Popeye he sang, along with Gus Wickie as Bluto, a song titled *King of the Mardi Gras* (Fleischer, 1935), from the cartoon of the same name.

[Bluto]
Oh, I'm king of the Mardi Gras!
In fact I'm the whole bloomin' show!
Oh, I'm king of the Mardi Gras!
I dare anyone to say no!

[Popeye]
I'm Popeye the sailor man.
I'm Popeye the sailor man.
I yam what I yam
And that's all what I yam.
I'm Popeye the sailor man.

[Bluto]
I run the whole works here at Coney,

What power supreme I enjoy!
Hey, speaking of kings,
I'm one of those things.
In fact I'm the real McCoy!
I'm Bluto the Great One and Only!
My army is made up of freaks!
My horses are found on the merry-go-round.
My slaves are Arabian sheiks.

[Popeye]
Oh, I'm king of the Mardi Gras!
What's more, I'm the whole bloomin' show!
Oh, I'm king of the Mardi Gras!
I dares anyone to say no!

Jack Mercer, in a sinister voice, sings at the opening of the Color Classic, The Cobweb Hotel *(Fleischer Studios, 1936)* as the menacing spider!

Jack Mercer, in a menacing voice, sings as the evil, fly-hungry spider, in the opening scene of *The Cobweb Hotel*, a *Color Classic* (Fleischer, 1936)

Spend a night at the cobweb hotel!
Argghhhhh
You'll find that the service is swell!
Argghhhhh
Now you need-dent be shy,
I won't harm a fly,
Spend a night at the cobweb hotel.

Come into my parlor, please do!
Argghhhh
In a while all of your cares will be through!
Argghhhh
There will be no rent to pay,
Because you'll be here to stay,
Spend a night at the cobweb hotel.

Jack Mercer first sang Popeye's complete theme song in *Popeye the Sailor Meets Sindbad the Sailor* (Fleischer, 1936), a two-reel special in color.

> *I'm Popeye the sailor man!*
> *I'm Popeye the sailor man!*
> *I'm strong to the 'finich,'*
> *'Cause I eats me spinach.*
> *I'm Popeye the sailor man.*
> *I'm one tough gazooka*
> *Which hates all palookas*
> *What ain't on the up and square.*
> *I biffs and I boffs them*
> *And always outroughs 'em*
> *But none of 'em gets nowhere.*
> *If anyone's dasses to risk me fisks*
> *It's "Bop!" and it's "Wham," understand?*
> *So keep good behav'or,*
> *That's your one lifesaver*
> *With Popeye the sailor man.*
> *I'm Popeye the sailor man!*
> *I'm Popeye the sailor man!*
> *I'm strong to the 'finich,'*
> *'Cause I eats my spinach.*
> *I'm Popeye the sailor man!*

Jack Mercer, as Popeye, sings about his new automobile at the beginning of the cartoon *The Spinach Roadster* (Fleischer, 1936). The song is called *At the Wheel of my Automobile.*

> *When I'm at the wheel*
> *Of my automobile,*
> *I feel just like a king!*
> *She's not much to see,*
> *But she's okay with me,*
> *She's got that certain swing!*
> *We take the bumps to'getter*
> *As easy as anything!*
> *When I'm at the wheel*
> *Of my automobile,*
> *I feel just like a king!*

Along with Bluto (voiced by Gus Wickie), Jack Mercer's Popeye sings a song called *Climb the Mountain with Me* at the beginning of *I –Ski Love-Ski You-Ski* (Fleischer, 1936).

> [Popeye]
> *Heidell dee, heidell ho, heidell day-hee-dee-ho.*
> *Day-hee-dee-ho, Day-he-dee-ho!*
>
> [Bluto]
> *Hedelly dee, hedelly ho, hedelly dee-tee-dee-do.*
> *Dee-tee-dee-do, dedelly dee!*
>
> [Popeye]
> *Won't you come and climb the mountain with me?*
> *O-lay-hee-dee-ho, don't say-ee no.*
> *Oh the air up there is fresh as can be.*
> *O-lay-hee-dee-ho, dee-ho.*
>
> [Bluto]
> *I'll take you up, up, up to the tip.*
> *It's a wonderful trip.*
> *I won't let you slip.*
> *Won't you come and climb the mountain with me?*
> *O-lay-hee-hey-ho, hee-ho.*

The Hot Air Salesman (Fleischer, 1937), a *Betty Boop* cartoon, features Jack Mercer singing in a nasal-sounding voice as Whiffle Piffle. The diminutive salesman knocks at Betty Boop's door to try and sell her his merchandise. Mae Questel sings along as the voice of Betty Boop.

> [Whiffle Piffle]
> *Would you like a chance to feast your eyes,*
> *Upon my stock of merchandise?*
> *You say "yes" if you are wise*
>
> [Betty Boop]
> *Nothing today kind sir!*
>
> [Whiffle Piffle]
> *Woolen hammers, rubber nails,*
> *A nice embroidered dinner pail*
> *Also knits and a bathroom scale*

[Betty Boop]
Nothing today kind sir!

[Whiffle Piffle]
Would you like a sink that never leaks,
A rug made by the hands of sheiks?
Or some nice brand new antiques.

[Betty Boop]
Nothing today kind sir!

In the classic Popeye theatrical, *Goonland* (Fleischer, 1938), Jack Mercer, as Popeye, sings a song at the film's opening regarding his search for his Pappy called *I Found Out Where to Find My Pappy*.

I found out where to find my pappy,
My pappy what got lost when I was born.
One look at me made him unhappy,
Forty years has gone since he was saw'n!
But I'll sail and sail and sail the sea,
And I'll never come back 'till he comes with me.
'Cause I found out where to find my pappy,
My pappy what got lost when I was born!

Jack Mercer often provided animal voices for animated cartoons. In *Fowl Play* (Fleischer, 1937), he sings a song to Olive Oyl as a parrot called *Shiver Me Timbers*.

Shiver me timbers, blow me down,
If you ain't the prettiest gal in town.
Tickle me starboard, scrape my paint,
I'll lick any 'lubber who says you ain't.
Sailors never tell a lie
And I says you got class.
I need but one good eye to see
That you are ship-shape lass.
Shiver me timbers, blow me down,
I'm sure gonna like it with you around.

A touching Fleischer Studio's Popeye theatrical is *Let's Celebrake* (1937), where the sailor can't stand to see Olive's elderly grandmother home alone on New Year's Eve. He takes her, as his date, to a party where eating spinach energizes the couple and they win a dance contest. This is also a rare cartoon as

Bluto and Popeye are depicted as friends. The pals share a song while heading to Olive's house in a horse-ridden sleigh. Jack Mercer's Popeye sings with Gus Wickie's Bluto, *New Year Comes But Once a Year.*

> [Bluto and Popeye]
> *New Year comes but once a year, now it's here, now it's here!*
> *Bringing lots of joy and cheer, tra la-la la la la!*
>
> [Horses]
> *You and me and he and she and we are glad because!*
> *Why, because we're here, because, because!*
>
> [Bluto and Popeye]
> *New Year comes but once a year, now it's here, now it's here!*
> *Bringing lots of joy and cheer, tra la-la la la la!*

As a parrot, Jack Mercer sings to Popeye (also Mercer) Leave Well Enough Alone (Fleischer, 1939) in the cartoon of the same name.

Jack Mercer, again sings as a parrot in *Leave Well Enough Alone* (Fleischer, 1939). The parrot sings to Popeye the folly of setting free all of the pets in Olive's store. The song is named after the title of the cartoon.

> *Leave well enough alone (squawk, squawk!)*
> *Leave well enough alone (snort, snort!)*
> *I've got my bottle and bread*
> *And a roof over my head.*
> *Leave well enough alone (honk, honk!)*
> *Why should I want to roam?*
> *I know me stuff*
> *And I'm smart enough*
> *To leave well enough alone!*

In the two-reel color special, *Aladdin and His Wonderful Lamp* (Fleischer, 1939), Jack Mercer as Popeye/Aladdin sings a song, *What Can I Do for You ?*, while striding on a white horse.

What can I do for you?
I'd do most anything you'd ask me to.
I'd go and get that pot of gold from the rainbow,
And bring it where you are,
And then I'd hitch your wagon to a star.
What can I do for you?
Hey, how'd you like to have your dreams come true?
I'd like to make you happy through and through.
'Deed I do!
So what can I do for you?

When the Fleischer Studios decided to add Popeye's father, Poopdeck Pappy, as a regular in the theatrical cartoons, the old sailor was given his own theme song, sung by Jack Mercer in *My Pop, My Pop* (Fleischer, 1940), called *Popeye's Poopdeck Pappy*.

Oh, I'm Popeye's Poopdeck Pappy,
A seagoing sun of a gun.
From bold Algiers to old Shanghai,
A seagoing sun of a gun am I.
I'm Popeye's Poopdeck Pappy,
Ahoy, ahoy, ahoy!
In building boats I'm never wrong.
I've built a million, short and long.
I'm ninety-nine and going strong!
Ahoy, ahoy, ahoy!
No swab alive can call me bluff.
In building boats, I knows me stuff.
I'm ninety-nine and plenty tough!
Ahoy, ahoy, ahoy!

For 1940's *Shakespearean Spinach*, produced by the Fleischer Studios, Jack Mercer (Popeye), Margie Hines (Olive Oyl) and Bluto (presumably Pinto Colvig) took on the roles as Romeo, Juliet and would-be Romeo. They all lent their voices to *Like a Beam From Above*.

{Popeye}
Like a beam from above.
Heavenly radiance, Juliet appears!

[Olive Oyl]
Blissful dream, star of love!
To my heart, remains endeared!

[Popeye]
Here's this heart, by your dart, only finds bliss by your side!
In your arms, by your charms, I'd have heaven in your light!
But your ray died away, fled as fades the cloud in air.
Let me 'lone here to moan, and has doomed me to despair,
To dark despair.
Like a beam, from above.

[Olive Oyl]
Heavenly radiance, Romeo appears!

[Popeye]
Blissful dream, star of love!
To my heart, remains endeared!
Juliet! Oh, Juliet! Why hast thou sunk this heart in love?

[Olive Oyl]
Thou didst leave me broken hearted.

[Popeye]
To my own grave I go!

[Bluto]
Ah! To your grave you go! Ah, you'll go!
Like a beam from above.
Heavenly radiance, Juliet appears!

[Olive Oyl]
Get out, scram! Clumsy ham!
You're a monkey with a beard!

[Bluto]
Here's this heart, by your dart, only finds bliss by your side!

[Olive Oyl]
I say go, better go, you will only spoil our show!

[Bluto]
But your ray died away, fled as fades the cloud in air.
Let me 'lone here to moan, and has doomed me to despair,
To dark despair.

[Olive Oyl]
On your way, you can't play!
Nay, nay! Oh, if Popeye'd only hear!

[Bluto]
Thou didst leave me broken hearted.
So, I'll go!

Popeye and Bluto act like they're in a Bob Hope and Bing Crosby *Road* picture with 1944's *We're On Our Way to Rio* (*We're* is spelled this way on the title card), produced by Famous Studios. At the cartoon's opening, Jack Mercer, as Popeye, and one of the unidentifiable voices of Bluto sing the film's title.

[Bluto and Popeye]
I'm on my way to Rio.

[Popeye]
To love and laughter, and soft guitars.

[Bluto]
It's always gay in Rio,

[Popeye]
With lovely ladies 'neath the stars.

[Bluto and Popeye]
Once there I'll sure try to be good.

[Bluto]
And I'll be good, so have no fear.

[Bluto and Popeye]
Tell all the girls in Rio

[Popeye]
That Popeye

[Bluto]
And Bluto

[Bluto and Popeye]
Are here.

In 1948's *Robin Hood-Winked*, produced by Famous Studios, Popeye played Robin Hood. In the opening of the film, Jack Mercer's Popeye, along with an unidentified voice performer playing a pint-sized Little John, sing *Little Bow and Arrow*. It is possible Jack Mercer was also Little John, but no vocal credits were provided.

[Robin Hood]
I'm Robin Hood from yonder wood with my little bow and arrow.
I hit with ease three out of threes, with my little bow and arrow.

[Little John]
I'm Little John, I've never gone on the road that's straight and narrow.
I get my pound of what's around with my little bow and arrow.

[Robin Hood and Little John]
Two busy little men are we, giving our gold away!

[Little John]
We take from the wicked,

[Robin Hood]
And give to the good,

[Robin Hood and Little John]
So happily on our way!
When they come tough, we treat them rough,
with our little bow and arrow!
Heigh-ho, heigh-ho, we fear no foe, with our little bow and arrow!

As previously mentioned, Jack Mercer often sang at the conclusion of either a theatrical or television Popeye film with dialogue relating to the plot of the cartoon. The lyrics would be adapted to the *I'm Popeye the Sailor Man* theme. Here is a selection of the closing songs, which were often followed by a *TOOT! TOOT!* of the sailor's pipe.

Jack Mercer sings as Popeye at the conclusion of Giddy Gold (Paramount Cartoon Studios, 1961), Oh yes in-deedy, doesn't pay to be greedy, says Popeye the Sailor Man! TOOT! TOOT! The pictured animated sequence was used in many of the TV Popeyes produced by Paramount Cartoon Studios when Jack Mercer would begin singing. The animation was carefully segued into the action of the cartoon. For example, if Popeye wasn't wearing a sailor's hat prior to singing his song, the animators removed it from the sequence.

I may be a shorty but I licked the forty I'm Popeye the Sailor Man!
From *Popeye Meets Ali Baba and His Forty Thieves*
(Fleischer, 1937)

Now I have proven no one can do movin' like Popeye the Sailor Man!
From *Lets Get Movin* (Fleischer, 1937).

Romance will be brighter when you have a fighter
like Popeye the Sailor Man!
From *Hold the Wire* (Fleischer, 1937).

A painting won't match you it must be a statue
by Popeye the Sailor Man!
From *My Artistical Temperature* (Fleischer, 1937).

I am the sickest cause I was the quickest I'm Popeye the Sailor Man!
From *Hospitaliky* (Fleischer, 1937).

As Olive's Parrot, Jack Mercer sings, *You'll learn a lesson if you start in messin' with Popeye the Sailor Man!* From *Fowl Play* (Fleischer, 1937).

There's no use in cryin' cause I'll keep on tryin'
I'm Popeye the Sailor Man.
From *The House Builder Upper* (Fleischer, 1938).

I am me and jus' me and there's no other me
cause I'm Popeye the Sailor Man.
From *Hello, How Am I?* (Fleischer, 1939).

If you spank kids I betcha, yer conscious will get ya
says Popeye the Sailor Man.
From *Never Sock A Baby* (Fleischer, 1939).

It's been proven through history that wimmins a myskery
says Popeye the Sailor Man.
From Wimmin Is a Myskery (Fleischer, 1940)

I guess he's not jokin' I shouldn't be smokin' as Popeye the Sailor Boy!
From *Popeye Meets William Tell* (Fleischer, 1940)

Although I am late with me girl for a date
I'm still Popeye the Sailor Man!
From *Many Tanks* (Fleischer, 1942)

Me ships I did 'finich' cause I ate me spinach
I'm Popeye the Sailor Man!
From *A Hull of a Mess* (Famous Studios, 1942).

He won at the 'finich' cause he ate his spinach
he's Frenchie the Fightin' Man!
From *Barking Dogs Don't Fight* (Famous Studios, 1949).

As Popeye's nephews, Jack Mercer sings, *We had spinach for chow now, we're cowboys en how on Popalong Popeye's ranch!* From *Popalong Popeye* (Famous Studios, 1952)

The Martians were hateful but now they are playful
cause of Popeye the Sailor Man!
From *Popeye, the Ace of Space* (Famous Studios, 1953).

I gave Bluto a whippin' and stopped all the drippin'
I'm Popeye the Plumbin' Man!
From *Floor Flusher* (Famous Studios, 1954).

I fights to the 'finch' on one whiff of spinach
I'm Popeye the Sailor Man!
From *Hag Way Robbery* (Gene Deitch/William Snyder, 1960)

Through space in an hour on pure spinach power
I'm Popeye the Sailor Man!
From *Astronut* (Gene Deitch/William Snyder, 1960).

I saved Olive's poodle cause I used me noodle
I'm Popeye the Sailor Man!
From *Dog-Gone-Dog-Catcher* (Gene Deitch/William Snyder, 1960).

I am weak to the 'fiinch' I gave Brutus me spinach
I'm Poop-eye the Sailor Man!
From *I've Been Sculped* (Gerald Ray, 1960).

Jack Mercer, as Wimpy, sang, *It's bad to be tardy*
to a hamburger party says Wimpy the Burger Man!
From *Egypt Us* (Gerald Ray, 1960).

He'll be warm to the 'finich' eatin' his spinach
says Popeye the Sailor Man.
From *The Big Sneeze* (Gerald Ray, 1960).

Jack Mercer as Poopdeck Pappy sang, *I may tell a whopper*
but I am the popper of Popeye the Sailor Man!
From *Jeopardy Sheriff* (Gerald Ray, 1960).

They were strong at the 'finich' cause they ate the spinach
of Popeye the Sailor Man!
From *Fleas A Crowd* (Gerald Ray, 1960).

At home or vacation spinach is me salvation says Popeye the Sailor Man!
From *The Last Resort* (Gerald Ray, 1960)

He'll juggle his spinach and fight to the 'finich'
says Popeye the Sailor Man!
From *Baby Phase* (Gerald Ray, 1960).

*I'm Popeye the Pizza man, I'm Popeye the Pizza Man, I beats 'em
and rolls 'em as fast as I can cause I'm Popeye the Sailor Man!*
From *Popeye's Pizza Palace* (Jack Kinney, 1960).

*Me spinach is pleasure it's better than treasure
I'm Popeye the Sailor Man!*
From *Aztec Wreck* (Jack Kinney, 1960)

*Cheese is strong to the 'finich' when mixed with some spinach
says Popeye the Sailor Man!*
From *Hits and Missiles* (Paramount Cartoon Studios, 1960).

*Yer edjumacation must start if ya wants to be smart
like Popeye the Sailor Man!*
From *The Spinach Scholar* (Paramount Cartoon Studios, 1960).

Even down to the end you're still the best friend of Popeye the Sailor Man!
From *From Rags to Riches to Rags* (Paramount Cartoon Studios,
1960).

Jack Mercer, as both Popeye and Poopdeck Pappy, sings,
*[Popeye] Now I am happy I've found I'm the Pappy
[Poopdeck Pappy] Of Popeye the Sailor Man!*
From *Me Quest For Poopdeck Pappy* (Paramount Cartoon Studios,
1960).

*They'll be strong to the 'finich' cause they've learned to eat spinach from
Popeye the Sailor Man!*
From *Valley of the Goons* (Paramount Cartoon Studios, 1960).

Jackson Beck, as Brutus, joined Jack Mercer's Popeye to sing,
[Popeye] *You're not a riff-raff*
[Brutus] *If ya fights and you laugh*
[Popeye] *says Popeye the Sailor Man!*
From *It Only Hurts When They Laugh* (Paramount Cartoon
Studios, 1960).

*Whether you're a giant or mite that's no reason to fights
says Popeye the Sailor Man!*
From *Popeye's Travels* (Paramount Cartoon Studios, 1960).

It may sound amusin' but women are confusin' to Popeye the Sailor Man!
From *Voo Doo to You, Too* (Paramount Cartoon Studios, 1960).

When I aims me arrows I make love birds of sparrows
I'm Cupid the Lovin' man!
From *Love Birds* (Paramount Cartoon Studios, 1961)

Entertainments not best fine food gets the guests
says Popeye the Sailor Man!
From *Boardering on Trouble* (Paramount Cartoon Studios, 1961).

Brutus was beaten because he was cheaten' says Popeye the Farmer Man!
From *County Fair* (Paramount Cartoon Studios, 1961).

A friend I am told is worth more than pure gold
says Popeye the Leprechaun!
From *The Leprechaun* (Paramount Cartoon Studios, 1961).

Ya has nothing ta fear if yer spinach is near
says Popeye the Sailor Man!
From *Scairdy Cat* (Paramount Cartoon Studios, 1961).

When ya goes to the zoo ya must know who's zoo
says Popeye the Sailor Man!
From *Who's Kidding Zoo* (Paramount Cartoon Studios, 1961).

There's only one 'poil' that's me goil Olive Oyl
says Popeye the Sailor Man!
From *A Poil for Olive Oyl* (Paramount Cartoon Studios, 1961).

We don't want to risk-o a year at the disco
says Popeye the Sailor Man!
From *Spinach Fever* (Hanna-Barbera, 1978).

Me seal of approval will stay his removal
says Popeye the Sailor Man!
From *A Seal With Appeal* (Hanna-Barbera, 1978).

I ain't no machine but me hearts pure and clean
cause I'm Popeye the Sailor Man!
From *Popeye Versus Machine* (Hanna-Barbera, 1978).

We both look downhearted because we've been outsmarted
says Popeye the Sailor Man!
From *Yukon County Mountie* (Hanna-Barbera, 1978)

I cants stop me Pappy as long as he's happy, says Popeye the Sailor Man!
From *The Decathlon Dilemma* (Hanna-Barbera, 1978)

There's no ifs or maybes he sleeps like a baby says Popeye the Sailor Man!
From *Popeye of the Jungle* (Hanna-Barbera, 1979).

It's never too late to improve a man's fate says Popeye the Sailor Man!
From *Bluto's Bike Bullies* (Hanna-Barbera, 1979).

As long as I gets me spinach I'll fight to the 'finich'
I'm no longer the lone legionnaire.
From *Popeye the Lone Legionnaire* (Hanna-Barbera, 1979).

If you haven't' hoid' this one's for the' boids'
says Popeye the Crow's Nest Man!
From *So Who's Watching the Bird Watchers* (Hanna-Barbera, 1980).

If yer windows are 'doity' I'll make them look 'perty'
says Popeye the Sailor Man!
From *Winner Window Washer* (Hanna-Barbera, 1980).

When I gets things movin' I'm really a groovin'
says Popeye the Sailor Man!
From *Olive's Moving Experience* (Hanna-Barbera, 1980).

Oh I sent Bluto out whailin' so we could go sailin' I'm Popeye the Sailor Man! TOOT! TOOT! *Popeye (Jack Mercer) sings this closing song to Olive Oyl (Marilyn Schreffer) in* Popeye Goes Sailing *(Hanna Barbera, 1978). Though the violence had to be toned down for the Saturday morning CBS Popeye series of films, the tradition of Jack Mercer singing at the close of the cartoons was retained.*

THEY CLAIMED TO BE POPEYE'S VOICE!

An unfortunate result of Jack Mercer being such a shy individual was the many people who publicly claimed to be the voice of Popeye the Sailor. Though Mercer received official credit for being the voice of Popeye on records during the 1960s, the public didn't associate the name with the voice. This led the field wide open for others to come out of the woodwork.

Wallace V. Clark
Old Lyme, Conn. Aug. 24

Wallace Vincent Clark, 63, who was the original voice of Popeye the Sailor and Betty Boop, died today in the Veterans Hospital, Rocky Hill. Clark entertained vaudeville after World War I naval service. He also was employed for a time by NBC. A member of the Debonair Quartet, Clark did most of the Popeye and Betty Boop soundtracks himself.

Daily News, Thursday, August 25, 1960.

The above obscure death notice is just one of many published over the years mentioning the voice of Popeye being an occupation. When the theatrical Popeye films were scoring huge ratings on television, TV personality Captain Allen Swift mimicked Popeye's voice for a few children's recordings. While Swift is a voice artist in his own right and emcee for a regional program of Popeye cartoons, his rendition of the sailor was weak.

Jack Mercer's wife, Virginia, recalled an incident with Swift. "Allen Swift was MC of the old Popeye cartoons for a while. He bragged that he was the voice. A show decided to have Popeye on for a guest appearance with Olive Oyl. They asked Jack to come and discuss it. When he went, they said they would have to choose either Jack or Swift. Jack turned and left! So Mae went on with Swift."

Virginia Mercer tried to help clarify the claim of Swift when the Long Island Press did a profile of the voice actor with the headline, "He's Popeye, Howdy Doody..."

Mr. Norman N. Newhouse, Editor
Long Island Press
Jamaica, Long Island
New York

Dear Mr. Newhouse:
It has occurred to me that I had better write to you to clarify a point that may come up again.

Last February 10th William A. Raidy wrote a full page article on Allen Swift. The sub-head read, "He's Popeye, Howdy Doody ..." So many people kept calling my husband about it and I'm sure, after reading the article, some began to doubt that Jack Mercer is the voice of Popeye and has been for the past twenty years, right up to less that two years ago when the last Popeye was made.

Jack is still with Paramount Cartoon Studios in New York. Still writing the cartoons and doing voices. These facts can be verified at Paramount. He has been written up as "The triple-threat man" (he draws, writes and does the voices), been shown on Paramount Newsreel, and has received much publicity during the past years, and it occurred to me that since Jack is a local product, you might find him an interesting subject.

At any rate, I would appreciate it so much if the subject should arise again that Jack receive the credit that is rightfully his.

Very Truly Yours,
Virginia Mercer
December 9, 1957.

When William Costello, who was the original voice of Popeye, passed on in 1971, at the age of 73, many newspapers reported that he was the voice of the sailor for much longer than his two-year period. While Costello continued to perform as a live Popeye act, the notices led many to believe that his tenure on the animated cartoon series was longer. Mrs. Mercer, again, had to correct this misinformation.

Popeye alive!

Poop...poop, well pickle my spinach, a favorite cartoon character from my cinemagoing days in the thirties has just come to life. In fact, following James Saunders article on Popeye the Sailorman, the Editor has received a letter from Virginia Mercer of Woodside, New York, USA, whose husband, Jack Mercer, is that world famous character's voice. She points out: "Mr. Saunders credits William Costello with doing the Popeye voice for decades and one would assume that he still does it. The fact is that he did only a few before my husband, Jack Mercer, took it over and improved it."

Mrs. Mercer explains that Jack has, in fact, being doing the voice for 44 years and since the article was published has recorded 33 additional cartoons, plus several commercials for various companies. I must admit that while I've always thought Popeye was great, he has been a character in his own right to me and I have never paused to speculate on who creates the voice. It's nice to know that in his 50th year he is more popular than ever. Poop, poop, good luck Popeye and to his voice, Jack Mercer.

Nottingham Evening Post, Dec 18 or 19, 1979

An outrageous, unbelievable piece, which leads one to wonder why reporters fail to verify information prior to publishing, came from the December 26 edition of *The Arkansas Gazette* in 1987 by Ethan Rarick, for the United Press International.

Popeye's voice still strong, complete with 'toot toot'

At first, Bill Fraser sounds like any other retiree, but the veteran vaudevillian's voice drops and he utters those famous words, "I'm gonna get ya, Bluto, Skiddle-dee-dee." "Anybody can do Popeye," said the man who invented the voices of the cartoon sailor, his lady love Olive Oyl and his perennial rival, Brutus (since renamed Bluto). "I did them all," said Fraser, who for the last 25 years has lived in the small town of Clackamas southeast of Portland. Fraser, 74, first recorded Popeye's voice at Yonkers, N.Y. in 1927, when the character only appeared in comic strips. A friend of his. who was both a policeman and a show business promoter, convinced Fraser to record the voice and then sent the recordings to Hollywood where the black and white Popeye cartoons were just starting to be made. "I use to put my head in the side of the horn and would put pillows around my side of my head," Fraser said of the early recording sessions, adding that the pillows improved the recording quality. Fraser recorded the cartoon soundtracks for three or four years and sang the Popeye song when it came out in 1931. He can still sing it, sounding exactly like a Popeye cartoon, even complete with the "toot" toot" at the end. Fraser even invented the stock Popeye phrases, "skiddle-dee-dee" "biddle-e-bee" and "whoa boy" to cover himself when he forgot his lines. "I used to do anything I could think of and they said leave that in," Fraser said. He didn't invent Popeye's love of spinach, although he said he does like the vegetable. "They said Popeye was brought up on spinach and I went along with it," Fraser said. In later years, when he performed at schools, children would often give him cans of spinach. "One day I got about 35 cans of spinach," Fraser said. Fraser is still a little bitter that he never was paid residual fees for each showing of the cartoons, as performers are today. "They duped me out of the whole thing," Fraser said. Even though he said anyone can do Popeye, Fraser maintains his version is still the best. "And I still look like Popeye too."

Had Mr. Rarick done his homework and learned Popeye was created in 1929, not "1927," and reached the theater screen in 1933, not "1931," that should have stopped this story dead in its tracks. It is an extreme example of literally anyone taking claim for the vocal talents of Jack Mercer and the failure of the media to research a claim. Fortunately, Virginia Mercer sent the following letter to the editor of *The Arkansas Gazette* shortly after the bogus article ran:

Mr. Carrick H. Patterson
Editor
The Arkansas Gazette
Little Rock, Arkansas

Dear Mr. Patterson:

I am the widow of Jack Mercer, the voice of Popeye. It has come to my attention that you ran a story about a Bill Fraser who claimed to be the voice of Popeye. If Jack hadn't dedicated his entire life to the character, I could be amused by the fabrication with his widely inaccurate use of dates, places, etc. However, Jack WAS the character--he wrote many of the stories, drew his own storyboards, even had the go-ahead to change many of the commercials he recorded. During the last six months of his life he recorded in the hospital and had delayed open-heart surgery until he completed the series.

If Fraser were an actor, he would have known that this work is covered under Screen Actors Guild, and their contracts in the early years did not include residuals--not even for full-length pictures. They required a minimum amount, plus by out for re-runs. However, this has changed and I receive residuals in his name and social security number. SAG made this rule so that the actor is always credited for his contribution to the arts and for a particular work.

Jack's death was covered by the press (you might have used the UPI item at the time) including Radio and TV, including Entertainment Tonight. Leonard Maltin of ET is an authority on animation and would be happy to verify my statements I'm sure. Los Angeles had a minute of silence for Jack and I have the plaque to prove it.

I hope you run a retraction. Jack deserves it.

Very Truly Yours,
Virginia Mercer
February 18, 1988

Then there are the supporters of the performers who indeed gave voice to Popeye, for the brief period that Jack Mercer was in the armed service, who embellish the resume of those who they support. In the winter 1994 issue of the *Official Popeye Fanclub* newsmagazine, the following letter was published:

My fellow Popeye-ites,

It is generally believed that Jack Mercer was the original voice of Popeye. I can assure he was not.

Though he continues to be the most recognized individual for his renditions of the old sailor, truth be known, he learned the voice of Popeye from none other than Harry Foster Welch himself.

Seems Harry met Mr. Segar in 1928, before Popeye entered the cast of characters in Mr. Segar's comic strip. When Popeye cartoons first went into production back in 1931, Segar called Harry and the voice of Popeye was born. In February of 1937, as Segar's personal representative, Mr. Welch attended (along with Dick Hyman of King Features and a host of other cartoonists, writers and executives), the Atlanta Georgian Newspaper's Silver Anniversary celebration in Atlanta, Georgia.

Harry Foster Welch was born with 4 and 1/2 vocal chords [and] in all the early cartoons of Popeye, he did all the voices. Disney owes much of its early success to Harry, who did all the voices of The Three Little Pigs, the Big Bad Wolf, Little Red Riding Hood, all of them. Lawrence Welk was made a believer of his abilities when Harry did [imitated] all 37 pieces of Welk's band instruments at intermission. Welch started out in vaudeville on the same bill as Bob Hope and his [Hope's] orchestra act got more play at the time. Harry Foster Welch was born on November 27th, 1898 at the US Naval Academy in Annapolis, Maryland. He died August 16th, 1973, in Blowing Rock, South Carolina. He is survived by his loving wife of some forty years, Dorothy, and his daughter, Mrs. Ruth Caine of Poughkeepsie, New York, along with two grandchildren. Harry Foster Welch was, is and always will be the original, one and only, "The Livin' Popcyc." Harry Foster "Popeye" Welch was the voice of Popeye and entertained as the living Popeye for more than 43 years. He was anything but "obscure."

Poet "Popeye" Horton

When I first heard of this letter, my immediate suggestion to Mike Brooks, who edits the newsmagazine, was not to publish it. It contained falsehoods and I was afraid of misinforming fans and historians. However, after much discussion, Mike and I decided to have it published to see if the audience was paying attention. Many were; some took the time to write, as these two letters, published in the spring 1995 issue of the Official Popeye Fanclub newsmagazine, show:

Dear Fanclub,

In response to Poet "Popeye" Horton's letter in the Winter 1994 issue of The Official Popeye Fanclub News Magazine, I checked the sources at my disposal, among them, The Fleischer Story (Leslie Carbaga), Of Mice and Magic (Leonard Maltin) and The World Encyclopedia of Cartoons (edited by Maurice Horn), Popeye: An Illustrated History by Fred Grandinetti and two books by John Cawley and Jim Korkis, Cartoon Confidential and The Encyclopedia of Cartoon Superstars. I simply cannot find a reference to Mr. Harry Foster Welch being the "original" voice of Popeye, nor do I find any evidence that he did the voices in Disney's

The Three Little Pigs or the unnamed cartoon that featured Little Red Riding Hood. All sources unanimously agree that William Costello originated the Popeye voice, and Jack Mercer took it over for many decades, until his untimely passing. Actors Det Poppen, Floyd Buckley and Jack Mercer are listed in more than one source as the radio voices for Popeye, and Mr. Buckley did some fill-in work between Costello and Mercer in the cartoons. In my interviews with the late Bud Sagendorf, Elzie Segar's only assistant, and the eventual successor to the Thimble Theatre strip, I asked if Mr. Segar had much input in the early cartoons. According to Mr. Sagendorf, Segar was somewhat surprised at hearing Popeye "speak" for the first time, which would indicate he was not familiar with the voice artists in Popeye the Sailor and the other early films. I must say that I do remember a newscast in the early 1970's which reported the passing of "the voice of Popeye," the "4 & 1/2 vocal chords" quote being the main fact lodged in my memory, rather than the name. I saw The Man Who Hated Laughter when it was televised on Saturday, October 7, 1972 and again on August 4, 1973 and naturally assumed it was the final performance of "the voice of Popeye," until I learned later that Mercer performed the voice. Mr. Horton will be glad to know that Mr. Welch made headlines in 1973! No doubt Harry Foster Welch was a very talented individual, and I have no resources available to research his involvement with Bob Hope or Lawrence Welk. It is entirely possible he might have been acquainted with Elzie Segar, and could very well made personal appearances as Popeye, but with respect to Mr. Horton and Mr. Welch's family, I find it very doubtful that he performed the voice for animated cartoons. Should members provide documentation that proves otherwise, I will stand corrected!

"Uncle Donnie" Pitchford
Carthage, Texas

Dear Fanclub,

First, let me congratulate you on the new fanclub newsletter. The publication looks better and better! The letter from Poet Horton demands a response. As someone who has worked for years documenting the life and career of Max Fleischer, and also as someone who revered the talent of the late Jack Mercer, I have

to challenge Mr. Horton's statements. I'm afraid that his assertion concerning Harry Foster Welch is, at the very least, misinformed. Thirty years ago, before the advent of both academic
scholarship and intense fan interest, animation history, like other
aspects of film studies, was something that was cared about by
relatively few. In this information vacuum, there were people
who took advantage of the ignorant. There seemed to be a number of people who solicited the attention of a wide-eyed newspaper reporter looking for an interesting feature story by making claims that were simply not true. The "original voice of
Popeye" was William Costello, a radio performer who was chosen by the Fleischer Studios to perform the voice first in "Popeye
the Sailor," nominally a "Betty Boop" cartoon that served as a
pilot for a new series. The cartoon appeared in 1933, not as Mr.
Horton says, in 1931. Mr. Segar had very little to do with the
production of the Popeye shorts, and there is no evidence that
Mr. Segar was involved with the selection of the vocal performers. The above is a statement of fact which has been confirmed
by studio records, and the statement of people who worked at the
Fleischer Studios. It is not opinion.

When a salary dispute signaled the exit of Costello in 1934, a
young inbetweener (animation term) named Jack Mercer auditioned for the job. With the exception of several cartoons recorded
during Jack's military service in World War II, Jack Mercer was
the "voice of Popeye the Sailor" in the theatrical and television
cartoons up until his death in 1984.

Jack perfected the voice and built upon the foundation left by Mr.
Costello. His vocal ability was more nimble than Costello's with
a greater facility for gentleness, humor, and ability for Popeye to
sing. The fact that Jack was a storyman with the studio also manifested itself in the wonderful ad-libs, which became Jack's trademarks. There were indeed other actors who performed the voice
for children's records and radio series, but no performer was as
identified with the role as Jack.

Ironically, few people outside of the industry knew who Jack
was, because of the lack of voice credit that was a norm in the
animation industry. The outcome of the lack of on-screen credit
unfortunately allowed a number of people to take credit for
Jack's work. Giving the late Mr. Welch credit for something he

did not do is bordering on the outrageous. Where is the proof for these claims?

Jack Mercer worked very hard nearly his entire adult life performing the voice for a character that won the hearts of millions of people. I would ask members of the fan club not to dishonor his achievements by believing these sad lies.

All my best,
Mike Dobbs
Springfield, Massachusetts

In the Summer 1995 issue of the *Official Popeye Fanclub* newsmagazine, Mr. Horton replied to criticism of his original letter stating, "My exuberance caused me to make, what has apparently been premature claims on Mr. Harry Foster Welch's behalf. For any ill feelings this may have caused I apologize. It was never my intention to lessen any credit due to Mr. Jack Mercer (for whom my admiration runs deep) for the role he played in the Popeye legacy." Mr. Horton maintained his claim that Mr. Welch and Mr. Segar met in 1931. Also, Segar called Welch to lend a hand in the production of "Fleischer Studios' newest cartoon venture." He insisted that Mr. Welch, Mr. Segar and Mr. Sagendorf knew each other, both professionally and personally.

Harry Foster Welch did indeed play a substantial role in the career of Popeye the Sailor. He made a number of personal appearances as the sailor, authorized by King Features Syndicate. This was especially true when a live Popeye was needed to perform for groups of children due to the success the theatrical cartoons were having on television. He also supplied Popeye's voice (and others) for several children's records based upon television scripts from the 1960-61 *Popeye* TV-cartoons. While no voice credit was given, it does sound like Welch's Popeye voice in a few of the Famous Studios *Popeye* films produced during the period Jack Mercer was in the service. As for Harry Welch lending a hand on the Fleischer Studio's *Popeye* series, I would think after so many years some record of this information would have turned up. To this date, no animation historian knows of Harry Welch's actual involvement in their production.

Though I tried to explain personally to Mrs. Virginia Mercer the reason why Mr. Poet Horton's original letter was printed, she was very upset. In the Winter 1995 issue of *The Official Popeye Fanclub* newsmagazine, her feelings on this issue were printed. They served to remind people the type of person Jack Mercer was:

I'm sick with the business of anyone can have an opinion. Here's mine, a fact not an opinion.

I've been in public relations all my life and know how self-per-
petuation works. Tell one reporter who doesn't check his facts,
who publishes as reported, and perpetrator shows that to another
reporter, and this continues until he has a fat file of clippings. As
for Welch, he did have KFS (King Features Syndicate) permission to appear as the Popeye character. Jack would tell me of times
some animators would be in line at the bank and Welch was telling one and all that he was the "voice of Popeye." They thought
it was absurd as to be hilarious. Jack didn't think so. He resented
it. There was a time when a nephew of mine saw Welch on stage
again taking credit for all the cartoons. Friends had to restrain
my nephew from confronting him right on stage. Even William
Costello's obit in Variety had him doing all, even going back and
forth from Hollywood (this was long before Hanna-Barbera, the
first time they were done on the West Coast). They printed a cor-
rection after I wrote and had letters from England. There's an
impostor in Oregon I still have to watch, and I think Captain
Allen Swift who did a record, has given up the claim. After Jack's
death, I saw a news program where some young guy dressed as
Popeye. I called King Features Syndicate anonymously and asked
who had been the voice for the cartoons. They told me it was the
same fellow I saw on TV. I told him to do his homework and
hung up. I trust their PR is better now?

As for the army, when they discovered who Jack was, they offered
him a transfer to the USO. He said, "No, I trained with these guys,
and I'm going over [Germany] with them."

I think that says a lot about his character! Jack liked to live a nor-
mal life. We had a house in New Jersey and five acres, where we
went weekends, mowing, rebuilding the garage, etc., There was
nothing he hated more than dinner with other voice men who
ordered in their character, so everyone knew who they were. In
1978, Hanna-Barbera hired him to write and do the Popeye voice.
They provided an apartment in the Hollywood Hills, furnished a
car, phone, etc. This one-year contract that H-B had (with Jack),
called for a certain number of cartoons, which kept him there
approximately five months. Since this contract was on a yearly
basis, they never knew if it would be renewed. Consequently, I did
not give up my job. But, I had enough vacation time to spend 10
days every month. He would come back to New York on a Friday
for any commercials that came his way.

When he was away, we spoke on the phone for hours, everyday (H-B must have had some phone bill!)

One week when I was there, he had unusual pains in the back, but he would not see a physician (I know it was because of his work schedule there). However, it was a heart attack. He needed to rest two weeks after leaving the hospital and H-B was very considerate of that fact. However, when the series was over and back in New York, he had more symptoms. The very top man in New York City said he needed a bypass right away. Jack said he had to return to H-B to do The Valentine Special. Although he was told that literally it was an extreme risk, he went, while I prayed a lot.

Early in 1984, he developed cancer (I had given up my job). This was after the completion of the 83 series and before 84.* He was in the hospital, just three days after the 15-hour operation, when H-B called him to go out and write. I confessed he was not able to go out. They said they had four stories ready. Could he do them? I didn't tell him that at that point, he could barely speak, but "yes" express the scripts ahead. Jack always changed the way Popeye says something, even commercials. So he had two days to get his voice to that point.

Jack said the recording had to be done in a room that didn't contain any "dead" sound (absolute no sound from the room). So it was recorded in the hospital auditorium in the other wing of the hospital. In they came, director, writer, and soundmen with equipment even a man from World Vision. And time was limited. If one could visualize this; Jack in wheelchair, IV (feeding tubes) running in his arm, nurse holding the IVs and me pushing the chair. Everyone stared in amazement, and all the doctors came to listen. And no one can tell those four (cartoons) from the remaining group for that year, which he did at a studio in New York then sent out to H-B for mixing with the other characters. Jack was very special. He was kind and good to humans

---

* The dates mentioned in the above letter do not correspond with the production dates of the Popeye cartoons produced by Hanna-Barbera (1978-81). I would assume the cartoons Jack Mercer worked on while in the hospital were the ones aired originally on the *Popeye and Olive Comedy Show* during 1980-81 television season. Immediately upon leaving the CBS network in September of 1983, all of Hanna-Barbera's Popeye cartoons began airing in syndication. Considering the courageous circumstances surrounding the recording of these cartoons one can understand why dates may fluctuate.

and animals, never took credit for anyone else's work. He suffered much those last years and it took great courage for him to complete that series. He would have been devastated if he could not have done that.

Mrs. Virginia Mercer

To make sure Popeye's primary voice artist would be recognized nationally I sent information to *The Guinness World Book of Records* in 1998 regarding Jack Mercer's record-breaking career as the voice of the sailor man. It was published in the 1999 edition and many times thereafter recognizing Jack Mercer's as *the longest working career for a cartoon-voice ever*. I notified Mrs. Virginia Mercer when her husband's record was first published. She was quite ill at the time but stated, "That clipping from *The Guinness World Book of Records* really picked me up and I need a picking up!"

For the decades of enjoyment Jack Mercer has brought to so many, it was the very least one could do!

APPENDIX

This is an Appendix to the section "Voice Characterizations From A to Z" (beginning on page 65) with a more detailed listing of films featuring characters Jack Mercer provided the voice for.

FELIX THE CAT

Jack Mercer gave Felix a high-pitched, squeaky-clean-sounding voice in all of the television films, produced between 1958 through 1962. These cartoons include: "The Magic Bag," "Into Outer Space," "Abominable Snowman," "Felix Out West," "Felix the Cat Suit," "Electronic Brainwasher," "Do-It Yourself Monster Book," "Blubberino the Whale," "Ghostly Concert," "Captain No-Kiddin'," "Felix in Egypt," "Detective Thinking Hat," "Balloon Blower Machine," "Friday the 13th," "Stone Making Machine," "Penelope the Elephant," "The Money Tree," "Oil and Indians Don't Mix," "The Glittering Jewels," "The Gold Car and County Fair," "Sheriff Felix vs. The Gas Cloud," "Felix's Gold Mine," "How to Steal a Gold Mine," "Private Eye Felix and Pierre Mustache," "The Gold Fruit Tree," "The Flying Saucer," "Felix Baby-sits," "Instant Money," "Master Cylinder - King of the Moon," "The Invisible Professor," "Venus and The Master Cylinder," "The Termites of 1960," "Moo Moo Island Oysters," "The Mouse and Felix," "King Neptune's S.O.S.," "Relax-A-Lawn Chair," "The African Diamond Affair," "Felix's Prize Garden," "Finally, the Magic Bag Is Mine," "Felix and the Rhinoceros," "Felix-Finder and The Ghost Town," "Snoopascope, A Magic Bag of Tricks," "Stone Age Felix," "The Gold Silkworms," "Felix and Vavoom," "The Jubilee Dime," "Movie Star Felix," "Youth Water," "Game Warden Felix," "Master Cylinder Captures Poindexter," "Atomic Drive Explosion of Master Cylinder," "Supertoy," "The Jewel Bird," "The Atomic Rocket Fuel," "The Hairy Berry Bush," "General Chang and The Secret Rocket Fuel," "The Rajah's Elephants," "The Exchanging Machine," "The Leprechaun," "The Master Cylinder's Spacegram," "The Leprechaun's Gold," "Felix and the Mid-Evil Ages," "The Capturing of the Leprechaun King," "Martin the Martian Meets Felix the Cat," "The Professor's Committed No Crime!," "The Martian Rescue," "The Portable Closet," "Redbeard the Pirate," "A Museum, The Professor and Rock Bottom," "The Professor's Instant Changer," "The Vacation Mirage," "Cat-Napped," "The Sea Monster and Felix," "The Diamond Tree," "King of the Leprechauns," "The Magic Apples," "Oysters and Starfishes," "The Haunted House," Gold Digger Vavoom," "The Wizard and Sir Rock," "The Coal Diamonds," "Out West With Big Browne," "Love-Sick Squirt Gun," "Mechanical Felix," "The Ski Jump," "Felix and the Beanstalk," "The Milky Way," "The Super Rocket Formula," "The

Weather Maker," "The Giant Magnet," "The Instant Truck Melter," "The Pep Pill," "Leprechaun Gold From Rainbows," "The Magnetic Ray," "The Instant Grower," "The Professor's Ancestor-The Wizard," "Luring the Magic Bag of Tricks," "The Uranium Discovery," "Chief Standing Bull," "The Strongest Robot in the World," "Stairway to the Stars," "Cleaning House," "Vavoom Learns How to Fish," "The Golden Nugget," "The Genie," "Felix and Poindexter Out West," "The Bad Genie," "The Rajah's Zoo," "The Loan Business," "A Treasure Chest," "The Essence of Money," "Mercury's Winged Sandals," "The $10,000 Vacation," "Brother Pebble Bottom," "The North Pole and A Walrus Hunt," "Cleopatra's Beauty Secrets," "The Trip Back From the North Pole," "The Golden Whale Babysitter," "North Pole Jail Hole," "Felix the Handyman" and "Public Enemies Number One and Two."

J. WELLINGTON WIMPY

Jack Mercer's voice for Wimpy was soft-pitched, but with air of sophistication, which worked well for his mooching attempts. J. Wellington Wimpy appeared in two 1960 cartoons produced by Larry Harmon, "Track Meet Cheat" and "Crystal Ball Brawl." Produced by Gene Deitch and William Snyder, in 1960, Wimpy appeared in "Hag Way Robbery," "Potent Lotion," "Astronut" (voice only) and "The Billionaire." Wimpy appeared in two cartoons produced by Gerald Ray in 1960, "Egypt Us" and "The Last Resort." He appeared in the following TV-cartoons produced in 1960 by Jack Kinney: "Battery Up," "Popeye's Service Station," "Popeye's Pep-Up Emporium," "Popeye's Pet Store," "Sea Hagracy," Popeye and The Dragon," "Popeye the Fireman," "Popeye's Pizza Palace," "Out of this World," "Madame Salami," "Skyscraper Capers," "Lil' Olive Riding Hood," "Frozen Feuds," "Golf Brawl," "Wimpy's Lunch Wagon," "Weather Watchers," "Popeye and the Giant," "Tiger Burger," "The Golden Touch," "Hamburger Fishing," "Popeye's Used Car," "Spinachonare," "Popeye's Tea Party," "Popeye in the Woods," "Popeye's Car Wash," "Camel-Ears," "Popeye and the Herring Snatcher," "The Square Egg," "The Super Duper Market," "The Golden Type Fleece," "Popeye the White Collar Man," "The Black Knight," "Mississippi Sissy," "I Yam Wot Yamnesia," "Popeyed Columbus," "Popeye Revere," "Forever Ambergris," "Uncivil War," "Popeye the Piano Mover," "Popeye's Testimonial Dinner," "Round the World in 80 Days," "Popeye's Fixit Shop" and "Barbecue For Two." Wimpy appeared in the following TV-cartoons produced by Paramount Cartoon Studios in 1960 through 1961: "Hits and Missiles," "Rags to Riches to Rags," "Quick Change Ollie," "Wimpy the Moocher," "The Baby Contest," "Duel to the Finish," "The Bathing Beasts," "County Fair," "Hamburgers Aweigh," "The Cure," "Autographically Yours," "See-ring is Believer-ring," "Strange Things are Happening," "Robot Popeye," "Sneaking Peeking," "The Whiffle Bird's

Revenge" and "Boing, Boing Gone." Mercer also voiced Wimpy in the hour-long special, "The Man Who Hated Laughter," which aired as part of *The ABC Saturday Superstar Movie* in 1972.

PIP-EYE, PUP-EYE, POOP-EYE AND PEEP-EYE

The nephews appeared in the following theatrical cartoons: "Me Musical Nephews" (Famous Studios, 1942), "A Jolly Good Furlough" (Famous Studios, 1943), "Cartoons Ain't Human" (Famous Studios, 1943), "Her Honor the Mare" (Famous Studios, 1943), which was the first color *Popeye* short subject, "Spinach vs. Hamburgers" (Famous Studios, 1948), "Popeye Makes a Movie" (Famous Studios, 1950), "Riot in Rhythm" (Famous Studios, 1950), which was a remake of "Me Musical Nephews," "Pilgrim Popeye" (Famous Studios, 1951), "Let's Stalk Spinach" (Famous Studios, 1951), "Lunch with a Punch" (Famous Studios, 1952), "Tots of Fun" (Famous Studios, 1952), "Popalong Popeye" (Famous Studios, 1952), "Big Bad Sindbad" (Famous Studios, 1952), "Popeye's Mirthday" (Famous Studios, 1953), "Greek Mirthology" (Famous Studios, 1954), "Gift of Gag" (Famous Studios, 1955), "Mister and Mistletoe" (Famous Studios, 1955) and "Patriotic Popeye" (Famous Studios, 1957).

POOPDECK PAPPY

Jack Mercer supplied Poopdeck Pappy's voice in the following theatrical cartoons; "My Pop, My Pop" (Fleischer, 1940) "With Poopdeck Pappy" (Fleischer, 1940) where Mercer also supplied the voice of a brutish dancing rival; "Problem Pappy" (Fleischer, 1941), "Quiet Pleeze",(Fleischer, 1941), "Child Psykolojiky" (Fleischer, 1941), "Pest Pilot" (Fleischer, 1941), "Popeye's Pappy"(Famous Studios, 1952), with a whistle in his speech pattern) and "Baby Wants a Battle" (Famous Studios, 1953), Mercer voices a young Pappy, sounding like Popeye. Returning to the voice he used in the 1940-41 Fleischer Studios "Popeye" theatrical films, Mercer voiced Poopdeck Pappy in the following cartoons produced for television in 1960-61; "Sheepich Sheepherder" (Larry Harmon,1960), Tooth Be or Not Tooth Be" (Gene Deitch/William Snyder, 1961), "Jeopardy Sheriff" (Gerald Ray, 1960), "Westward Ho-Ho" (Jack Kinney, 1960), "Popeye's Folly" (Jack Kinney, 1960), "Popeye Revere"(Jack Kinney, 1960), "Me Quest for Poopdeck Pappy"(Paramount, 1960) and "Myskery Melody"(Paramount, 1961). When Hanna-Barbera began production on a new series of "Popeye" television cartoons for Saturday mornings in 1978, Mercer voiced Poopdeck Pappy, in an older sounding vocal based on his characterization from the Fleischer Studios in, "Shark Treatment" (H-B, 1978), "Popeye's Roots"(H-B, 1978), "The Spinach Bowl" (H-B, 1978), "A Whale of a Tale" (H-B, 1978), "The Decathlon Dilemma" (H-B, 1978) and two "Popeye's Treasure Hunt" cartoons (H-B, 1978).

POPEYE THE SAILOR

Jack Mercer provided Popeye's voice in the following cartoons, which the Fleischer Studios produced from 1935 to 1942: "King of The Mardi Gras" (1935), "The Spinach Overture" (1935), "Adventures of Popeye" (1935), "Vim, Vigor and Vitaliky" (1936), "A Clean Shaven Man" (1936), "Brotherly Love" (1936), "I-Ski Love-Ski You-Ski" (1936), "Bridge Ahoy!" (1936), "What-No Spinach?" (1936), "I Wanna Be a Lifeguard" (1936), "Let's Get Movin'" (1936), "Never Kick a Woman" (1936), "Little Swee' Pea" (1936), "Hold the Wire" (1936), "The Spinach Roadster" (1936), "I'm in The Army Now" (1936), "The Paneless Window Washer" (1937), "Organ Grinder's Swing" (1937), "My Artistical Temperature" (1937), "Hospitaliky" (1937), "The Twisker Pitcher" (1937), "Morning, Noon and Night Club" (1937), "Lost and Foundry" (1937), "I Never Changes My Altitude" (1937), "I Likes Babies and Infinks" (1937), "The Football Toucher Downer" (1937), "Proteck the Weakerist" (1937), "Fowl Play" (1937), "Let's Celebrake" (1938), "Learn Polikeness" (1938), "The House Builder Upper" (1938), " "Big Chief Ugh-A-Mugh-Ugh" (1938), "I Yam Love Sick" (1938), "Plumbin' is a Pipe" (1938), "The Jeep" (1938), "Bulldozing the Bull" (1938), "Mutiny Ain't Nice" (1938), "Goonland" (1938), "A Date to Skate" (1938), "Cops is Always Right" (1938), "Customers Wanted" (1939), "Leave Well Enough Alone" (1939), "Wotta Nitemare" (1939), "Ghosks is the Bunk" (1939), "Hello-How Am I?" (1939), "It's the Natural Thing to Do" (1939), "Never Sock a Baby" (1939), "Shakespearean Spinach" (1940), "Females is Fickle" (1940), "Stealin' Ain't Honest" (1940), "Me Feelins is Hurt" (1940), "Onion Pacific" (1940), "Wimmin is a Myskery" (1940), "Nurse Mates" (1940), "Fightin' Pals" (1940), "Doing Impossikible Stunts" (1940), "Wimmin Hadn't Oughta Drive" (1940), "Puttin' on the Act" (1940), "Popeye Meets William Tell" (1940), "My Pop, My Pop" (1940), "With Poopdeck Pappy" (1940), "Popeye Presents Eugene the Jeep" (1940), "Problem Pappy" (1941), "Quiet! Pleeze" (1941), "Olive's Sweepstakes Ticket" (1941), "Flies Ain't Human" (1941), "Popeye Meets Rip Van Winkle" (1941), "Olive's Boithday Presink" (1941), "Child Psykolojiky" (1941), "Pest Pilot" (1941), "I'll Never Crow Again" (1941), "The Mighty Navy" (1941), "Nix on Hypnotricks" (1941), "Kickin' The Conga Around" (1942), "Blunder Below" (1942), "Fleets of Stren'th" (1942), "Pip-eye, Pup-eye, Poop-eye and Peep-eye" (1942), "Olive Oyl and Water Don't Mix" (1942), "Many Tanks" (1942), "Baby Wants a Bottleship" (1942), and three two-reel color specials, "Popeye the Sailor Meets Sindbad the Sailor" (1936), "Popeye the Sailor Meets Ali Baba and His Forty Thieves" (1937) and "Aladdin and His Wonderful Lamp" (1939).

Jack Mercer supplied Popeye's voice in the following films which came out of Famous Studios, through mid-1957: "You're a Sap, Mr. Jap" (1942), "Alona on the Sarong Seas" (1942), "A Hull of a Mess" (1942), "Scrap the Japs" (1942), "Me Musical Nephews" (1942), "Spinach Fer Britain" (1943), "Seein' Red, White 'n' Blue" (1943), "Too Weak to Work" (1943), "A Jolly Good Furlough" (1943), "Ration for the Duration" (1943), "The Hungry Goat" (1943), "Happy Birthdaze" (1943), "Woodpeckin'" (1943), "Cartoons Ain't Human" (1943), "Her Honor the Mare" (1943, the first color *Popeye* short), "Marry-Go-Round" (1943), "W'ere on Our Way to Rio" (1944), "Anvil Chorus Girl" (1944), "Spinach-Packin' Popeye" (1944), "Puppet Love" (1944), "Pitchin' Woo at the Zoo" (1944), "Moving Aweigh" (1944), "She-Sick Sailors" (1944), "Pop-Pie Ala Mode" (1945), "Tops in the Big Top" (1945), "Mess Production" (1945), "Rocket to Mars" (1946, Mercer voices Popeye until he begins battling the Martians, here Harry Welch takes over), "I'll Be Skiing Ya" (1947), "Popeye and The Pirates" (1947), "The Royal Floor Flusher" (1947), "Wotta Knight" (1947), "Safari So Good" (1947), "All's Fair at the Fair" (1947), "Olive Oyl for President" (1948), "Wigwam Whoopee" (1948), "Pre-Hysterical Man" (1948), "Popeye Meets Hercules" (1948), "A Wolf in Sheik's Clothing" (1948), "Spinach vs. Hamburgers" (1948), "Snow Place Like Home" (1948), "Robin-Hood Winked" (1948), "Symphony in Spinach" (1948), "Popeye's Premiere" (1949), "Lumberjack and Jill" (1949), "Hot Air Aces" (1949), "A Balmi Swami" (1949), "Tar with a Star" (1949), "Silly Hillbilly" (1949), "Barking Dogs Don't Fight" (1949), "The Fly's Last Flight" (1949), "How Green is My Spinach" (1950), "Gym Jam" (1950), "Beach Peach" (1950), "Jitterbug Jive" (1950), "Popeye Makes a Movie" (1950), "Baby Wants Spinach" (1950), "Quick on the Vigor" (1950), "Riot in Rhythm" (1950), "Farmer and the Belle" (1950), "Vacation with Play" (1951), "Thrill of Fair" (1951), "Alpine for You" (1951), "Double-Cross Country Race" (1951), "Pilgrim Popeye" (1951), "Let's Stalk Spinach" (1951), "Punch and Judo" (1951), "Popeye's Pappy" (1951), "Lunch With a Punch" (1952), "Swimmer Take All" (1952), "Friend or Phony" (1952), "Tots of Fun" (1952), "Popalong Popeye" (1952), "Shuteye Popeye" (1952), "Big Bad Sindbad" (1952), "Ancient Fistory" (1952), "Child Sockology" (1953), "Popeye's Mirthday" (1953), "Toreadorable" (1953), "Baby Wants a Battle" (1953), "Fireman's Brawl" (1953), "Popeye the Ace of Space" (1953), "Shaving Muggs" (1953), "Floor Flusher" (1954), "Popeye's Twentieth Anniversary" (1954), "Taxi Turvy" (1954), "Bride and Gloom" (1954), "Greek Mirthology" (1954), "Fright to the Finish" (1954), "Private Eye Popeye" (1954), "Gopher Spinach" (1954), "Cookin' With Gags" (1955), "Nurse to Meet Ya" (1955), "Penny Antics" (1955), "Beaus Will Be Beaus" (1955), "Gift of Gag" (1955), "Ka-Razy Drivers" (1955), "Mister and Mistletoe" (1955), "A Job for a Gob" (1955), "Cops is Tops" (1956), "Hillbilling and Coo-ing" (1956), "Popeye for President" (1956), "Out to Punch" (1956), "Assault and Flattery" (1956), "Insect to Injury" (1956), "Parlez-Vous-Woo" (1956), "I Don't Scare" (1956), "A Haul in One" (1956), "Nearlyweds" (1957), "The Crystal Brawl" (1957),

"Patriotic Popeye" (1957), "Spree Lunch" (1957) and "Spooky Swabs" (1957).

Jack Mercer continued to provide the sailor's voice for the Popeye cartoons produced for television by King Features Syndicate.

Jack Mercer voiced Popeye in the following films produced by Larry Harmon Productions in 1960: "Muskels Shmuskels," "Hoppy Jalopy," "Dead-Eye Popeye," "Mueleer's Mad Monster," "Caveman Capers," "Bullfighter Bully," "Ace of Space," "College of Hard Knocks," "Abominable Snowman," "Ski Jump Chump," "Irate Pirate," "Foola-Foola Bird," "Uranium on the Cranium," "Two-Faced Paleface," "Childhood Daze," "Sheepish Sheepherder," "Track Meet Cheat" and "Crystal Ball Brawl."

Mercer voiced the one-eyed sailorman for the following TV-cartoons produced by Jack Kinney in 1960: "Barbecue for Two," "Battery Up," "Deserted Desert," "Skinned Divers," "Popeye's Service Station," "Coffee House," "Popeye's Pep-Up Emporium," "Bird Watcher Popeye," "Time Marches Backward," "Popeye's Pet Store," "Ballet De Spinach," "Sea Hagracy," "Spinach Shortage," "Popeye and the Dragon," "Popeye the Fireman," "Popeye's Pizza Palace," "Down the Hatch," "Lighthouse Keeping," "Popeye and the Phantom," "Popeye's Picnic," "Out of this World," "Madame Salami," "Timber Toppers," "Skyscraper Capers," "Private Eye Popeye," "Lil' Olive Riding Hood," "Hypnotic Glance," "Trojan Horse," "Frozen Feuds," "Popeye's Corn Cherto," "Westward Ho-Ho," "Popeye's Cool Pool," "Jeep-Jeep," "Popeye's Museum Piece," "Golf Brawl," "Wimpy's Lunch Wagon," "Weather Watchers," "Popeye and the Magic Hat," "Popeye and the Giant," "Hill Billy Dilly," "Pest of the Pecos," "The Blubbering Whaler," "Popeye and the Spinach Stalk," "Shoot the Chutes," "Tiger Burger," "Bottom Gun," "Olive Drab and the Seven Swea'peas," "Blinkin' Beacon," "Azteck Wreck," "The Green Dancin' Shoes," "Spare Dat Tree," "The Glad Gladiator," "The Golden Touch," "Hamburger Fishing," "Popeye the Popular Mechanic," "Popeye's Folly," "Popeye's Used Car," "Spinachonare," "Popeye and the Polite Dragon," "Popeye the Ugly Ducklin'," "Popeye's Tea Party," "The Troll That Got Gruff," "Popeye the Lifeguard," "Popeye in the Woods," "After the Ball Went Over," "Popeye and Buddy Brutus," "Popeye's Car Wash," "Camel Ears," "Plumber's Pipe Dream," "Popeye and the Herring-Snatcher," "Invisible Popeye," "The Square Egg," "Old Salt Tale," "Jeep Tale," "The Super-Duper Market," "The Golden Type Fleece," "Popeye the White Collar Man," "Swee'pea Through the Looking Glass," "The Black Knight," "Jingle Jangle Jungle," "The Day Silky Went Blozo," "Rip Van Popeye," "Mississippi Sissy," "Double-Cross Country Feet Race," "Fashion Fotography," "I Yam Wot Yamnesia," "Paper-Pasting Pandemonium," "Coach Popeye," "Popeyed Columbus," "Popeye Revere," "Popeye in Haweye," "Forever Ambergris," "Popeye DeLeon," "Popeyed Fisherman," "Popeye in the Grand Steeplechase," "Uncivil War," "Popeye the Piano Mover," "Popeye's Testimonial Dinner," "Round the World in 80 Days," "Popeye's Fixit Shop" and "Bell Hop Hop Popeye."

Gene Deitch and William Snyder produced the following TV-cartoons starring Popeye during 1960 and 1961, where Mercer provided the sailor's voice: "Interrupted Lullaby," "Sea No Evil," "From Way Out," "Seeing Double," "Swee'pea Soup," "Hag Way Robbery," "The Lost City of Bubble-On," "There's No Space Like Home," "Potent Lotion," "Astronut," "Goon with the Wind," "Insultin' the Sultan," "Dog-Gone-Dog Catcher," "Voice from the Deep," "Matinee Idol Popeye," "Beaver or Not," "The Billionaire," "Model Muddle," "Which is Witch," "Disguise the Limit," "Spoil Sport," "Have Time Will Travel," "Intellectual Interlude," "Partial Post," "Weight For Me," "Canine Caprice," "Roger" and "Tooth Be or Not Tooth Be."

Gerald Ray contributed to the *Popeye* TV-cartoon series, producing the following films in 1960 in which Jack Mercer voiced Popeye: "Where There's a Will," "Take It Easel," "I Bin Sculped," "Fleas a Crowd," "Popeye's Junior Headache," "Egypt Us," "The Big Sneeze," "The Last Resort," "Jeopardy Sheriff" and "Baby Phase."

The remaining batch of television cartoons produced for the *Popeye* TV-cartoon series were produced by Paramount Cartoon Studios in 1960 and 1961. Mercer supplied the one-eyed sailor's voice in the following titles produced by Paramount: "Hits and Missiles," "The Ghost Host," "Jeep is Jeep," "The Spinach Scholar," "Psychiatricks," "Rags to Riches to Rags," "Hair Cut-ups," "Poppa Popeye," "Quick Change Ollie," "The Valley of the Goons," "Me Quest for Poopdeck Pappy," "Mobey Hick," "Mirror Magic," "It Only Hurts When They Laugh," "Wimpy the Moocher," "Voo Doo to You, Too," "Popeye Goes Sale-ing," "Popeye's Travels," "Incident at Missile City," "Dog Catcher Popeye," "What's News," "Spinach Greetings," "The Baby Contest," "Oil's Well That Ends Well," "Motor Knocks," "Amusement Park," "Duel to the Finish," "Gem Jam," "The Bathing Beasts," "The Rain Breaker," "Messin' Up the Mississippi," "Love Birds," "Sea Serpent," "Boardering on Trouble," "Aladdin's Lamp," "Butler-Up," "The Leprechaun," "County Fair," "Hamburger's Aweigh," "Popeye's Double Trouble," "Kiddie Kapers," "The Mark of Zero," "Myskery Melody," "Scairdy Cat," "The Cure," "Seer-ring is Believer-ring," "William Won't Tell," "Pop Goes the Whistle," "Autographically Yours," "A Poil For Olive Oyl," "My Fair Olive," "Giddy Gold," "Strange Things Are Happening," "The Medicine Man," "A Mite of Trouble," "Who's Kidding Zoo," "Robot Popeye," "Sneaking Peeking," "The Whiffle Bird's Revenge," "Boing, Boing Gone" and "Popeye Thumb."

Jack Mercer provided the voice of the venerable old salt in the following Popeye cartoons for *The All New Popeye Hour*, produced by Hanna-Barbera and airing from 1978 to 1980: "Merry Madness at the Mardi Gras," "Ships That Pass in the Fright," "Peask and Quiet," "Popeye's Self-Defense," "Popeye's Perilous Pursuit of A Pearl," "Olive Goes Dallas," "Sparing Partners," "Abject Flying Object," "Top Kick in Boot Camp," "Pappy Fails in Love," "The Umpire Strikes Back," "W.O.I.L.," "Tough Sledding," "Getting Popeye's Goat," "Close

Encounters of the Third Spinach," "Popeye's Finest Hour," "Popeye and The Pest," "Popeye Meets the Blutostein Monster," "Ship Ahoy," "Here Stew You," "Popeye and the Pirates," "Popeye Goes Hollywood," "Popeye's Roots," "Popeye Snags The Sea Hag," "The Three Ring-Ding-A-Lings," "Unidentified Fighting Object," "I Wouldn't Take That Mare to the Fare on A Dare," "Popeye of Sherwood Forest," "Bad Company," "A Goon Gone Gooney," "Popeye of the Jungle," "Alpine for You," "Tour Each His Own," "Popierre the Musketeer," "The Great Speckled Whale," "Popeye the Carpenter," "A Day at the Rodeo," "The Decathlon Dilemma," "Chips Off the Old Block," "Popeye of the Klondike," "Popeye Goes Sightseeing," "Shark Treatment," "Mother Goose is On the Loose," "Bluto's Bike Bullies," "Steeple Chase At Ups and Downs," "A Camping We Will Go," "Take Me out to the Brawl Game," "Popeye vs. Machine," "The Spinach Bowl," "Ballet Hooey," "The Big Wheel," "Popeye the Sleepwalker," "A Whale of A Tale," "Olive's Shining Hour," "A Bad Knight For Popeye," "Popeye Goes Sailing," "A Seal With Appeal," "The Crunch For Lunch Bunch," "A Day at Muscle Beach," "Wilder Than Usual Blue Yonder," "Popeye Out West," "Popeye the Plumber," "Spinach Fever," "Heir Brained Popeye," "Popeye and Bigfoot," "Popeye's Engine Company," "Olive's Bugged House Blues," "Boo Who," "The Game," "Free Hauling Brawl," "Wotsa Matterhorn," "Pedal Powered Popeye," "Popeye's Aqua Circus," "Take It or Lump It," "Popeye's Poodle Problem," "Westward Ho-Ho," "Bad Day at the Bakery," "Popeye the Painter," "Bully Dozer," "Popeye the Robot," "Swee'pea Plagues a Parade," "Paddle Wheel Popeye," "Yukon County Mountie," "Queen of the Load," "Love on the Rocks," "Popeye the Lone Legionnaire," "Roller-Rink-a-Dink," "Old McPopeye Had a Farm," "Polly Wants Some Spinach," "The Loneliness of the Long Distance Popeye," "Popeye's High School Daze," "On Mule-itary Detail" and "Building Blockheads."

Featured on *The All New Popeye Hour* were longer cartoon segments where Mercer voiced the spinach-eating sailor called *Popeye's Treasure Hunt*. These titles were: "Dublin or Nothin'," "Around the World in 80 Hours," "Hail, Hail the Gang's All Here," "Beyond the Spinach Brick Road," "In a Little Spinach Town," "Forum or Against 'Em," "I Wants Me Mummy," "The Terrifyink Transylvanian Treasure Trek," "Sword of Fitzwilling," "Play it Again Popeye," "Captain Meno's Sunken Treasure," "The Delmonica Diamond," "The Treasure of Howe's Beyou," "Spring Daze in Paris," "Coldfinger," "A Horse of a Flying Color," "Mask of Gorgonzola," "I Left My Spinach in San Francisco," "A Trio in Rio," "Popeye at the Center of the Earth," "Boola-Boola Hula," "Treasure of Werner Schnitzel," "Plunder Down Under" and "The Reel Hollywood Hunt." In addition to the treasure hunt series, "Popeye's Sports Parade" was added for the 1979-80 season where Mercer voiced Popeye in the following cartoons, "King of the Rodeo," "Sky High Fly Try," "The Great Decathlon Championship," "Popeye in Wonderland," "Fantastic Gymnastics" and "Water Ya Doin?"

Popeye returned to the CBS Saturday morning schedule in a half-hour series called *The Popeye and Olive Comedy Show* in September of 1980. In addition to new cartoons featuring Olive Oyl and Alice the Goon in the army, Jack Mercer voiced Popeye as a caveman in "Prehistoric Popeye" for the following films: "Reptile Ranch," "Chilly Con Caveman," "Come Back Little Stegosaurus," "Neanderthal Nuisance," "The First Resort," "Vegetable Stew," "Snow Fooling," "Bronto Beach" and "Up a Lizard River." In addition, Mercer voiced the sailor in new *Popeye* adventures that debuted in 1980: "So Who's Watching the Bird Watchers," "Olive's Devastating Decorators," "Cheap Skate Sate," "The Incredible Shrinking Popeye," "Winner Window Washer," "Hot Wash at the Car Wash," "The Midnight Ride of Popeye Revere," "Popeye Stumps Bluto" and "Olive's Moving Experience." This half-hour series aired on CBS, Saturday mornings until September of 1983.

ABOUT THE AUTHOR

Fred M. Grandinetti has been writing about Popeye's career since 1983. He has four books and over fifty articles published on the spinach-eating sailor. He has written articles on numerous figures from popular culture including *Bozo The Clown, I Dream of Jeannie, The Avengers,* The Batman Family, *The Mighty Hercules,* and *Sabrina the Teen-Age Witch.*

The Big Reel, Comics Buyers' Guide, Filmfax, Antiques and Collecting Magazine, The New England Entertainment Digest and *Animato* are some of the publications featuring Fred's writings.

Since 1992 he has been the host and producer of the award-winning *Drawing with Fred* cable series, aired in Massachusetts. Fred contributed his talents to the critically-acclaimed anthology series, *The Popeye Show.* This program aired new episodes on the Cartoon Network for three years. He was also a dilligent force in making sure that the theatrical *Popeye* series would be preserved on DVD for future generations.

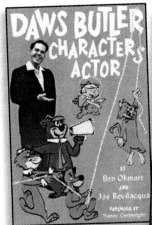

LaVergne, TN USA
04 April 2011
222748LV00004B/151/A